OXFORD HISTORICAL MONOGRAPHS

Conscription and the Attlee Governments

THE POLITICS AND POLICY
OF NATIONAL SERVICE
1945–1951

WITHDRAWN

L. V. SCOTT

CLARENDON PRESS · OXFORD
1993

Oxford University Press, Walton Street, Oxford OX2 6DP

Oxford New York Toronto
Delhi Bombay Calcutta Madras Karachi
Kuala Lumpur Singapore Hong Kong Tokyo
Nairobi Dar es Salaam Cape Town
Melbourne Auckland Madrid
and associated companies in
Berlin Ibadan

Oxford is a trade mark of Oxford University Press

Published in the United States
by Oxford University Press Inc., New York

British Library Cataloguing in Publication Data
Data available

Library of Congress Cataloging in Publication Data
Scott, L. V. (Leonard Victor), 1957–
Conscription and the Attlee governments : the politics and policy
of national service, 1945–1951 / L. V. Scott.
p.   cm.—(Oxford historical monographs)
Revision of thesis (D.Phil.)—Oxford, 1983.
Includes bibliographical references and index.
1. Draft—Great Britain—History—20th century.   2. Great Britain—
Politics and government—1945–1964.   3. Labour Party (Great
Britain)—History—20th century.   I. Title.   II. Series.
UB345.G7S28.   1993.   93–24904
355.2'2363'094109044—dc20
ISBN 0–19–820421–3

1 3 5 7 9 10 8 6 4 2

Typeset by Graphicraft Typesetters Ltd., Hong Kong

Printed in Great Britain
on acid-free paper by
Bookcraft (Bath) Ltd., Midsomer Norton, Avon

TO THE MEMORY OF
MY MOTHER AND FATHER

And to the memory
of my friend, Stephen,
and the courage of his parents,
Ron and Olive

Preface

Books of theses are, perhaps, as much rites of academic passage as the theses themselves. Yet I have enjoyed writing this book rather more than I enjoyed producing the thesis. In part this reflects changing professional and personal circumstances; in part it is because I spent some years away from academic life, in Westminster and Whitehall, between finishing the thesis and starting the book. That Aberystwyth has proved a congenial environment for this enterprise is not to suggest that Nuffield College, Oxford, was inhospitable. Nor is it to imply anything other than profound gratitude to Michael Howard and the late Philip Williams, whose inspiration, kindness, and patience sustained and motivated my efforts as a graduate student.

Michael Howard was indeed instrumental in persuading me to publish a version of the thesis, and it is to him that I am most greatly indebted. I am also grateful to my colleagues at Aberystwyth, not least the Principal, Kenneth Morgan, who compounded the folly of passing my D.Phil. as an Oxford examiner in 1983 by offering me a lectureship at Aberystwyth in 1990. The Department of International Politics has provided a most congenial and engaging place to complete the book, and I am especially grateful to John Baylis and Colin McInnes for their valuable comments on the draft manuscript. Colin Matthew of the Oxford Historical Monographs Committee also made a number of constructive suggestions. None of these people is to blame for any errors of fact or interpretation that remain.

The subject of National Service attracted my interest as a graduate student in the early 1980s because it combined my twin interests in the British Labour Party and in British defence policy. The period of my initial research was a time when defence and nuclear weapons, and Labour's attitude to nuclear disarmament, were matters of great political significance. The rhetoric and policies of the first Reagan administration, and the deployment of cruise and Pershing missiles in Western Europe, led to a period of great tension in international politics. My own response to this was a 'dual-track' strategy in itself: protesting against the arrival of the missiles while burying myself in the Public Record Office. The principal focus of the research was what the Labour Party did in government; my own views on the contemporary security and disarmament issues reflected the opposition attitudes of the labour and peace movements, which I supported. Equipped with the benefits of this dialectic, and some of the historian's empathy for the situation confronting the policy-maker, I left Oxford to serve as Denis Healey's aide for four years, working in the hope (more often than the expectation) of a Labour victory in 1987.

The issue of National Service may appear little more than a historical anachronism in the debates on security of the 1980s and 1990s. Yet I hope that this study is of value, not just to historians of the Attlee governments, but also to those concerned with the wider issues of the post-war consensus on national security and the challenges this posed to political as well as military leaders. Labour arrived in power in 1945 in the unique circumstances of having served in office under Churchill since 1940. Indeed, this was one of the foundations of the dramatic and radical reform of British society affected by Attlee and his colleagues. Subsequent Labour governments promised in opposition what they did not deliver in office (whereas, on conscription, at least, Attlee delivered what he had not promised).

The political culture—and, moreover, the international environment—have changed since 1945–51. Yet for the Labour Party the problem of expectations and disillusionment remains. The creation of a domestic consensus, while managing radical reforms, often in the face of a hostile economic environment, was Attlee's great achievement, and is the challenge for the Labour Party and Labour governments of the 1990s. A study of National Service 1945–51 is intended as a work of historical interest; yet, as Machiavelli reminds us, to understand the future, we must understand the past.

The bulk of the research was conducted in the Public Record Office at Kew, and I wish to record my gratitude to the PRO and its staff. I am also grateful to the trustees of the Liddell Hart Centre for Military Archives at King's College, London, for permission to quote from the following collections: the papers of General Sir Ronald Adam; the diaries and papers of Viscount Alanbrooke; the papers of Lord Ismay; and the papers of Sir Basil

Liddell Hart. I wish also to thank the then Secretary of the Parliamentary Labour Party, Bryan Davies, for access to PLP files. I am also grateful to the following institutions and their staff for access to various collections and archives: Bodleian Library, Oxford; British Library of Political and Economic Science, London School of Economics; Churchill College, Cambridge; Imperial War Museum; Labour Party archives; Liddell Hart Centre for Military Archives, King's College, London; Nuffield College, Oxford.

Finally, I wish to thank Anne Gelling, my extremely helpful editor at OUP, and Elaine Lowe, my extremely efficient typist in Aberystwyth. Most of all, I wish to thank my wife, Frances, without whom this book, along with all the important things of the last four years, would not have been possible.

L.V.S.

Aberystwyth
1993

Contents

I

Introduction

WHEN the Chamberlain government introduced military conscription in April 1939 it was bitterly opposed by the Labour Party. Eight years later the 1947 National Service Act was passed by a Labour government under the same leaders who had denounced Chamberlain in 1939. How that came to happen and the consequences for British defence policy are the subjects of this study.

In sponsoring the 1939 Military Training Act the government abandoned its previous pledges not to introduce military conscription in peacetime in haste and without the consultation that the opposition had come to enjoy. The Labour Party did not oppose the principle of compulsory military service in wartime, but found peacetime conscription unacceptable. It rejected Chamberlain's argument that the present represented neither peace nor war; and its opposition to the measure was exacerbated by the speed and style with which the government abandoned its pledges. In December 1938 the party, and moreover the unions, had promised their support for the government campaign to raise voluntary recruits. Ernest Bevin, the General Secretary of the Transport and General Workers' Union, sat on the national committee that organized that campaign. This support was given on the assurance that compulsory service would not be introduced, and in the face of bitter left-wing criticism led by Aneurin Bevan, who denounced the Labour leaders and, with ten other Labour MPs, voted against the national register.[1]

On 29 March 1939 Chamberlain announced that the government was still committed to the voluntary principle in service recruitment.[2] He was unwilling to introduce compulsion because he felt the need for Labour, and especially union, support for rearmament in general and the recruitment drive in particular.[3]

[1] Michael Foot, *Aneurin Bevan*, i: *1897–45* (MacGibbon and Kee, 1962), 284–5.
[2] *House of Commons Debates* (*HC deb.*), vol. 345, 29 Mar. 1939, cols. 2048–50.
[3] Peter Dennis, *Decision by Default* (Routledge & Kegan Paul, 1972), 192–3.

However, in the next month he changed his mind[4] and on 26 April he announced the 'temporary and limited' measures that would conscript twenty-year-olds for a period of six months' military training.[5]

Chamberlain changed his mind for a mixture of diplomatic and military reasons. The diplomatic argument for conscription derived partly from the guarantees given to Poland, Greece, and Romania, principally from the need to reassure the French. According to Dennis this was because 'rightly or wrongly French public opinion wanted large numbers of British troops in Europe and rational military arguments could not prevail over desires that had deep psychological and historical roots'.[6] In the spring of 1939 French pressure on the British to commit land forces was not great, though the French government did urge Chamberlain to introduce conscription,[7] which they saw as the symbol of Britain's will to send its army to the continent.[8]

The military reason for conscription was that the government, and particularly Chamberlain, became obsessed with the fear of a sudden German knockout blow from the air. Chamberlain wanted the air defences at a high state of readiness and, under pressure from the Secretary of State for War, Leslie Hore-Belisha, accepted that conscription was needed to effect this. The services (particularly the Army General Staff) did not oppose compulsory military service but in early 1939 were well aware of the enormous problems that another expansion of the army would cause; they were already grappling with Hore-Belisha's sudden increase in the field army after Munich. Labour's front-bench spokesmen focused on this, pointing out that the War Office was incapable of equipping the existing army, let alone another 200,000 conscripts. Basil Liddell Hart, the *Times'* defence correspondent, wrote: 'Don't enlist men before there is adequate equipment to train them.'[9]

In Parliament Attlee argued that as Britain was providing a fleet, an air force, and munitions it could not also provide a great

[4] For accounts of this see Dennis, *Decision by Default*, chs. 9–11; Brian Bond, *British Military Policy between the Wars* (Oxford University Press, 1980); and Norman Gibbs, *History of the Second World War*, i: *Grand Strategy* (HMSO, 1976), ch. 8.

[5] *HC deb.*, vol. 346, 26 Apr. 1939, cols. 1150–8.

[6] Dennis, *Decision by Default*, 159.

[7] Denis Hayes, *Challenge of Conscience: The Story of the Conscientious Objectors of 1939–45* (Allen & Unwin, 1949), 380.   [8] Bond, *British Military Policy*, 295.

[9] Quoted in Kenneth Harris, *Attlee* (Weidenfeld & Nicolson, 1982), 162.

continental army.[10] The voluntary system of recruitment would produce all the men that Britain could usefully put into the field. Rejecting the view that the obligation of recent treaties with Poland, Romania, and Greece entailed the provision of new forces, Attlee argued that a better gesture to warn enemies and encourage friends would be to conscript wealth to strengthen the moral solidarity of the nation. In domestic terms this may well have been commendable; in foreign policy terms it was of little value, as Britain's European allies could only be interested in the provision of military forces. Attlee concluded his initial attack on the government by arguing that 'the voluntary efforts of a free people are far more effective than any regimentation by dictators'.

The real reasons for Labour's opposition were quite different. Fear of industrial conscription was a principal one. The former Labour leader and celebrated pacifist, George Lansbury, argued that as the government of the day could call up men to prevent a general strike, the government of the day would 'always have a terrific political weapon with which to destroy the economic claims of the workers'.[11] Whether or not this was true, a general strike was the last thing on the minds of the union leaders at the time. Yet industrial conscription was a genuine and widespread fear within the party. Attlee himself argued:

The feeling behind this bill is not the desire to meet the immediate needs of this country, but the desire for conscription. That desire will grow; it will not stop short of this demand. Behind it all looms the spectre of industrial conscription. In the name of defence of liberty our liberties may be destroyed and the members of the present government are the very last people we should trust.[12]

Residual pacifist sentiment was a significant factor in the Parliamentary Labour Party (PLP); but such feelings could hardly be attributed to Ernest Bevin, who had played such a crucial role in weaning the party away from pacifism and getting it behind the government's rearmament programme. Yet Bevin's opposition to conscription remained and he was reluctant to use industrial powers of direction when Minister of Labour in the Coalition

[10] *HC deb.*, vol. 346, 27 Apr. 1939, cols. 1352–61.
[11] *HC deb.*, vol. 346, 27 Apr. 1939, col. 1424.
[12] *HC deb.*, vol. 347, 8 May 1939, col. 152.

government until public attitudes to compulsion had changed.[13]
There is no evidence that he, unlike either Dalton or Attlee, later
thought that the party had been wrong in 1939.

Nevertheless, residual pacifism does appear to have played a
role in Labour's attitude. Richard Crossman, a young Oxford
don, assistant editor of the *New Statesman*, and one of the few
Labour critics of the party line, wrote in the summer of 1939; 'It
became clear last April that Labour's conversion to the use of
armed force was only skin deep. Underneath all the trappings of
collective security a pacifist heart still beats.'[14] This was undoubtedly true of many in the PLP.

Compounding this attitude were the strong traditional sentiments of non-conformity and a widespread bitterness within the
party about the domestic policies of the 1930s. The failure to
'conscript wealth' (by levying a wealth tax) was seen as a double
standard. If Chamberlain could argue that the present represented
neither peace nor war there was no reason why that logic should
not be applied to this other aspect of mobilization. Despite government assurances on armaments profiteering it was the case, as one
embittered Labour MP argued, that 'we are talking today about conscripting flesh and blood in peacetime and dealing with finance in
war'.[15] When, as Naylor argues, Bevan spoke as if the main enemy
were Chamberlain, his government, and his class rather than the
Germans, he reflected strong feelings within the party.[16] As Attlee
himself said, 'At the back of it all—and we cannot forget this—is
the resentment which is felt at the means test and the miseries of
unemployment and the existence of poverty in the midst of plenty.'[17]

Nevertheless, there was a handful of people in the Labour Party
who believed that whatever the justification for such resentments,
they should not take priority over defence and foreign policy at
this time. After Munich the future party leader, Hugh Gaitskell,
was particularly anxious that the party give unequivocal support
to the government's rearmament programme. He advocated 'the
conscription of wealth' as a *quid pro quo* for the conscription of

---

[13] Alan Bullock, *The Life and Times of Ernest Bevin*, ii: *1940–5* (Heinemann,
1967), 42–9.
[14] Richard Crossman, 'Labour and Compulsory Military Service', *Political Quarterly*, 10 (1939), 315.
[15] E. G. Hicks, *HC deb.*, vol. 346, 27 Apr. 1939, col. 1393.
[16] John Naylor, *Labour's International Policy* (Weidenfeld & Nicolson, 1969), 286.
[17] *HC deb.*, vol. 346, 27 Apr. 1939, col. 1357.

manpower.[18] Then, according to Douglas Jay, he, Gaitskell, and Evan Durbin went to see Attlee to persuade him to support conscription on this basis.[19] They were received in the opposition leader's room by Attlee, Morrison, Dalton, Alexander, and Shinwell, who were persuaded by their arguments. Attlee duly recommended this course to the PLP in the name of the Shadow Cabinet, only to be defeated. Whatever Attlee's own views, he was not in a sufficiently strong position to sway the party. The contrast with his post-war position will become evident. There was no public indication of this manœuvring within the party.

In Parliament peacetime compulsion brought a flood of embittered rhetoric from Labour members: 'the beginning of our enslavement',[20] 'a capitalist innovation to secure soldiers to protect private property',[21] the state making 'vassals of its citizens',[22] 'the destruction of "the spirit of our people"'.[23] The view that the government was sacrificing essential liberties in an attempt to defend freedom was not just Labour Party rhetoric. Liddell Hart was quoted as saying that conscription 'would be like committing suicide to escape a fear'.[24]

Nevertheless, the Labour Party became increasingly isolated in its hostility. The Liberal Party, despite the initial opposition of its leader, Sir Archibald Sinclair, to the first reading of the bill, quickly accepted the need for the Military Training Act and voted with the government. During the week following the initial debate the Liberals came to accept that conscription had become the touchstone of relations with France.

Most of the press supported the government and in this they reflected and probably assisted the movement of public opinion. Claims about public support made by the two sides in the debate appear exaggerated. There was, however, a definite shift of opinion: in January 1937 a poll showed only 25 per cent in favour of compulsory military training and 75 per cent against.[25] By

[18] Philip Williams, *Hugh Gaitskell* (Cape, 1979), 88.
[19] Douglas Jay, *Change and Fortune* (Hutchinson, 1980), 78–9.
[20] W. Lunn, *HC deb.*, vol. 346, 27 Apr. 1939, col. 2155.
[21] A. Sloan, *HC deb.*, vol. 346, 27 Apr. 1939, col. 2163.
[22] P. Grenfell, *HC deb.*, vol. 346, 27 Apr. 1939, col. 2198.
[23] W. Wedgwood-Benn, *HC deb.*, vol. 347, 8 May 1939, col. 55.
[24] Quoted by T. E. Harvey, *HC deb.*, vol. 346, 27 Apr. 1939, col. 2177.
[25] H. Cantril, ed., *Public Opinion 1933–46* (Princeton: Princeton University Press, 1951), 458–61.

April 1939, in the wake of the government's announcement that the field army was to be expanded to thirty-three divisions, 39 per cent favoured this on 'a planned and compulsory basis', 52 per cent on the voluntary principle. After the announcement of the Military Training Act in May, 58 per cent supported the government's decision, while 38 per cent were opposed. By July only 18 per cent favoured the abolition of compulsory training; 42 per cent wanted the provisions of the act left as they were, and 34 per cent wanted an extension beyond the twenty- to twenty-one-year-old range. It thus appears that after Munich, over the winter of 1938–9, public opinion moved only gradually behind conscription, swinging decisively in favour in the summer of 1939, when war looked imminent.

By then Labour's position was clearly unrepresentative. But was it wrong? M. R. Gordon describes the party's attitude to the bill as 'an acid test of Labour's true state of mind', echoing Crossman's contemporary criticism.[26] More damning was Eden's view that it represented the 'worst mark' in Labour's history.[27] Certainly opposition to conscription did not take account of the political and psychological need to demonstrate Britain's commitment to West European defence and in particular to reassure the French. Indeed, this was one of the fundamental problems with the whole idea of British 'limited liability' as developed in Liddell Hart's writing and taken up by the Labour Party.

Yet in purely military terms Labour's criticisms of the 1939 Military Training Act were not without foundation. There was a contradiction between introducing conscription to demonstrate Britain's resolve to fight on the continent and calling up men to ready the anti-aircraft defences. Six months' military training was not sufficient preparation for an army to be sent to France (although the French were delighted with Chamberlain's decision). Moreover, the army was already in a state of disorganization after its recent expansion; the influx of conscripts did little to strengthen it and might even have been counter-productive. Brian Bond has argued:

In the short term the introduction of conscription served only to exacerbate rather than solve the War Office's problems of raising divisions for

---

[26] M. R. Gordon, *Conflict and Consensus in Labour's Foreign Policy 1914–65* (Stanford: Stanford University Press, 1969), 81.

[27] Anthony Eden, *The Reckoning: Memoirs of Anthony Eden* (Cassell, 1965), 52.

war, since it set impossible targets for all kinds of equipment, uniforms, weapons and accommodation. In political terms the gesture doubtless helped to cement the belated Anglo-French entente, but there is no evidence that it deterred Hitler: on the contrary it may even have encouraged him to attack Poland while his western opponents were still disorganised.[28]

With the German invasion of Poland on 1 September the government extended the call-up, with Labour's support. In May 1940 Chamberlain resigned and Churchill formed a national coalition in which Attlee and other key Labour leaders served for the next five years. Bevin became Minister of Labour and National Service and was responsible for administering the wartime system of conscription. This was extended to include the conscription of industrial labour and, more controversially, the conscription of women. With the Labour Party now in office, and under conditions of total war against Nazi Germany, criticism within the movement was muted.

French and other European socialists remained unable to understand or sympathize with Labour's attitude. France, Belgium, Switzerland, and the Scandinavian countries all had compulsory military service—a fact which undermined British views that totalitarianism and compulsion were synonymous. These European countries were of course land powers which traditionally had looked to large armies for their military security. Yet different experiences of civil–military relations had led many among various parts of the European left to see military service as a defence of democracy and liberty against militarism. At the end of the nineteenth century Engels had believed that conscription would even advance the cause of socialism. In 1891 he wrote:

Contrary to appearance, compulsory military service surpasses general franchise as a democratic agency. The real strength of German social democracy does not rest in the number of its voters but in its soldiers. One becomes a voter at twenty-five, a soldier at twenty; and it is youth above all from which the party recruits its followers. By 1900, the army, once the most Prussian, the most reactionary element of the country, will be socialist in its majority as inescapably as fate.[29]

[28] Brian Bond, 'Leslie Hore-Belisha at the War Office', in Ian Beckett and John Gooch, eds., *Politicians and Defence: Studies in the Formulation of British Defence Policy* (Manchester University Press, 1981), 122–3.
[29] Sigmund Neumann and Mark von Hagen, 'Engels and Marx on Revolution, War, and the Army in Society' in Peter Paret, ed., *Makers of Modern Strategy* (Princeton: Princeton University Press, 1986), 277.

8 *Introduction*

Engels' view resonated with an important strand of thought in the English radical tradition, reflecting in part the reasons for which the English civil war had been fought in the seventeenth century.[30] In 1675 the English radical James Harrington had written:

The same might be said concerning the only Ancient and true Strength of the Nation, the Legal Militia, and a standing Army. The Militia must, and can never be otherwise than for English Liberty, because else it doth destroy itself; but a standing Force can be for nothing but Prerogative, by whom it hath its idle living and Subsistence.[31]

Yet to the British left in the inter-war period of the twentieth century these sentiments were anathema. During the Great War Labour leaders opposed compulsory military service and were instrumental in gaining public support for the voluntary scheme, whereby men attested their willingness to serve, but were not conscripted.[32] When Asquith did introduce the Military Service Act in January 1916 the Labour movement's leaders stood opposed, but quickly acquiesced. Socialist and radical intellectuals grappled with the issue of conscription as they and other Labour leaders had grappled with the decision to go to war itself. Bertrand Russell, for example, was prominent in the No Conscription Fellowship, which was formed in November 1914.[33] Sidney Webb advocated the 'conscription of riches' in much the same terms as Hugh Gaitskell was to use in 1939.[34]

The carnage of 1914–18, and the British casualties of the Somme and Passchendaele, profoundly affected the thinking of a generation. Appeasement and pacifism were each a consequence of the terrible losses of the Great War. The rise of fascism and the growing military threat of Nazi Germany posed great challenges to radical opinion and to the labour movement in the 1930s. Until 1935 the Labour Party was led by a committed pacifist, George Lansbury, and remained wedded to the ideals of a socialist foreign policy which abhorred balances of power and threats of military

[30] For a discussion of the issues see J. G. A. Pocock, *The Machiavellian Moment: Florentine Political Thought and the Atlantic Republican Tradition* (Princeton: Princeton University Press, 1975), esp. ch. 12.   [31] Quoted ibid., 410.
[32] A. J. P. Taylor, *English History 1914–45* (Pelican, 1975), 86–9.
[33] Martin Ceadel, *Pacifism in Britain 1914–45* (Oxford University Press, 1980), 33.
[34] J. M. Winter, *Socialism and the Challenge of War* (Routledge & Kegan Paul, 1974) ch. 7.

force, even while it proclaimed the principles of collective security. The reality of Nazi Germany challenged many of the party's assumptions and shibboleths, and Lansbury's views came under increasing criticism. This culminated in a ferocious personal assault on Lansbury by Ernest Bevin at the 1935 party conference, an event which marked the turning-point in Labour's attitude. Lansbury resigned and the PLP elected Attlee as leader, a man who had volunteered to fight for 'King and Country' in 1914, who had risen to the rank of major, and who harboured none of the anti-military sentiment which pervaded the ranks of his parliamentary colleagues. Nevertheless, the principal parliamentary figure involved in changing the attitude of the PLP and the person responsible for getting Labour to stop voting against the defence estimates was Dalton. Few expected Attlee to be more than a caretaker leader. Yet within five years he was Deputy Prime Minister, and Bevin and Dalton were members of Churchill's War Cabinet. Labour ministers were to play a decisive role in mobilizing the country for war, and later, when victory loomed, in preparing the country for peace.

National Service was not only a key issue in the transition from war to peace; it was at the heart of Britain's post-war defence and foreign policy, and indeed at the centre of the conflict between economic and national security objectives. National Service presented the 1945–51 governments with a number of difficult dilemmas which occurred in differing forms on several occasions during Attlee's term of office. The most important of these are briefly outlined below, along with the other principal themes of this study.

The central dilemma facing the Attlee government lay in the allocation of resources between domestic and foreign/defence policy objectives. The war had left the United Kingdom economically and financially disabled, and with an economy more geared to total mobilization than any of the other protagonists apart from the Soviet Union. During Attlee's period of office economic crises were to be a recurrent feature. The war had also left Britain with military obligations stretching across the globe. These were a mixture of occupational commitments (of varying size and duration) and more long-standing responsibilities. Some of the latter were to disappear—most notably in India and Palestine. Nevertheless,

foreign commitments on a worldwide scale remained, traditional
Imperial concerns fusing with the strategic, largely 'negative sum'
concepts of the Cold War, where British withdrawal was perceived as an invitation to communist expansion.

In 1945 the question of conscription involved two separate
issues: the continuation of the call-up in the immediate few years
after the war and the idea of permanent conscription. There was
universal and enduring agreement on the former, but political, and
at certain points military, disagreement on the latter. In the
Labour Party permanent conscription remained anathema and the
party's leaders took care to equivocate on the period for which
National Service would be needed.

The essentially incompatible, and indeed divergent, aims of
domestic recovery and foreign/defence policy were evident in
both the short- and the long-term considerations of conscription.
Conflict was evident in the inter-departmental and ministerial
battles over defence expenditure, the manpower budget, and the
specifics of National Service policy—particularly the period of
service each man had to undertake. The Treasury was to persist in
the belief that the scale of the defence effort should be determined
in the first instance by what the country could afford, and military
strategy and foreign policy hammered out thereafter. Eventually
the Cabinet agreed to this in principle, but in practice the defence
effort remained in excess of what the economic ministries wanted
—even on the occasions when crisis led the government to impose severe financial and/or manpower cuts on the services. The
Chiefs of Staff, on the other hand, argued that defence requirements could be determined only by the tasks and roles that the
forces were expected to perform. The experience of the 1930s
added weight to their case, although the post-war defence burden
was far heavier than any pre-war set of commitments. Moreover,
their position was weakened, and indeed the problem confronting
the government increased, by the failure of the services to reach
agreement on a strategic doctrine and the policies and resource
allocations that would follow from that.

Manpower was one of the crucial economic issues. At a time of
enormous industrial shortages the diversion of productive manpower to the forces was directly at the expense of industrial production, the export drive, and the balance of payments. The Board
of Trade, at least under Stafford Cripps, became the principal

protagonist on the domestic side when conscription was considered. The conflict focused on the length of service and, later, on the size of the conscript intake. The period of full-time service produced repeated conflict in both short- and long-term considerations, and led to several changes of policy by the government.

While the government remained strongly committed to the principle of universal military service, the impositions of financial and manpower ceilings led to reductions in the number of men called up each year. During the passage of the 1947 act, with its overriding emphasis on universal liability, this was not foreseen. The services continued to be short of men. They nevertheless preferred to have fewer troops for a longer period in preference to larger numbers of men, from whom little productive service could be obtained. Adjusting the size of the intake and the length of service to try to accommodate changing military needs within the manpower ceilings became a preoccupation after the convertibility crisis of 1947.

Attention focuses in this study on how these issues developed within government and in particular on the ministerial conflict over and opposition to National Service. The roles of Cripps and Dalton, and later Morrison and Shinwell, are of especial interest in this context. The crucial roles played by Attlee and Bevin are persistent themes.

The politics, and in particular the Labour Party politics, of National Service are closely examined. As has been seen, Labour opposed the 1939 Military Training Act. By 1945 the crucial perspectives of the Labour leaders, and their position in the party, had been transformed. Yet for many Labour MPs, the sorts of sentiments and beliefs they held before the war had not been changed by their experiences. Opposition to National Service emanated from a wide spectrum of opinion and interest in and outside the Labour Party, voiced by pacifists and economists alike. In the particular circumstances of the spring of 1947, that opposition was to lead to a large-scale backbench revolt and an immediate volte-face by the government on the issue of the length of service in response. The traditional and specific reasons for the actions of MPs and the circumstances of the government's reaction are analysed.

The book is to a large extent a study of defence policy. As it developed during the Attlee government, British defence policy had two principal objectives. The first was to provide the military means for the pursuit of foreign policy; armed force was necessary in peacetime to preserve British influence and authority in Europe, the Middle East, the Far East, and elsewhere. When the Brussels and NATO treaties were signed, British forces were seen as bolstering the confidence of the allies. The second was the preparation of forces which would be required in the long term to fight a major war. By 1957, the date when it was deemed that a nuclear-armed Soviet Union might be prepared to go to war, the services would need to be ready. In addition, they would have to retain a residual capability to 'fight with what they had' should 'unpremeditated' war occur before that time.

In theory there was no reason why both these goals could not be attained, although each did imply a somewhat different set of priorities. However, as was to become evident in the later years of the Attlee administration, the financial and manpower restrictions imposed by the government meant that the services were faced with choices between short- and long-term designs. As the Cold War intensified, that dilemma became increasingly apparent.

Compulsory military service was designed to secure both principal objectives. National Service would provide the embodied forces in peacetime that would be necessary for overseas commitments; and it would provide the means by which trained reserves would be available on mobilization. The latter—the need to be prepared for war—was widely accepted as the main military lesson to be learned from 1939, if not, indeed, from 1914. Yet although conscription was seen as the basis on which Britain would be able to fight at the outset in a major war, it was not specifically linked to a particular strategy. The inter-service conflict over strategy and the gradual and reluctant acceptance of a limited continental commitment were notable features of the development of defence in this period, and their relationships with National Service policy are examined.

Conscription continued to lie at the heart of British defence policy. Strategic requirements for the Middle East and, as they emerged, for the defence of Western Europe, meant that the original function of providing large reserves of trained manpower on the outbreak of war still held, although there did emerge some discussion of whether full-time training was essential for this. Initially the use of National Servicemen to provide embodied forces for peacetime commitments had been viewed as a second-ary purpose—a temporary expedient until the regular strength of the forces should be sufficient to meet what was assumed to be a lower level of commitment. Some commitments were eliminated, but as others persisted, as new ones arose, and as the rate of regular recruiting remained below requirements it became increasingly evident that conscription was unavoidable without a major revision of foreign policy.

Nevertheless, as the economic pressures on the forces mounted, there was increasing reason to believe that conscription was not able to provide effective forces at the outset of a war on the sort of manpower and financial provision that the government was prepared to make. The military criticisms of the outsiders like Liddell Hart, which are examined in some detail, pointed in any case to certain important weaknesses in the government's position. Yet as the purely military objections gained ground the demand of the peacetime services for sheer numbers of men persisted and, as the Cold War developed, began to increase.

The military preference for regular forces was apparent. As the Chiefs of Staff argued:

Regular forces backed by the necessary auxiliary formations and reserves provide undoubtedly the most economical and efficient method of meeting our commitments in peace and the requirements of our strategy in the early stages of a war. To use the National Servicemen as we must at present to supplement the regular forces in their peacetime tasks is both expensive and inefficient because it results in an undue proportion of manpower being absorbed by training establishments at the expense of the front line.[35]

Yet only in the navy, where manpower problems were least serious, did this attitude lead to opposition to conscription. In the RAF and the army the need for trained reserves at the outbreak of war and the increasing numerical imperative of peacetime requirements exacerbated their respective dependence on National Service. There were some voices within the services and familiar ones outside government (notably those of Liddell Hart and Giffard Martel) who argued in favour of all-regular forces. Sentiment within the forces began to develop against conscription as the problems of training National Servicemen and the implications

[35] DO (49) 50, 22 Jun. 1949, CAB 131/7.

for the allocation of resources within the defence budget began to be understood. Conflict between the services was fuelled by personal differences, but more importantly by profound disagreements over strategy and the allocation of resources that were never adequately reconciled; the struggle between the services and the role of ministers in those debates forms an important theme.

2

The Coalition Government and Post-war Conscription

BY the end of 1944 it was clear that the defeat of Germany was only a matter of time. However, the nature of post-war Europe and the post-war world in general was far from clear. There were also fundamental differences between the Labour and Conservative Parties, and in particular between Churchill and Attlee, about Britain's role in world affairs, and especially about the nature of the British Empire. But whatever the disagreements, there was a common recognition of the enormity of the problems of reconstruction.

The extent of Britain's war effort and the mobilization of its population had surpassed those of almost all the other belligerents. The problems of demobilizing millions of troops and ammunition workers were immense, and many people could remember the disastrous manner in which Lloyd George's government had attempted this after the Great War.[1] The use of manpower was clearly a central concern in Britain's industrial recovery, and planning soon began to require decisions with huge implications. The *demandeurs* were the armed forces, the economic planners, and the civilian ministries such as education, who needed to know how many people they would have, when, and for how long. Yet changes in the post-war world presented formidable challenges to planners and policy-makers.

As the war drew to an end it was clear that the question of conscription involved two separate issues: the continuation of the call-up to meet occupational commitments and ensure the success of the demobilization scheme, and the long-term issue of permanent conscription. This chapter focuses on how these issues were seen in government before the war ended, and on the reaction of

---

[1] See Andrew Rothstein, *The Soldiers' Strikes of 1919* (Journeyman, 1980).

the Labour Party. The outcome, in both government and party, was acceptance of compulsory service in the short term, but deferment of the more controversial decision on the long term.

In October 1944 Churchill decided, on the advice of the Chief of the Imperial General Staff (CIGS), Field-Marshal Sir Alan Brooke, to begin consideration of post-war National Service.[2] On the advice of the Cabinet Secretary, Sir Edward Bridges,[3] and under pressure from Attlee,[4] Churchill referred the matter to the Armistice and Post-war Planning (APW) Committee, which was chaired by Attlee, and which considered the issue in the spring of 1945. The APW Committee was designed to provide preliminary discussion of post-war issues, before decisions were taken by the War Cabinet. Its members included the Labour ministers Bevin and Alexander and the leader of the Liberal Party, Sir Archibald Sinclair.

All three service ministries wanted a quick decision on permanent conscription in order to plan the reconstruction of the post-war armed forces. The Chiefs of Staff were already engaged on a study of the whole framework of post-war Imperial strategy, but it was recognized that as this was bound up with so many incalculable factors, its conclusion could not be expected for a long time.[5] Yet post-war manpower planning was unavoidable and necessarily entailed assumptions about post-war commitments and post-war strategy.

The main proposals, and the driving Whitehall force behind conscription, came from the War Office, which submitted its views in a memorandum to the APW Committee.[6] The paper was followed, and its conclusions supported, by similar contributions from the Admiralty,[7] the Air Ministry,[8] and notably the Foreign Office.[9]

[2] COS (44) 819, 7 Sept. 1944, memorandum by CIGS. Discussed at COS (44) 304th, 11 Sept., DEFE 7/146.

[3] Bridges to Churchill, 28 Oct. 1944, DEFE 7/146.

[4] Attlee to Churchill, Oct. 1944, DEFE 7/146.

[5] APW (45) 4, 5 Jan. 1945, CAB 87/69. For a systematic account of the development of post-war planning see Julian Lewis, *Changing Direction: British Military Planning for Post-war Strategic Defence 1942–7* (Sherwood Press, 1988).

[6] APW (45) 4, 5 Jan. 1945, CAB 87/69.

[7] APW (45) 9, 23 Jan. 1945, CAB 87/69. For an account of the development of post-war naval policy see Eric Grove, *Vanguard to Trident: British Naval Policy Since World War II* (Bodley Head, 1987).

[8] APW (45) 20, 19 Feb. 1945, CAB 87/69.

[9] APW (45) 8, 21 Jan. 1945, CAB 87/69.

The Ministry of Labour and National Service provided a hurried and limited appreciation of the overall manpower situation, which Bevin did not have time to study beforehand.[10]

There were serious limits to the value of the APW Committee's work, and it is worth noting the private view of the Deputy Military Secretary to the Cabinet, General Sir Hastings Ismay, that 'so far as the Fighting Services are concerned all the better brains are required to deal with our immediate affairs and post-war problems have perforce to be left to lesser lights who are long past their best'.[11] Yet, as he himself noted, 'the problems are so nebulous and complicated as to be almost insoluble'.

The Army General Staff identified the following commitments: occupation forces for ex-enemy territories; formations at an appropriate degree of readiness to re-occupy those territories if there were an infringement of the Peace Treaty; an appropriately located strategic reserve; forces necessary to fulfil obligations to the nascent world security organization; Imperial garrisons for the protection of bases and for the maintenance of internal security; the necessary base and training organizations at home to support these; the means of expanding land forces for a major war.[12] All but the last two of these would be decided on the basis of the inter-service appreciation of Imperial strategy being undertaken by the Chiefs of Staff.

The War Office's outline of commitments did not provide a breakdown of the numbers involved in each area. But even after making due allowance for any re-allocation of defence responsibility among the services, it was apparent to the General Staff that the size of the army in peacetime would demand a larger number of soldiers than could be obtained by voluntary enlistment. While it was recognized that the post-war rate of regular recruiting would depend on many imponderable factors, it was assumed that inducements to serve in the regular army would be greater than before the war. From 1934 to 1939 a maximum of only 207,000 enlistments had been achieved (in 1939), despite mass unemployment and the rise of fascism. In 1945 the War Office took as its planning assumption a figure of 275,000 regular engagements, and indeed it was believed that if sufficient inducement were offered

[10] APW (45) 22, 2 Mar. 1945, CAB 87/69.
[11] Ismay to R. G. Casey, 14 Mar. 1944, Ismay papers IV/CAS/2.
[12] APW (45) 4, 5 Jan. 1945, CAB 87/69.

it might be possible to exceed that figure. Subsequent experience shows these views to have been extremely optimistic.

It was estimated that this figure of 275,000, together with the output of one year's military service, would produce an army capable of providing a garrison throughout the Empire for the protection of bases and the maintenance of internal security on a scale approximating to that before the war; a strategic reserve of some two divisions abroad; a force of some four divisions at home; a nucleus of anti-aircraft defence; the necessary cadres for an auxiliary army; and base installations and training staff.

On the basis of this estimate the War Office concluded that the forces needed eighteen months' to two years' conscript service. Indeed, it was argued that if the number of regulars fell below the pre-war level of 207,000 it would be necessary to extend the period of service by another six months. It was thus apparent at this very early stage that the final post-war army would be very much larger than its pre-war counterpart: A total of 275,000 regulars and an annual intake of 150,000 National Servicemen would, on the basis of eighteen months' to two years' service, provide an army of 500,000. This compared with the 1939 figure of 176,000 embodied troops which included 47,000 men in India and 9,500 Colonial soldiers.

Inescapable post-war commitments were sufficient grounds for compulsory army service. The War Office listed additional reasons. First there was the need to distribute the burden of national defence in an equal manner throughout the nation. The notion of equality was to play an important part in the Attlee government's attitude towards National Service. Yet while political leaders were concerned with equality of sacrifice, the War Office was keen to secure more efficient forces, drawn from across society.

The second reason was to ensure that officers came from all backgrounds. This meritocratic ideal reflected both the experience of war and profound dissatisfaction with the military qualities of the pre-war voluntary Territorial Army (TA). Leadership in the land forces in peace and war now had to be open to men of ability from 'all levels of the community', and not just to public-spirited amateurs with public-school backgrounds.

Third, the War Office was keen to ensure that manpower was allotted, both quantitatively and qualitatively, in accordance with the requirements of the services rather than with their popularity.

This reflected the army's concern that the other two services would have few difficulties in recruiting sufficient numbers, and would tend to cream off the more able and technically proficient men. In sharp contrast, the Admiralty and the Air Ministry argued that the conscripts should be allowed to choose which service they entered.

Fourth, the War Office wanted conscription to create an organization that would permit easy expansion on mobilization at the outbreak of a major war. At this time the Army did not lay particular stress on what was subsequently emphasized as the principal rationale for conscription. Nevertheless it was occupied with the long-term nature of the post-war forces. Although the precise length of full-time service was still to be fixed, the War Office assumed a total period of seven years (including reserve liability). This, the Secretary of State for War, Sir James Grigg, told the APW Committee, would enable the War Office to plan the shape and construction of the army for the next twenty years.[13]

Just as the army emphasized the need to give proper support to a world security organization, and to convince prospective allies that Britain 'meant business', so the Air Ministry argued that 'strong forces will be necessary to restore and preserve international order'[14] in what the Secretary of State for Air, Sir Archibald Sinclair, called the 'critical formative period after the war'.[15] He, at least, did not see that period as anything like twenty years. The Air Ministry also recognized that the various assumptions of post-war planning would have to be revised and adjusted in the light of the Chiefs of Staff's evaluation of post-war commitments. Like the Admiralty it gave little indication of the scale of forces it envisaged, or of how many National Service Airmen it needed. It did, however, estimate that the probable intake for the regular air force, and its reserves, would be 70,000–80,000. A decision on the retention of National Service was seen as essential for a number of other decisions in the personnel, organization, and training fields.

It was emphasized that the Royal Air Force and its non-regular services would continue to depend on voluntary recruiting. Of interest was the belief that conscription would assist regular recruiting as experience of air force life would encourage men to

13 APW (45) 7th, 22 Mar. 1945, CAB 87/69.
14 APW (45) 20, 19 Feb. 1945, CAB 87/69.
15 APW (45) 7th, 22 Mar. 1945, CAB 87/69.

stay on. Voluntary recruiting was essential. In particular the service 'could not contemplate employment on aircrew duties either
in the regular or non-regular air forces except on a voluntary
basis'. The bulk of the ground personnel would also have to be
volunteers, although these objectives were eroded as the manpower situation of the RAF deteriorated.

None the less, it was clear to the Air Ministry that the retention
of National Service was essential as a complementary measure to
regular voluntary recruiting. Yet unless the period of service was
some three to four years, conscripts would not be able to serve
as aircrew without a significant loss of efficiency caused by the
high turnover. If they did serve as aircrew they would have to be
supernumerary to squadron establishment. With regard to ground
personnel, tradesmen in the higher skill groups needed fourteen
months' training; men in lower skill groups needed a minimum of
six. The productive value of conscripts was therefore limited.

On the period of service, twelve months would mean that many
categories of maintenance and other ancillary personnel would
complete their technical courses but not gain the necessary practical experience. Only a proportion of aircrew would complete
basic flying training. Eighteen months' service would ensure all
aircrew finished basic training, with some available for supernumerary service with their squadrons. All ground personnel
would complete basic technical training and could be posted to
units. With two years' service, all ground personnel would be
capable of productive employment, and aircrew would be available for short periods of squadron service.

The preference of the Air Ministry for the longer periods was
clear. But they did not press the point, arguing that 'a period of
national service of eighteen months would accord with the technical requirements of the air force but if it is decided that the period
should be twelve months the Air Ministry would wish to make
provision for volunteers to extend beyond that period'. In the
APW Committee Sinclair explained that one year's conscription
was the minimum acceptable, and added that the Air Ministry
might have to press for eighteen months. As with the army proposals, a total seven-year engagement was envisaged, with entry
at age eighteen.

The position of the Admiralty was that given proper conditions
of service, it expected to be able to man the fleet on a voluntary

basis. The navy's requirements were smaller. Furthermore, unlike the other two services it had continued with regular recruiting during the war. Conscription would not be necessary to man the fleet in peacetime, but 'a form of conscription' would probably be needed to provide the large numbers of reservists required on the outbreak of war. The Admiralty was 'in favour of the principle that compulsory service for men should be retained as a permanent feature after the war and an early decision on this proposal would greatly assist post-war planning'.[16] The Admirals were anxious that so far as possible conscripts should choose which service they joined. It was considered 'highly important that the Fleet should be manned by men who had voluntarily chosen service at sea'.

The navy wanted the period of full-time training to be one year, with an extension of one or two months for some classes of ratings. Beyond that the Admiralty could see little advantage to the navy of extending service beyond twelve months, unless it was extended to between three and a half and four years. This was recognized to be politically impractical.

The use of short-service conscripts as part of the complements of ships in service seriously reduced the efficiency of those ships, owing to the rapid turnover of personnel. The use of conscripts on foreign stations for the very short period that would be possible within the eighteen months to two years service period envisaged by the War Office would be impracticable. It would mean the constant movement to and fro of large numbers of men who would be employed abroad for less than a year. The Admiralty therefore considered that the period of conscription should not be fixed above twelve months. On the other hand, it should not be fixed below twelve months. That would be insufficient even for naval training on peacetime standards and would yeild an uneconomic return on the effort expended. As training at sea should form some part of a conscript's service, twelve months was the minimum acceptable.

In anticipation of the argument subsequently used in the navy to oppose conscription in October 1946, the Admiralty warned that the introduction of a permanent scheme of conscription would entail a considerable increase in the navy estimates. This would be

[16] APW (45) 9, 23 Jan. 1945, CAB 87/69.

necessary to provide for instructors and administrative staff and the very large capital outlay on buildings and other material facilities. It would also involve the provision and maintenance of a seagoing training squadron or squadrons that would provide the sea-training of the conscripts. This would constitute a 'second Fleet'. As Alexander told the APW Committee, this would mean extra resources.

Neither the Air Ministry nor the Admiralty spelled out its commitments in detail. It was simply argued that military force was necessary for foreign policy. In this the service ministries were strongly supported by the Foreign Office, which argued that conscription was of the greatest importance to Britain's foreign policy on two grounds. First, it was bound to affect the numbers of armed forces available to carry out foreign commitments and responsibilities, which would inevitably be greater than before the war. Second, the maintenance or abandonment of compulsory military service would have a direct influence on the authority of the country throughout the world and thus upon the strength and success of Britain's foreign policy. These two views were accepted and repeated by Bevin when he became Foreign Secretary.

The Foreign Office paper summarized the country's post-war responsibilities as follows: to provide for the obligations assumed in the Four Power Pact signed at Moscow in October 1943 to co-operate with allies to maintain international peace and security until that responsibility could be taken over by a world organization; to provide the quotas of forces for that organization; to maintain, for an indefinite period, forces of occupation in north-west Germany and Austria and possibly a permanent force in the industrial Rhine basin; to provide for treaty commitments to various allies, notably Egypt, Iraq, and Portugal; to maintain sufficient forces for the defence of the Empire and Britain's 'vital interests', which included the Near and Middle East and the defence of communications and oil supplies.

This greater elaboration of the scope of Britain's post-war burden clearly reinforced the position of the War Office. Although modified by events in the next few years, this outline and the corresponding assumptions on which foreign policy was based were eventually accepted by the Labour government—not, as far as the Middle East was concerned, without a struggle. Nevertheless, the guiding principle was to be a strong element of continuity in foreign policy, which facilitated an essentially bipartisan approach in foreign affairs.

The Foreign Office wrote of the lessons of the pre-war period, of the disastrous consequences of having tried to play a part in the world without the necessary backing of armed force, and of the need to possess the means to fulfil commitments. Between the wars, it was argued, there had grown an impression that the British people had lost 'the will and the self-discipline to protect themselves and to enforce their voice in world affairs'. The failure to adopt compulsory military service demonstrated both to potential allies and to foes Britain's lack of determination, and this helped to undermine British policy on the continent.

These views were not challenged either in the APW Committee or in the War Cabinet.[17] Moreover, when the length of National Service was examined in 1946, 1948, and 1950, the relationship between conscription and foreign policy formed an essential argument. Criticisms of the Foreign Office view were voiced in some areas of Whitehall (and certainly elsewhere). It could, for example, be argued that the failure to act over Abyssinia was a failure of political rather than of military will. Military critics of conscription, such as Liddell Hart and Giffard Martel, argued that far from providing Britain with an effective instrument of military force, conscription was a burden that weakened the services and inhibited action. A subtle variation on that idea obtained in the Treasury, where Britain's post-war economic plight was increasingly recognized. Commenting on the Foreign Office paper, Sir Wilfred Eady, Joint Second Secretary to the Treasury, wrote:

In APW (45) 8 the Foreign Secretary says that our defence must *seem* to be strong. This, as an argument in support of the political principle of conscription, has its value. Beyond that it may beg some dangerous questions. The war has shown that there are inescapable physical limits to the size of the war effort however far willingness goes. This is not much less true about continuing measures for defence. We cannot simultaneously seem to be strong in the Navy and the Air by reference to USA standards, and on the land by reference to Russian and possibly French standards, or maintain sufficient strength for all contingencies in the European centre and also at the periphery of British possessions. We cannot simultaneously afford effective strength and prestige. No defence

[17] WM (45) 48, 20 Apr. 1945, CAB 65/52.

is weaker than one that appears to be stronger than it is eg France and Italy in this war.[18]

These were far-sighted heresies, though certainly few would have questioned the view that a credible defence policy was one that could be maintained over a long period of time.

On the issue of the continental commitment, Eden argued in forthright and unequivocal terms. Since the beginning of the century Britain had been committed to defence policies which implied action on the continent with large forces in certain contingencies. Now that Britain had taken its frontier to be on the Rhine, that meant taking responsibility which could only be met by larger forces than a voluntary system could provide. With Europe overshadowed by a huge 'Russian' army based upon the most severe system of compulsory military service, more explicit and greater commitments to the continent than before the war were now necessary. Power would continue to be assessed on the continent largely in terms of land forces. On this basis it would be inconceivable that Britain should succeed in persuading Continental opinion that it retained and was determined to retain its position as one of the Great Powers if compulsory military service was given up. The Soviet Union was the principal consideration here. Separate, but related to this, was the view that unless Britain was determined to guarantee a military presence to prevent a revival of German militarism, the French would gravitate towards the Soviet Union in search of guarantees for their security.

These views were not challenged. Bevin was to agree on the basic premiss of requiring military forces for international diplomacy; yet, as will be seen, the Labour leaders were unhappy with the prospect of a long-term commitment to the defence of Western Europe. This might suggest an area of potentially significant difference between the parties. Certainly the India Secretary, Leo Amery, supported Eden. He believed that extra-European commitments would be met by regular forces but that conscription should be used to meet continental commitments.

The Foreign Office paper did not even allude to the economic burdens of Britain's post-war defence efforts. Moreover, the Treasury was not invited to submit any estimate of the likely cost of

[18] Eady to Sir A. Barlow (Joint Second Secretary to the Treasury), Mar. 1945, T. 247/71.

the forces envisaged. The Ministry of Labour was brought in at a relatively late stage and could not provide a considered appreciation of the industrial consequences of the loss of manpower to the armed services. However, Attlee's committee and the War Cabinet did not agree to permanent conscription as the services wanted. Attlee argued in his report to the Cabinet that it should be the ultimate aim to reduce the burden of British responsibilities, and the armaments required for their fulfilment, 'by the strongest possible support for international arrangements that would contribute to those ends'.[19] Until the future could be seen more clearly compulsory military service should be maintained. Attlee wanted to delay the more controversial decision about a permanent scheme. He argued that the question of conscription had to be related both to post-war defence policy as a whole and to the general economic position. A complete picture of Britain's future strategy should be examined by the Defence Committee before any conclusion on such an important question could be reached.

In Cabinet the discussion concentrated on the continuation of the call-up in the immediate post-war period. Nevertheless, it is interesting to note Bevin's position and the difference between the two Labour leaders in the APW Committee. Bevin had been thinking about the retention of compulsory military service after the war as early as 1942.[20] He was clear in his mind that the committee should be considering the matter as a long-term policy, as the various memoranda had done. He stressed that this was his personal view as the Labour Party had not yet been consulted.

On the question of permanent conscription, he recognized that it would be preferable if decisions could first be reached on the defence organization and overseas commitments. Nevertheless, there were strong arguments for reaching a decision on National Service soon. In addition to the military, the educational and industrial authorities needed to know the government's long-term plans. Bevin's personal opinion was that 'as the State had now undertaken so many commitments to the citizens (i.e. full employment, social security etc.) it would be right for the citizen in return to accept the obligation of Military Service'. This was a theme to which he was to return. This support for permanent

[19] WP (45) 242, 12 Apr. 1945, CAB 66/64.
[20] Alan Bullock, *The Life and Times of Ernest Bevin*, ii: *1940–5* (Heinemann, 1967), 198.

conscription was contradicted by a later statement that he made to Labour leaders in May 1945 (see below), but was fully in accord with subsequent remarks as Foreign Secretary.

He was especially concerned that the system of conscription had to be applied to everyone. Indeed, he went so far as to indicate support for the conscription of women. Along with Churchill he was anxious that National Service should not become an issue of party controversy. By this Bevin meant both inter- and intra-party controversy, and with the latter in mind he pressed for ministers to consult with their parties before any announcement.

The Cabinet accepted Attlee's report. Conscription was to continue until the war against Japan and the occupation of enemy countries was completed and until there was a 'reasonable measure of stability in the world'. However, in his paper Attlee suggested that the industrial burden might prove too great. He argued that it had always been assumed that security and freedom from unrest in the Middle East was a vital interest of the British Empire. However, he warned, its maintenance in the future might well require association with the United States and it was clear that in this he had more in mind than the sort of financial support that the Truman doctrine would eventually provide in Greece and Turkey. Subsequently he was to advocate effective British withdrawal from the region.

In the spring of 1945 it was Attlee who was responsible for the deferment of the decision on a permanent scheme of compulsory military service in peacetime. He was well aware how sensitive the issue was for the Labour Party. In February, at a meeting with senior Labour politicians, he and Morrison had both been inclined for Labour to come out in favour of a permanent scheme.[21] On 11 April (after he had written the report for the Cabinet) he assembled a larger number of Labour ministers. According to Dalton the general feeling of that meeting was in favour of permanent conscription.[22] Several future ministers, however (notably Ellen Wilkinson and Philip Noel-Baker), were against and, as will be seen, there were a great many in the Labour Party outside the government who were resolutely opposed.

Attlee must have been aware of the likely reaction of the pacifist

---

[21] Diaries of Hugh Dalton (London School of Economics), 9 Feb. 1945.
[22] Dalton Diaries, 11 Apr. 1945.

elements of his party. It is possible that after February he became aware of non-pacifist opposition, although there was no discussion of the issue in the PLP. He may well have listened to Dalton. Although in 1946 Dalton's support for National Service was crucial, in the spring of 1945 he doubted whether a decision was necessary 'beyond what seems the inevitable . . . continuation of the call-up for another two or three years'.[23] This was to facilitate the demobilization scheme while a large army was still needed in Europe.

Dalton was undoubtedly correct in judging it imprudent to agree on the long-term question of conscription until a clearer picture had emerged, not just of the post-war settlement in general but of British defence policy in particular. It was only sensible to await the outcome of the Chiefs of Staff's examination and to consider the financial and industrial implications of an agreed strategy.

In the field of defence policy considerable changes had to be digested, most obviously in the area of technological development. Even in conventional terms there were grounds for believing that changes in military technology and tactics had undermined the case for large conscript armies. Martel and Liddell-Hart were to argue that the development of modern armoured warfare meant that large, unwieldy, conscript forces were obsolete. The development of ballistic missiles and jet aircraft also posed fresh challenges to military ideas and practices.

Potentially of much greater significance was the emergence of the atomic bomb. In the spring of 1945 the dawn of the atomic age was still some time away. Neither Bevin nor Attlee was aware of the development of the A-bomb when conscription was being discussed. It was to become evident that weapons of mass destruction could make an enormous impact on war. After the first explosion Churchill initially believed the A-bomb would tilt the post-war balance firmly to the West.[24] Yet Churchill himself, who knew of the development of the bomb, was (and remained) committed to conscription. Although the destruction of Hiroshima and Nagasaki may have changed some attitudes towards conscription and conscript armies, it was not to have any significant effect

[23] Ibid.
[24] Brooke, Notes on My Life and Diary for 23 Jul. 1945, Alanbrooke 3/B/XVI and 5/11.

on the key military or political leaders. As will be seen, the Chiefs of Staff saw no inconsistency in possessing both atomic bombs and conscription. Yet even though atomic weapons did not have a direct impact on manpower policy and even though their emergence was, in early 1945, still in the future, Attlee's reticence was sensible. Implications of technological changes and tactical innovations at the conventional level had yet to be understood. Moreover, Attlee's remarks about the Middle East indicate that he already had in mind the reorientation of British Imperial strategy which he was later to attempt.

Bevin was to recall in 1947 that when he had accepted the case for permanent conscription, it had been as a *quid pro quo* for Indian independence.[25] Before the war the Indian Army had represented the Empire's strategic reserve. Although withdrawal from India would free some 47,000 British troops in peacetime, the loss of the Indian Army was a serious blow. Brooke was to describe it as rendering Britain impotent in the region.[26] There is, however, no record of any discussion in the APW Committee or the War Cabinet linking the two issues. The War Office was not planning on Indian independence. Indeed, when India was granted its freedom the Chiefs of Staff were not consulted beforehand.[27] Furthermore, Bevin did not attempt to use his acceptance of conscription as a lever to get Churchill to accept change in India. More significantly, there was no attempt to use the question of Indian independence as an argument to convert senior Labour and trade union figures to military conscription. This may well suggest that Bevin's awareness of the relationship between the subjects developed with hindsight and particularly with Attlee's assault on the Middle East strategy.

Although it was apparent that the post-war regular army would be insufficient to meet expected post-war commitments, the General Staff did not provide the Cabinet with an analysis of the manpower consequences of their planning. However, one estimate was that the forces envisaged in APW (45) 4 would require 847,000 embodied troops and 1,050,000 reserves.[28] The APW

[25] Bevin to Attlee, 15 Aug. 1947, PREM 8/833.
[26] Brooke Diaries, 5 Apr. 1946, Alanbrooke Papers, 5/12. Later he recognized that withdrawal was unavoidable: see Diaries, 5 Apr. 1946, 3/B/XVIII.
[27] DO (47) 23, 7 Mar. 1947, CAB 131/4.
[28] Lt.-Col. Mocatta to Lt.-Col. Norman, 23 Mar. 1945, DEFE 7/146.

Committee was not given these extraordinary figures which demonstrated the economic and political vacuum in which the War
Office was thinking. Instead, Grigg gave details of what the army
could expect from regular recruiting and one year's compulsory
service: some 408,000 troops.[29]

Even for a government committed to the preservation of a
Middle East strategy it should have been evident that the War
Office was planning forces on a scale unprecedented in peacetime.
All three service departments wanted a decision on the long-term
question. While they recognized that the 'ultimate case for conscription' rested on the 'final assessment of our strategic requirements' it would not be possible to postpone planning until that
time. In any case 'inescapable commitments' in peacetime could
not be provided for by regular recruiting alone. However, for the
government to have taken a decision which begged so many
questions about the size and nature of the forces involved, and
with no idea of how much they would cost, would have bordered
on folly. That is not to suggest that conscription in itself determined either the size of the forces or the strategy for which they
were designed. Nevertheless, given the assumption of a universal
scheme the scale of the forces involved would be greater than ever
before envisaged in peacetime.

The Treasury was not asked to submit a paper to the APW
Committee. When the issue of conscription was examined by the
Attlee government it was similarly excluded from the working
party which designed the National Service scheme. In part this
reflected the division of responsibilities on financial and economic
issues. In the case of conscription it was the Board of Trade and
the Ministry of Labour that were responsible for the manpower
needs of industry. In 1946 the Board of Trade was the services'
main opponent on conscription. The Treasury was responsible for
expenditure and in the ensuing years under both Dalton and
Cripps was engaged in long-running battles with the service
departments over the defence estimates.

Although the War Office emphasized that its projections were
based on tentative assumptions, and although a whole series of critical decisions on defence and equipment priorities lay ahead, it is
evident that the cost of the forces contemplated was economically

[29] APW (45) 7th, 22 Mar. 1945, CAB 87/69.

and politically prohibitive. When the Chiefs of Staff's designs were costed in 1947 ultimate defence expenditure was estimated at £1,200 million per annum, including atomic energy and excluding civil defence.

The early discussion of conscription ought to have brought home to ministers the scale of the defence burden. A provisional estimate by the Treasury would have shown that the forces envisaged were well beyond what the country could afford. At this time the Treasury was thinking of an eventual annual defence expenditure of some £500–550 million.[30] By 1946–7 this had risen to £600 million. By 1947–8 it was desperately trying to keep it down to £700 million, though without success. From the military point of view these figures were wholly arbitrary and not based on a considered appreciation of what was needed.

There was one economic perspective which held that high defence expenditure was not necessarily a bad thing. Eady's view about the dangers of trying to appear strong has been noted. Yet, on the other hand, the new Keynesian belief in public expenditure suggested that 'within reason anything is possible financially in the way of domestic expenditure'.[31] Keynes believed that 'defence expenditure might prove one of the methods of reaching full employment and thereby partly at least pay for itself as compared with other alternatives, at least in the short run'. For a Labour government committed to massive social and economic reform those other alternatives were inherently preferable. Moreover, this argument took no account of the industrial consequences of the loss of productive manpower, which was one of the crucial economic problems in the early years of reconstruction. However, Keynes, in keeping with the rest of the Treasury, was well aware of the need to distinguish between expenditure at home and expenditure overseas. The latter was recognized as the real burden of defence spending as it exacerbated the balance of payments problem.

The conversion of the Treasury to Keynesian thinking may well have played some part in a reluctance to press the economic opposition to conscription. Pre-war experience of the role of the Treasury in defence policy decision-making might also have

---

[30] Eady to Barlow, Mar. 1945, T. 247/71. Attlee later described this figure as no more than guesswork: CM (47) 13, 28 Jan. 1947, CAB 128/9.

[31] Keynes to Sir Edward Bridges, 3 Mar. 1945, T. 247/71.

contributed to its reluctance to become embroiled in issues which were not seen as primarily economic. Despite his own pre-war involvement in defence in the Labour Party, Dalton was keen to keep the Treasury out of inter-service battles.[32]

Sir John Anderson, Chancellor of the Exchequer in the Coalition government, was aware of the need to plan the post-war economy within the country's means and had already made this plain to his colleagues. However, although he recognized that the financial implications had yet to be examined, he suggested that there were two principles on which the need for conscription should be judged.[33] One of these was Britain's inescapable defence commitments. The other was 'social justice'. If conscription was required then it should be applied to everyone, and indeed he argued that compulsory training for women deserved full consideration.

Anderson's views are interesting for two reasons. The notion of universal service was to remain one of the crucial characteristics of the British system of military conscription. Anderson's argument was important as it shows that the view of universal liability as a political prerequisite for peacetime conscription was not confined to the Labour Party. When the Labour government came to consider National Service, universal liability was considered essential. The guarantee of equal treatment was regarded as vital to secure and maintain the support of the Labour movement and of public opinion in general. The inherent egalitarianism of Labour's position was clearly shared by people outside the party. It was one of the principles on which the demobilization scheme was based, and indeed reflected a major feature of the post-war consensus on a wider range of social issues.

Second, Anderson's arguments indicate that the Treasury did not see a scheme of selective service as offering a practical political option for reducing the size and the financial cost of the conscript intake. That position did not alter when Dalton became Chancellor. It was only after Cripps took over, when economic conditions had deteriorated, that there was any significant Treasury support for a reassessment of the principle of universality.

At no point in the discussions of spring 1945 was the question asked: 'How much is conscription going to cost?' For the Chiefs

[32] CM (46) 82, 17 Sept. 1946, CAB 128/6. For an account of the pre-war Treasury role, see G. G. Peden, *British Rearmament and the Treasury 1932–1939* (Scottish Academic Press, 1979).   [33] APW (45) 7th, 22 Mar. 1945, CAB 87/69.

of Staff and the service departments the framing of that question
would have been misleading. When estimates were made they
should be based on what the armed forces were expected to do.
The scale of the defence effort should be shaped by the commitments and functions that the services were to perform, not
by the money available. This underestimated the bearing of the
system of manpower provision on both the size and the cost of
the services. Yet in 1945 it did reflect the fact that crucial decisions
had yet to be taken—for example on the size and nature of the
conscript intake, and on how much conscripts should be paid.
While it is true that conscription did not determine the size or cost
of the forces, the principle of universal military service went a
considerable way towards shaping the manpower of the services.
There was no attempt to compare and contrast regular and
conscript forces—in Whitehall it was assumed from the outset that
the former would be insufficient. Nor was there any attempt to
estimate the economic cost of the loss of manpower. When this
was considered in 1946 it led to conflict within government on the
length of National Service.

On 20 April Churchill and the War Cabinet accepted Attlee's
view. Despite opposition from Sinclair, Bevin succeeded in
getting the announcement of the decision on the continuation of
the call-up for the next few years delayed until the Labour Party
was consulted. Churchill had wanted an early decision on both the
short- and the long-term questions. Yet he still entertained hopes
of keeping at least some members of the Labour Party in his
government. Perhaps he also remembered his personal attacks on
Chamberlain for having failed to consult with the Labour Party in
1939.[34] He agreed to Bevin's proviso and declared himself gratified
that agreement should have been reached on the principle of
conscription—a disingenuous remark given that the decision on
permanent conscription had yet to be taken.

Given the Labour Party's past, persuading it to accept military
conscription was not going to be easy. The task fell to Bevin as
Attlee was in San Francisco at the negotiations over the United
Nations charter. On 9 May, the morning on which victory in
Europe was saluted, the key sections of the Labour movement
were assembled to discuss in strictest confidence the continuation

[34] *HC deb.*, vol. 346, 27 Apr. 1939, cols. 1370–1.

of compulsory military service after the war.[35] It was through this joint meeting of the General Council of the Trades Union Congress (TUC), the Labour Party's National Executive Committee (NEC), and the Administrative Committee of the Parliamentary Labour Party that Bevin gained the support of the crucial elements of the labour movement.

Bevin argued that it was the tentative conclusion of the Coalition government that, until the form of the world organization was known, it would be necessary to retain military conscription modified in the light of peacetime conditions. He said that it was a terrible state of affairs for the army to have to depend upon unemployment as its chief recruiting agency.[36] Given that Labour was committed to full employment, the number of men wanting to make it their career would be very limited and inadequate. If social services were to be made universal and if there were to be full employment there arose, so he said, the question of whether defence should also become a social obligation. Moreover, international collective security could not be made effective unless each nation had its quota of power put into a pool to stop any aggressor. He believed that as the navy and the RAF were unable to defend against the German V1 and V2 rockets, until scientists found ways of attacking countries other than by means of invasion the army was the only 'insurance premium'. Conscription was also necessary to relieve the burden on those already in the forces.

These were the various arguments that formed the major part of the case for conscription in the ensuing debates, though subsequently the army and the government drew a more precise distinction between embodied forces required to fulfil existing commitments and the provision of trained reserves ready for expansion on the outbreak of war. Bevin's emphasis was significant. The stress on armed collective security was a dominant theme in the case to the party. That would obviously strike a less discordant note than the idea of policing the Empire. The issues of armed collective security and the provision of a large

[35] Minutes of meeting in 'National Service 1947–59', unsorted defence papers, Labour Party archives.
[36] The link between unemployment and regular recruiting was widely accepted, although the evidence was not so clear. See the report of the Advisory Committee on Recruiting, Cmnd. 545 (HMSO, 1958).

army were nevertheless separate. Noel-Baker, for example, firmly backed the former but in early 1945 argued that Britain's contribution should be provided by air and naval forces.

The argument about the V1 and V2 is more curious. At an earlier meeting Bevin had said that if the Russians were on the Oder in the future they might be able to fire rockets at Britain from that distance. 'These are not good thoughts', Dalton reflected in his diary.[37] The claim that an army was the only defence against long-range missile attack clearly implied the stationing of significant land forces on the continent that would presumably have to carry the attack to the Soviet Union. On 9 May this question was not addressed expicitly; Bevin did not mention the Oder or indeed the defence of Western Europe.

This was a peculiarly abstract argument which drew upon selective military and technical experience. The implications had not been thought out and certainly not discussed. It was not until 1949 that the Chiefs of Staff even began to consider the defence of Western Europe as a priority for the defence of the United Kingdom. If Western Europe were overrun then the principal threat would come from medium-range bombers rather than from missiles.[38] As will be seen, Bevin himself was reluctant to guarantee to send British divisions in the event of a Soviet attack. Yet in 1945 the justification of conscription to prevent long-range bombardment could mean nothing other than an army on, or east of, the Rhine.

This was an argument propounded with London's recent experiences in mind. Bevin conflated fundamental questions about British security and subsumed them under an emotional and misleading idea in order to persuade a Labour Party audience who would have shared the emotional reaction but understood little of the wider issues.

Bevin was primarily concerned with the short-term continuation of the call-up although he expressly wanted this to be effected under the auspices of a new National Service Act. Indeed, he stated that he would not be a party to putting the country under long-term National Service. This was in contradiction to what he had already said in the APW Committee and would go on

[37] Dalton Diaries, 11 Apr. 1945.
[38] COS (50) 316, 14 Mar. 1950, discussed at COS (50) 43rd, 16 Mar. 1950, DEFE 4/29.

to say as Foreign Secretary. It clearly raised many questions about the nature of the post-war world. Yet throughout this and subsequent debates, he and his colleagues were to emphasize the temporary nature of the measures. The duration of National Service was clearly problematic and for many in the meeting the crucial concern. Noel-Baker stated that the transitional period would be some two or three years and supported it on that basis. Bevin described this as optimistic.

Yet despite his stated hostility to permanent conscription, to a large extent Bevin put forward the case for a much longer, indeed indefinite, period. Whatever the uncertain conditions of international affairs in the next few years, the provision of troops for world security was a long-term requirement. Discussion of armed collective security was approached differently in the Labour Party than in the military. The latter did not see a world security organization as an alternative to British strategy. Provision of forces for the United Nations (UN) organization was seen as a possible additional commitment which would not displace the British strategic role in the Middle East, for example. This was at variance with pre- and post-war Labour sentiment which perceived a dichotomy between collective security and the pursuit of a balance of power and an imperial role. Attlee in particular attached great importance to the UN. Indicative of how other Labour leaders had discarded the traditional Labour perspective on international relations was Morrison's view. Although he was primarily concerned with the provision of the necessary forces for the military occupation of Germany, he chose to make the point in the bluntest terms of power politics. He argued that 'the rise and fall of Great Britain in foreign affairs would be according to . . . military power . . . Diplomacy is weakened if a nation is unable to make material contribution on the land on the sea and in the air.'[39]

Bevin might have said this himself. Yet he was concerned to make the pill as palatable as possible. It is interesting, in the light of subsequent events, that he said that it was his personal view that men would have to give one years' service with five years' reserve liability. This was in spite of his knowledge of the previous discussions and the War Office's belief that eighteen months' to two years' service was necessary.

[39] 'National Service 1947–59'.

With traditional union concerns in view, he assured the meeting that it was possible to have compulsory military service without industrial conscription and the compulsory direction of labour (which indeed he himself had introduced during the war). War-time provisions in the industrial field would have to go. The Labour MP Ellis Smith clearly spoke for many when he declared that he 'had no hesitation in saying that he would support the continuation of National Service provided that there were adequate industrial safeguards'.

Despite assurances on this, and despite guarantees on conscientious objectors and on the universality of the scheme, Bevin nevertheless made clear his resolve. In forthright fashion he told the meeting that 'if the General Council and the Executive of the Labour Party did not agree with the principle, he was afraid the government would have to go on with the matter and if a Labour Government were in power that is what they would have to do'. He wanted the Coalition to announce a decision and hence remove it from the realm of party politics and avoid labelling Labour as the party of conscription. As Bevin was well aware, a quick decision by the 'Three Bodies' would effectively circumscribe the issue within the movement, and the party conference later that month would be presented with what amounted to a *fait accompli*.

As the meeting had been called in strictest confidence there were no formal prior consultations. Not surprisingly, a number of those present wanted time to consult the movement. Despite this feeling, and the claim of some that even the short-term continuation of the call-up represented a fundamental reversal of party policy, Bevin succeeded in winning the meeting's support. Nevertheless, Noel-Baker made it clear that while he accepted that Bevin's arguments were conclusive for the continuation over the transitional period, he was not satisfied that conscription was the best contribution that could be made to an eventual system of collective security.

The opposition came from Bevan, Shinwell, and Greenwood (the acting leader of the PLP) and two of the trade unionists— Dukes (of the General and Municipal Workers) and Hallsworth (of the Distributive and Allied Workers). None of them was a member of the government. They argued that a decision was not possible until they had more information and/or had consulted the party. Of these Bevan, Shinwell, and Dukes spoke against conscription. Bevan argued on principle, on both the short- and the long-term questions. He accepted that it should continue until the end of the war against Japan but said that it would be a grave mistake to prolong it after then. Organized strength was no substitute for a wise international policy. If the labour movement agreed to the principle of conscription it would, he claimed, be making a present to the Conservative Party at the election. At this stage Bevan was more strongly opposed than many on the left of the party who, like the Liberals, accepted the short-term continuation but rejected anything more. Bevan's declared position was to change in government. At this stage it is clear that he was unaware of the relationship between the continuation of the call-up and the equal treatment of men waiting to be demobilized under the 'age and service' scheme (see Appendix 2).

Shinwell did not unequivocally oppose conscription, but the tenor of his argument was clear. He drew attention to the 'central manpower issue' and pointed to the weaker position of Britain in relation to the Soviet Union and the United States, with which he believed Britain would be engaged in a 'competitive peace'. This would necessitate raising the productive capacity of the country to the maximum. While he accepted that National Service should apply until the end of the Japanese war, and for some time afterwards in order to get the men home from the Far East, he warned that if it were accepted without limit there would be serious opposition in the ranks of the Labour movement. He described the considerable resentment and hostility aroused in Canada over the issue during the war[40]—a weak argument as the problems there were rooted in cultural divisions which did not exist in the United Kingdom, except in Northern Ireland. It did not always follow, Shinwell argued, that 'a conscripted country was a successful one', and he claimed that conscription could not be imposed in Great Britain with any success unless it was simultaneously imposed in the Dominions.

Despite these doubts Bevin succeeded in securing the support of the NEC and the TUC. The latter laid down conditions, and spelled out the reasons, for their acceptance. They agreed in principle the need for a revised National Service Act to operate for a

---

[40] For an account of this see R. V. Dawson, *The Conscription Crisis of 1944* (Toronto: University of Toronto Press, 1961).

limited period for the purposes 'of giving undertakings for the
fullest co-operation of Britain in a system of collective security;
assisting in the problem of demobilisation; and in the guidance of
industry in post-war planning'. The last point referred to the requirements of industrial and educational planning. Assurances on
'industrial implications' (the conscription and direction of labour)
were among the guarantees that the unions required before they
would approve the continuation of compulsory military service
after the end of the Japanese war. The other guarantees were a
revision of the Royal Warrant, the democratization of the armed
forces, and assurances on the precise period and commitments of
military service.

Bevin had thus secured agreement on the short-term continuation of conscription. This, so he told Dalton, was all that he
wanted;[41] and he had stated his opposition to a permanent scheme.
Yet many of his arguments could be used for the long-term case.
Indeed, his claims about vulnerability to rocket attack only made
sense in the context of a long-term commitment. Whatever he
told his colleagues in the labour movement, he himself was in
favour of conscription as a long-term policy. Yet, as he was well
aware, feeling in the party could not be moved quickly.

It is clear that Bevin no longer shared the feeling that conscription was an evil, necessary or otherwise. As already noted, he had
told the APW Committee of his personal opinion of the reciprocal
duties of citizenship that full employment and social security
entailed—domestic policies of the Coalition government, not of
the Labour Party.

Moreover, unless the post-war world were sufficiently devoid
of armed threat, arguments about collective security and British
commitments were effectively arguments for permanent conscription, even before it became necessary to plan for a major war
against the Soviet Union. To some extent the question could
be reduced to how long 'transitional' was. Yet whatever the
distinctions between the various commitments—the occupational
(Germany, Austria, Japan, and Venezia Guilia), the terminable
(Greece, Palestine, and India), and the seemingly perpetual (the
Middle East and the Imperial garrisons)—a number of things were
evident. It was clear that, as it had done after the Great War,

---

[41] Dalton Diaries, 9 May 1945.

Britain was expanding its obligations while its industrial and economic base was (and would become even more) precarious. It was
also clear that the perspective from which some of the key Labour
leaders viewed those international obligations was only partially
congruent with pre-war socialist conceptions of foreign policy and
the role of military force in international affairs.[42] This transformation was to have serious implications for the Labour Party
and indeed profound implications for the post-war international
settlement as a whole.

By gaining the support of the key sections of the Labour Party
the government defused effective, immediate political opposition.
Yet feeling in the party was discernible. The subject was not
specifically debated at the May 1945 conference, reflecting both
the pre-election concern with unity and the fact that conscription
had yet to emerge as an issue within the party. Traditional party
sentiment was nevertheless in evidence and found a voice in the
backbench MP Frederick Bellenger.[43] While accepting that the
short-term continuation of National Service was necessary, he
warned the platform that as a long-term policy conscription was
not tolerable to the Labour Party and especially not to the unions.
It would result in the lowering of wage standards and labour
conditions in industry. Moreover, he argued, 'conscript military
forces foster total war and total war will lead to total destruction
both spiritual and physical'. This is particularly ironic as Bellenger
went on to become the Secretary of State for War, departmentally
responsible for the 1947 National Service Act and the introduction
of peacetime military conscription. It is therefore interesting to
note that two of the men who were subsequently in charge
of the War Office (the other being Shinwell) were opposed to
National Service at this time.

An even more implacable opponent of conscription who spoke
at the 1945 conference was Rhys Davies. This former conscientious objector and committed pacifist was to play a part in
the opposition to conscription in 1946, 1947, and indeed whenever
the issue arose. In 1945 he argued that unless it was abandoned
after the end of the Japanese war, Britain would have 'embraced
the Nazi philosophy in industry, the very philosophy against

---

[42] For an analysis of this see M. R. Gordon, *Conflict and Consensus in Labour's
Foreign Policy 1914–65* (Stanford: Stanford University Press, 1969).
[43] Labour Party Conference Report, 23 May 1945, 113.

which we set out to fight'[44]—a vitriolic hyperbole reminiscent of
Labour attacks on Chamberlain in 1939. He reminded delegates of
the wartime industrial courts which had prosecuted 'thousands
of working class people' of whom some three thousand had been
sent to prison.[45]

Bevin, in reply, set about convincing the party of the need for
conscription, outlining some of his previous arguments. Again he
emphasized collective security: 'In our foreign policy we stand . . .
for collective security. Collective security involves commitments
and I do beg Labour not to bury its head in the sand. It is no use
talking about an international police force unless you supply
policemen and decide the means by which you will supply them.'
This of course was a far more harmonious chord to strike than
that of backing British diplomacy with military force. It was at
least in accord with the party's pre-war rhetoric and reflected and
reinforced the hopes and aspirations of the party with regard to
the UN.

He was also keen to emphasize that before the war the voluntary method of recruiting had been dependent upon unemployment. As there would now be conditions of full employment, that
method would no longer be adequate. In addition, conscription
would need to be continued until those who had been doing the
fighting had been brought home. This argument was central to
the short-term policy and was accepted by many who were
opposed to the long-term policy.

On the other hand, Bevin stressed the changes required in the
conditions of military service. He argued that the present act left
the state power to impose an unlimited liability on the citizen.
This would be ended at 'a very early stage' by an act limiting that
period. He promised to 'tear up the Royal Warrant' and prepare
afresh proper and adequate rates of pay. The scheme would be
universal, without the industrial deferments and exemptions that
wartime industrial demands had required. In reply to Rhys Davies
he stated that industrial conscription would have to go.

Since Bevin had already got the unions on his side it was inevitable that the conference would support the platform. The result
was that in the 1945 election both parties agreed that conscription

[44] Ibid.
[45] For an account of conscientious objectors in the Second World War see Rachel
Barker, *Conscience, Government and War* (Routledge & Kegan Paul, 1982).

should continue until the end of the Japanese war and until the world security organization had been established. Not surprisingly, conscription was not an election issue. Only 10 per cent of Conservative candidates and 1 per cent of their Labour counterparts mentioned it in their election addresses.[46] The Labour manifesto, *Let Us Face the Future*, gave no indication of support for a long-term scheme. When that was subsequently introduced, opponents were able to argue that the government lacked a mandate.[47] This was a potentially sore point as the same charge had been levelled by Labour at Chamberlain in 1939.

It was hardly surprising that opposition to conscription immediately after the war was limited even within the labour movement, and even more so when Labour won the election. A whole range of short-term government powers were retained, from rationing to the direction of labour. Many of these were inherently unpopular, although some measures, such as food rationing, were seen as the fairest means of distributing vital resources in conditions of scarcity. The principle of equal treatment had been the basis on which such policies had been pursued during the war, with Labour ministers playing a crucial role in its establishment. In the post-war period the social philosophy of Attlee's government was firmly rooted in that idea. Equality of treatment was to form the basis of both the demobilization scheme and the system of compulsory military service adopted by the Labour government.

Thus, while conscription touched raw nerves in the labour movement, it was but one of a package of controls and privations which were the unavoidable consequences of the transition from total war to peacetime conditions. There is little reason to believe that conscription was especially unpopular. Indeed, there is evidence that both parties overestimated the extent to which public opinion was opposed to permanent conscription. The indications are that public opinion tended to follow the parties. W. P. Snyder argues that it was 'transient and sensitive to pronouncements by national leaders'.[48] In September 1945 65 per cent approved of one year's conscription for all young men, while 27 per cent

[46] R. B. McCallum and A. Readman, *The British General Election of 1945* (Frank Cass, 1947), 98.
[47] Victor Yates, *HC deb.*, vol. 430, 12 Nov. 1946, col. 600.
[48] W. P. Snyder, *The Politics of British Defense Policy 1945–62* (Columbus, Ohio: Ohio State University Press, 1964), 54–6.

disapproved.[49] By March 1946 55 per cent approved of compulsory military service in peacetime and 38 per cent disapproved—the highest figure for those against conscription in the period 1945–51. In April 1947 58 per cent thought National Service was necessary at the present time; 29 per cent thought it unnecessary. By January 1949 57 per cent believed conscription should be continued and 33 per cent felt it should not; 60 per cent disapproved of a longer period of service while only 28 per cent approved, an indication of the way public opinion tended to accept the *status quo*. One interesting question is to what extent popular opposition would have been higher if there had not been a bipartisan political approach to the issue. Equally intriguing is the question of whether the principle of universality could have been abandoned without substantial popular opposition.

It is unquestionable that Churchill would have proceeded with the continuation of National Service in the immediate post-war period if he had been re-elected. The question of whether or not permanent conscription would have been necessary requires consideration of the likely development of foreign policy. This in turn raises enormous questions about the development of international affairs and the Cold War, which are far beyond the scope of this study. There is no reason to believe that a Conservative government would have produced a dramatic improvement in relations with the Soviet Union or that Imperial strategy would have been so altered as radically to reduce the need for armed forces. In the APW Committee Eden and Amery had seen conscription explicitly in terms of a continental commitment. A solution to the political and military problem of Germany might have allowed for a significant reduction in troops needed there in peacetime. Whether that solution would have removed the perceived need for an army designed to fight in the early stages of a major war is less clear. Although the early reflections of Eden and Amery might have changed in a different international environment, it is worth noting that Eden's thinking was not simply concerned with an effective military defence against a full-scale Soviet attack on Western Europe. It was deeply rooted in the view of military force as an indispensable element in the conduct

---

[49] G. H. Gallup, ed., *Gallup International Public Opinion Polls: Great Britain 1937–75*, i (New York: Random House, 1976).

of foreign policy. Happier relations with Stalin would not have altered that. Nor, indeed, would the military have abandoned its concern with the worst-case view of the long-term Soviet threat. A very radical change in the outlook of the British government would have been necessary.

If these generalizations were true of Europe, they were even more true of the Middle East. It is extremely difficult to imagine Churchill or his colleagues contemplating withdrawal from that arena. Even allowing for a more successful outcome in Palestine, British requirements in peace and the early stages of a war were considerable. Without a major readjustment of those requirements, conscription was a numerical imperative. As far as the services were concerned, whereas they were not in agreement over the continental commitment, they were united on the need for Britain to preserve its position in the Middle East. This attitude would not have changed simply because the Conservatives were in power.

Furthermore, Churchill's reluctance to relinquish India would have had serious consequences for army manpower. Whatever the conceivable long-term benefits to be drawn from the use of Indian troops as a strategic reserve, in the short term it would have meant keeping a substantial number of troops in the country. Amery and the Indian Office had said that at least 40,000–50,000 would be required for some time, and this took little account of how a British declaration to remain in India would have affected internal political stability with obvious implications for the size of the Imperial garrison.

Churchill balanced a professed reticence in criticizing Attlee's security policy with the happy opportunism of opposition politics. Yet it is significant that while he attempted to make political capital out of the demobilization scheme (which he had approved in office) he remained resolutely committed to the principle of conscription even when it was becoming unpopular in circles outside the Labour and Liberal parties in later years. Although opposition parties can gain some political advantage in being seen to support an unpopular government policy, Churchill's commitment appears to have been based on genuine support for the principle of National Service. There were in any case sufficient specific targets for him to attack, not least the government's handling of the National Service Act and the dramatic change of policy over

the length of service. This provided ample opportunity for the
expression of doubts about Labour's credibility and competence.
Churchill remained committed to the longer period of service
or indeed to whatever the government decided on the advice of
the Chiefs of Staff. There were occasional ambiguities in the
opposition's view of selective service which grew as time went
on. In their 1950 election manifesto *This is the Right Road*, the
Conservatives suggested that 'by wise arrangements it would
be possible to reduce the burden of conscription'. Churchill did
recommend fewer men for a longer period, though he stopped
short of a commitment to introduce a ballot. The principle of
universal liability nevertheless remained a bipartisan commitment.

In 1949 the government had confidential talks with the opposition.[50] Churchill, critical of the effects of National Service on the
army, wanted to reduce the numbers of men called up drastically.
He drew attention to other nations' use of a ballot and was clearly
attracted to the idea. Yet this was not translated into a public
commitment. The bipartisan approach certainly did not entail a
blank cheque for the government's defence policy. There were the
inevitable opposition claims of 'we can do better' on military
manpower efficiency, and a furious attack on the government for
the condition of the forces. In December 1948 Churchill was to
claim that 'there has never been a time when a more complete gulf
has existed between the two parties so far as national questions
common to us all are concerned'.[51]

However, Churchill remained committed to National Service
and it is clear that he and Attlee manœuvred their parties to facilitate and maintain a bipartisan approach. Chamberlain's reluctance
to introduce conscription in 1938–9 was largely based on Labour's
attitude and his need to secure the support of the unions for the
rearmament drive. When Labour went into opposition after 1951
the party adjusted its position to maintain the appearance of
responsibility while attempting to gain political advantage by
advocating a review of the period of service. Both parties were
anxious not to be trapped by the other party's abandonment of
conscription into supporting an electorally unpopular policy alone.
Despite Bevin's belief that a new National Service Act would

[50] See Gen 293 series, CAB 130/147.
[51] *HC deb.*, vol. 458, 1 Dec. 1948, col. 2031.

be an 'absolutely essential' priority for a Labour government it did not happen immediately, partly because of the massive legislative programme but largely because a new act required fuller consideration of the long-term issues. In keeping with Bevin's assurances, the more significant wartime industrial restrictions were gradually removed, although in the wake of the 1947 convertibility crisis powers for the control of labour were re-introduced. As far as military conscription was concerned the wartime legislation, amended and renewed, was to form the basis for the continuation of the call-up until the end of 1948. When the Coalition government broke up in May 1945 ministerial consideration of permanent conscription lapsed. Meanwhile the Chiefs of Staff, initially through the Post Hostilities Planning Staff and then through the Joint Planning Staff (JPS), began the task of shaping the long-term strategy of Britain's armed forces. Agreement on that strategy would take several years. Agreement on a strategy that was financially feasible and politically acceptable became the Holy Grail of post-war British defence policy. The decision on National Service was to predate these agreements. Therein lay one of the problems for the formulation of defence policy, the defence budget, and the system of National Service in the post-war period.

3

The Continuation of the Call-up 1947–1948

THE Attlee administration faced a massive burden of social and industrial reform. The government had to organize the transition from total war to peacetime conditions and at the same time tackle the short- and long-term problems of the size and shape of the armed forces. It was also committed to reorganizing the machinery for higher defence policy, including the creation of a new Ministry of Defence (MOD). The long-term issues of defence policy would have to be addressed with great energy and imagination if Britain's military and political roles were to be founded on a secure economic and industrial base.

As the Chiefs of Staff's review of Imperial strategy would not be completed for some time, the government was wise to avoid a decision on the issue of permanent conscription. However, it was more than apparent that the scale of commitments would require significantly larger forces in the immediate post-war period than could possibly be provided by regular engagements. In early 1946 the occupation of Germany alone accounted for over 200,000 men and another 60,000 were needed in Austria.[1] On 1 April 1947 British military personnel garrisons overseas totalled 476,000, including 72,000 in Palestine, 58,000 in India, and 100,000 in Germany.[2] A continuation of the call-up was unavoidable unless the government was prepared to abandon those tasks. In the early years after the war that was simply unthinkable.

One reason for the continuation of the call-up was the government's pledge on releases. Men would be released from the forces at the same time irrespective of whether they served at home or abroad. By early 1946 there was ministerial agreement that conscription would have to continue in the immediate future. Exactly how long it would be needed was not clear. Nor was

[1] DO (46) 1st, 11 Jan. 1946, CAB 131/1.
[2] Sir Harold Parker (Permanent Secretary, MOD), brief for Prime Minister for debate on National Service, 30 Nov. 1948, DEFE 7/506.

it evident how long the conscripts would have to serve when called up. Also, the issues of industrial and educational deferments and exemptions were raised as industry and society embarked on reconstruction.

The winter of 1945–6 had seen the first battles over the defence budget and the size of the forces. The initial requirements of the Chiefs of Staff were re-examined and cuts in manpower and defence spending imposed. In the face of union pressure in December 1945 the Cabinet decided to speed up the rate of demobilization.[3] These were the first of many reductions that the services would have to accept in post-war planning. Of much greater potential significance was the attempt by Attlee, begun in early 1946, to redirect British strategy away from the Middle East. One motive for Attlee's behaviour was economic, and Dalton was already warning his colleagues of economic disaster if the scale of the defence effort were not significantly reduced.[4]

The question of the continuation of the call-up was first considered by the Cabinet Manpower Committee, which was chaired by Bevin, the architect of the wartime scheme of conscription. In 1946 it was agreed that men would be called up under wartime National Service legislation; there would be no new act, despite Bevin's promise to the Labour party conference. As the policy was a continuation of existing procedures (though with important modifications) a number of issues pertaining to permanent conscription (e.g. reserve liability) did not require consideration. However, a number of crucial issues were raised, including the enormous scale of the service requirements. The continuation of the call-up was therefore a rehearsal, though not a dress rehearsal, for the decision on permanent conscription.

The discussions within government demonstrated the enormous problems facing the government in reconciling its domestic and foreign policy objectives. The Chiefs of Staff estimated that over a million servicemen would be needed for some considerable time, and it was immediately apparent that a lengthy period of service would be necessary for those called up under the transitional scheme. Subsequently, the issue of length of service was to emerge as the main focus of conflict over the National Service Act.

---

[3] CM (45) 58, 3 Dec. 1945, CAB 128/2.
[4] DO (46) 1st, 11 Jan. 1946, CAB 131/1.

After discussion in the Manpower Committee, in March 1946
Bevin forwarded a paper to Cabinet for a decision on the transitional scheme in May. This was quickly published as a White
Paper. The debate within government focused on two main issues:
the length of military service and the question of whether
apprentices and/or students should be allowed to defer their call-
up. To determine the length of service three proposals were put to
ministers, known as schemes A, B, and C. (see Appendix to this
chapter; Table 1). These involved different periods of service for
the various groups of registrations. All three were designed to
reduce the period of service below two years for those conscripted
by the end of 1949. In the light of subsequent events it is worth
noting Bevin's comment:

the period covered by the tables i.e. up to 1951 will be a period during
which abnormal commitments will persist (They will probably continue
beyond 1951). In particular, there will, throughout this period, be occupational forces in enemy territory. If this is so, it would be out of the
question to reduce the period of service below eighteen months. Regular
strength will not have been completely built up even by the end of this
period and if service were reduced to one year, none of the conscripts
would be used abroad. The Service Ministers consider that it will be hard
enough during this period to manage on a period of one and a half years.[5]

Initially Scheme A meant three years' service, Scheme B two and
a half years, and Scheme C two years. The main issues raised were
the size of the armed forces and the period of service/rate of
demobilization of those already in the armed forces. The implications of the three schemes for the size of the forces are shown
in Table 3A. 2 in the Appendix to this chapter.
    For the government the proposals raised problems which they
were also to face on the issue of long-term conscription. Three
principal needs had to be met: first, military manpower requirements for the pursuit of foreign policy and unavoidable post-war
commitments; second, the civilian sector's need for productive
manpower, particularly in manufacturing industry, and for the
export-led growth that was a central economic objective of
the government; third, a period of military service which would
be politically acceptable. Balancing these divergent objectives was
to remain the central problem for the government, not only for the

[5] CP (46) 121, 22 Mar. 1946, CAB 129/8.

transitional period but even more acutely when the National Service Act was designed.

The Chiefs of Staff reacted unfavourably to the proposals. They explained in detail why they needed the manpower and immediately rejected the working party's claim that at least Scheme A would provide sufficient forces to meet military requirements.[6] It would 'have serious implications on all three services and in the case of the Army amount to inability to meet certain major commitments'. So serious were the implications that they did not even bother to consider Schemes B or C.

Even assuming that the forecast rate of regular recruiting was achieved, it was evident that the army in particular would be well short of its stated requirements. After the winter battles over defence manpower, the Defence Committee had reduced the target strength of the army to 650,000 (excluding trainees). In order to achieve this the government had to accept a series of implications spelt out by the Chiefs of Staff: the withdrawal of British forces from Italy, Venezia Guilia, and Greece by the end of December 1946, and the absence of any reserves to meet unforeseen demands.

Scheme A was based on the assumption that the 650,000 target would be reached and that there would be sharp reductions in the army in early 1947 and then during 1949–50. The strength of the army would fall to 389,000 by 1951 (when there would still be occupational commitments), compared with existing War Office assumptions of a final post-war army of 408,000. The Manpower Committee envisaged a regular strength of only 180,000 by 1951, compared with the long-term aim of 275,000. The Chiefs of Staff argued that the successful liquidation of the commitments in Italy, Venezia Guilia, and Greece was dependent largely on political issues and might not be possible in all cases. According to the service chiefs Scheme A meant further and quite dramatic reductions and withdrawals: the occupation forces from Austria, a division from the Middle East, most of the division from Southeast Asia, and at least half the occupation forces from Germany or all British troops from India. This would mean major changes in key areas of foreign policy.

Although the effects of Scheme A (and the other proposals) would fall most heavily on the army, the other services were also

[6] DO (46) 52, 11 Apr. 1946, CAB 131/2.

affected. The navy would remain at a strength of 194,000 for 1947 and 1948, but from then until 1951 reductions in the number of ships would be necessary. The Admiralty was confident of achieving its permanent strength of 144,000 by 1951. The consequences of the reductions were less dramatic than for the army. The fleet, and particularly the naval air arm (which accounted for about a third of the navy's manpower) would be reduced to a low level of efficiency and be inadequate in the latter part of the period as a basis of expansion in war. The Admiralty believed 'that it would be possible to maintain sufficient ships in commission to cover the purely policing duties of the navy, but there would be no margin for any deterioration in the general situation'.[7] Furthermore, the training programme would have to be restricted, particularly in 1949–50 when more ships would be paid off into the reserve. This would affect the build-up of a body of adequately trained long-service personnel.

The consequences for the RAF were not initially seen to be any more significant than the cuts imposed by the Defence Committee in January 1946. It was anticipated that at least until mid-1949, providing there was no marked deterioration in the general situation, the RAF would be able to discharge its peacetime policing functions with a strength of 305,000 (agreed in February). By making fullest use of its existing reserves it could also consider this level 'a reasonable basis for expansion for war'. However, from mid-1949 to 1951, with numbers falling to a minimum of 266,000 (in 1950) the front-line strength would become seriously depleted and the number of trained reserves would also fall. In the view of the Chiefs of Staff: 'The result may be a general inability to carry out essential policing duties and the force must moreover be considered quite inadequate as a basis for expansion in war.' As all the auxiliary units (such as the meteorological and Air/Sea Rescue squadrons) had been disbanded to get within the target of 305,000, failure to recruit and retain the required number of regulars (210,000 by 1951) would necessitate further cuts in the overall strength.

Preliminary discussion of the proposals and the views of the service chiefs took place in the Defence Committee on 15 April 1946. Alanbrooke explained that under Scheme A the release of all

[7] Ibid.

the men with three years' service within so short a period of time would denude the army of the large majority of its officers and NCOs. The central issue for the services was the shortage of some 134,000 men in the 'most critical period' of the first six months of 1947. He suggested that the government should spread the release of the men by extending the 'age and service' release scheme to cover all men already serving on 1 January 1947. The Defence Committee deferred a decision until after the Easter recess and further consideration by the Manpower Committee.

When the Defence Committee met again on 17 May it had before it a further memorandum from the Foreign Office which drew attention to the 'serious implications' for foreign policy of the future state of the armed forces under the proposed schemes. The memorandum repeated the Chiefs of Staff's warning about the consequences for the efficiency of all three services: the reduction of the army to below what was required and the inadequacy of the navy and the RAF during 1949–51 to provide an adequate basis for expansion in war.

Bevin spelled out the implications for foreign policy. Withdrawal from Venezia Guilia and other Italian commitments was likely to be affected by the forthcoming Paris conference; Bevin argued that, if no settlement on the Trieste question could be reached, it was essential not to withdraw for reasons of manpower at such an unpropitious time. Likewise, withdrawal from Greece should not take place in the unsettled international conditions prevailing so long as Soviet troops were in Bulgaria and a comparatively large Bulgarian army remained in being.

Bevin's approach to the use of military force as a foundation of foreign policy was clear. He argued that

our presence in the Mediterranean area serves a purpose which is vital to our position as a Great Power. Without our physical presence there, we should cut little ice with the remaining states in this area who have not fallen under the totalitarian yoke, and overhasty withdrawal might mean that we should lose our political position particularly in Greece, with repercussions upon other countries such as Turkey and Italy which we can ill afford at the present moment.[8]

The withdrawal of a division from the Middle East would weaken British influence, a development the Soviet Union would not be

[8] DO (46) 64, 7 May 1946, CAB 131/2.

slow to exploit. In addition, the Anglo-American Commission's report on Palestine had only recently been published and it was recognized that this might have significant repercussions for the Chiefs of Staff's estimates. While that report was under discussion the service chiefs and the Foreign Secretary were adamant that no withdrawal was possible. Moreover, the Chiefs of Staff warned that if the report of the Commission were accepted the scale of the ensuing disorder would be beyond the capacity of existing forces in the Middle East to control. They calculated that the necessary reinforcements would be some two divisions (one as a reserve), an armoured brigade, and three infantry battalions, together with air and naval contingents. These reinforcements would be at the expense of other commitments and would have to be maintained for a prolonged period. Hence, they believed, American aid would be essential.

Bevin was also concerned with the occupation forces in Germany and Austria. The Chiefs of Staff argued that if Scheme A went ahead, unless all British forces were withdrawn from India in early 1947 it would be necessary to reduce the troops in Germany by about a half. The War Office was considering some reduction in Germany—from 126,800 at the end of 1946 to 97,910 by June 1947. Bevin regarded the forces of occupation as necessary not only to carry out agreed measures of disarmament and demilitarization but also to prevent Germany falling under exclusive Soviet domination. Even the revised War Office estimate was contingent on 'a very considerable improvement in conditions in Germany', about which the Foreign Office was not optimistic. Bevin believed that 'unless we can maintain a sufficiency of strength in Austria until a reduction of the Russian forces has been achieved and the Yugoslavian threat has been removed we shall risk losing Austria to Russian influence'.

With an already overwhelming Soviet military predominance further reductions by the Western allies would weaken the West's political position to a dangerous degree. Bevin warned that

complete Russian domination of Austria would result in increased Russian pressure on Western Europe, both through the American zone of Germany and Czechoslovakia and through Italy. It would also bring the Soviet Union into direct physical contact with the French zone of Germany, so that France herself would be even more open to direct Russian influence. It would also complete the economic isolation of the Danube basin and the countries in Central and South East Europe since Vienna is a natural link for trade and communications between these countries and the West.

It was thus necessary to keep sufficient forces in Austria until the Russians made substantial reductions. Yet as he himself noted, existing plans assumed the withdrawal of all British troops by 30 June 1947, with no provision for re-occupation at the expense of other commitments.

In the light of these various considerations Bevin argued that the first requirement for a successful foreign policy was that the call-up scheme should produce a flexible manpower situation. He emphasized: 'We must not be put in a situation where we will be forced to give up commitments by mid-1947 or even at the end of the current year unless developments in foreign affairs permitted.' He concluded by urging the participation of the Dominions, which should be informed of the facts and 'called upon to play a part commensurate with their population and their resources in bearing the burden for these commitments'.

Bevin's arguments about the need for military forces in the various countries and regions were not challenged by his colleagues. In the Defence Committee there was no attempt to criticize his 'domino theory' of Soviet influence spreading through the French zone of Germany if the military balance around Austria were radically altered. Moreover, when the Cabinet discussed the proposals for the call-up scheme on 20 and 27 May they were not even provided with the foreign policy assumptions on which the estimates were based. The absence of a Cabinet committee on foreign affairs and the limited information available to ministers strengthened the hand of the Foreign Office, at least where Attlee and Bevin were in agreement.

Yet the conclusions of the service chiefs and the Foreign Secretary did not go entirely unchallenged, as the economic costs of the defence burden were considerable. In a brief for the Prime Minister, his economic adviser Douglas Jay pointed out that if the calculations of the Chiefs of Staff, the Board of Trade, and the Ministry of Supply were all correct in their examination of Scheme A then 'it would follow that the United Kingdom cannot carry out its military commitments and achieve economic recovery and independence'.[9]

[9] Jay to Attlee, 13 Apr. 1946, PREM 8/609.

As noted, the Chiefs of Staff and the Foreign Secretary had put forward a strong case which had not been criticized on its own terms. And they had attempted to remove Schemes B and C (the two-and-a-half- and two-year length of service proposals) from ministerial consideration. The economic side of the argument was put by the Board of Trade. Discussion focused on the length of service, the commitments of the armed forces, and the issue of whether apprentices and students should be allowed to defer service.

The Board of Trade concentrated its support on Scheme A. The economic arguments were put to Cabinet in a paper by Morrison (Cripps, the President of the Board of Trade, was in India). The memorandum began by noting that

the amount of manpower that Britain can afford to devote to the needs of the forces during the next few years must be a decision of nice balance between military and economic advantage. Economic recovery is a matter of operational urgency and on a long view there may be little gain from maintaining large armed forces if the result is that in the economic field we become a second class power.[10]

The idea of a defence budget that was so great that it would cripple the economy and therefore be militarily counter-productive had become a familiar line used by the economic and civilian ministries, and indeed by the government itself. This sort of argument enabled reductions in, or opposition to, greater military expenditure at least to be couched in a form that the service ministries and the Chiefs of Staff could accept. This rather disguised the practical issue, which was not whether economic recovery would happen but how quickly and in what areas it would occur. Ministers talked of the economy being crippled; but the real issue was how long and how bad the limp was going to be.

The figures presented by the Board of Trade made very gloomy reading. The manpower target for direct employment on manufactured exports at the end of 1946 was only some 50 per cent above the pre-war level. Morrison warned that 'as production expands and capacity becomes available it will be necessary to increase the manpower on exports during 1947–8 by a further 250,000–300,000 in order that a balance of payments may be achieved'. The manpower that would be available to meet the

[10] CP (46) 138, 4 Apr. 1946, CAB 129/8.

requirements of the home market would be 16,090,000 at December 1946. If Scheme A were adopted, by December 1948 this would have fallen to between 15,850,000 and 15,900,000, and the number would be further reduced if it were found necessary to increase the 500,000 workers producing military supplies and equipment as existing stocks became exhausted. Under Scheme A there would thus be a reduction rather than an increase in manpower available in the next two years, at a time when the volume of investment in industrial reconstruction was expected to rise.

Only Scheme C would enable the maintenance of even the end-1946 position, which hitherto had been regarded as the 'first instalment' in the improvement of standards of life. The preference for this proposal was not based solely on the numerical difference between Schemes A and C. The nature of the manpower involved was an equally important consideration: 'They represent the young and fit age groups in which mobility and adaptability are highest and their loss would reduce our powers to break important bottlenecks and to achieve the expansion of manufacturing industry that is essential to the achievement of our export targets and the recovery of economic strength and equilibrium.' The quality of manpower was also the basis on which the Board of Trade supported the Ministries of Supply and Labour, who argued for the right of apprentices to defer their military service. The Board of Trade argued:

As to the possible effects on professional and technical training it is already abundantly clear that our future economic standards and our chances of achieving an economic equilibrium rest primarily on the possibility of increasing output per head. While more and better capital equipment will contribute to this objective an increase of individual personal efficiency is an essential element. A gap of seven years during which technical and professional training can be acquired cannot be extended without limit and a call-up for three years makes very heavy inroads into the vital few years when training is effectively possible.

The deferment of some apprenticeships would mitigate the danger. None of the three proposed schemes made allowance for this. If such determent were accepted then the manpower levels of the forces would fall even shorter of the service chiefs' and Foreign Office requirements. Bevin was strongly opposed to the suggestion.

As the Board of Trade was departmentally responsible for export trade, which was a fundamental priority of government economic policy, it was this body which most strongly voiced opposition to the longer periods of service and especially Scheme A. The Ministry of Supply (under John Wilmot) was especially concerned to secure the deferment of apprentices and received support from the Board of Trade and the Ministry of Labour (under George Isaacs). The Chairman of Labour's Education Committee, Harold Clay, also wrote to Morrison urging the government to allow deferment.[11]

All three schemes had assumed complete exemption in coal-mining and agriculture, and deferment on industrial grounds in building and building materials. Apprentices in other industries would be called up from 1 January 1947. Deferment on grounds of apprenticeship in certain sections of the engineering and shipbuild-ing industries would continue until the end of 1946, and by the end of 1947 all apprentices in these areas would be allowed to defer their service if they so wished.

Although the War Office undertook to consider apprenticeships in the forces, it was evident that this could only apply to a small number of men in a limited range of engineering trades. The number of civilian apprentices was much larger, although not all of these would opt to postpone their military service. During the war only some 12,000 apprentices had deferred their service out of a possible 75,000. It was expected that the proportion would grow in peacetime. In 1947 there would be some 63,000 apprentices liable for call-up; it was impossible to predict how many would opt for deferment. During the war 12,000 out of 75,000 appren-tices deferred their service.[12] By May it was believed that post-war deferments would be well over 30,000.[13]

When the proposals were initially discussed in the Manpower Committee the loss of this manpower was described by William Leonard, the Parliamentary Secretary to the Minister of Supply, as inflicting 'a lasting injury on the engineering industry'.[14] The Ministry of Supply told the Cabinet that it would not only re-move apprentices from industry before they had completed their

[11] Clay to Morrison, 13 Apr. 1946, PREM 8/609.
[12] MP (46) 19, memorandum by Isaacs, 13 Mar. 1946, PREM 8/609.
[13] CP (46) 206, memorandum by Bevin, 24 May 1946, CAB 129/10.
[14] MP (46) 6, 18 Apr. 1946, PREM 8/609.

training, but would seriously interfere with the effectiveness of that training and, so he claimed, deter new apprentices by driving young men into 'blind alley occupations'.[15]

From the industrial point of view the general manpower shortage was exacerbated by the government's decision to raise the school leaving age to fifteen. This further reduced the possibility of readjusting the system of apprenticeships to facilitate the completion of training before call-up. That readjustment had been strongly favoured by Bevin, who urged that the government should, when announcing the call-up scheme, press industry to give further consideration to reorganizing that system. Having gained the support of the Manpower Committee on this point, he argued that 'intensive industrial training has proved successful during the war and with modern methods of instruction, it should be possible to adjust the age of apprentices up and to reduce materially the period of apprenticeships for the great majority of trades'.[16] However, whatever the intrinsic merits of reducing the period of industrial training—and Wilmot thought it 'open to serious doubt' whether this was possible 'without violence to existing standards'— there was little possibility of industry being able to redesign its system of apprenticeships virtually at a stroke.[17]

The deferment of students in higher education was raised, as it was when the deferment of apprentices was again considered in the autumn. This did not raise problems. During the war, scientific and medical students had been able to defer their military service while arts students had been called up.[18] What was now proposed was that deferment would continue for scientific and medical students and be extended to cover students in teacher training colleges. Priority for university places would be given to men and women who had served in the forces and who now wished to undertake higher education. Arts students would also be allowed to defer their service, subject to gaining a place. As it was assumed that there would be a large number of existing service personnel who particularly wanted to do arts degrees it was estimated that there would be about 7,000 (mainly arts) students who would not have places and who would be called up. The

[15] CP (46) 126, 28 Mar. 1946, CAB 129/8.
[16] CP (46) 121, 22 Mar. 1946, CAB 129/8.
[17] CP (46) 126, 28 Mar. 1946, CAB 129/8.
[18] MP (46) 19, memorandum by Isaacs, 13 Mar. 1946, PREM 8/609.

more promising students, who had obtained scholarships or exhibitions, would be given preference among those who had not served in the forces and effectively guaranteed a place. In contrast to the 'needs' of industry the 'needs' of the universities (to utilize their teaching facilities to the fullest) were to be met. This was ironic as the universities were initially enthusiastic at the prospect of receiving maturer students who had completed their military service. The scheme was designed to allow those in the forces the opportunity of taking up their university careers and the proposal was endorsed without opposition.

The economic arguments about apprenticeships and about the size of the forces in 1947 fell on receptive Prime Ministerial ears. Attlee was at this time already engaged in a vital and protracted fight with the Chiefs of Staff over the Middle East. According to Dalton he had become increasingly aware of Keynes's warnings on the overseas deficit.[19] And whatever his support for the broad thrust (and indeed specific details) of Bevin's foreign policy, the prospect of maintaining a million men in the forces throughout 1947 was an alarming one. This was far in excess of any pre-war figure and it threatened the economic reconstruction of the country.

On Jay's advice, but guided by his own increasing awareness of the problems, Attlee did not initially back the Chiefs of Staff when the Defence Committee first considered the issue on 15 April. Instead he insisted that the expansion of trade to meet financial obligations meant that the country could not afford armed forces over a million strong, and indeed he went so far as to say that 'there must be a reduction in the size of the armed forces within this period to something approaching pre-war strength'.[20]

There was another purely political argument—the unpopularity of the longer periods of service. This was especially important as far as Labour Party opinion was concerned. Jay advised the Prime Minister that a call-up for three years in the second half of 1946 (reduced to two and three quarter to three years by the first half of 1947) would come as a shock to Parliament and the public who, he believed, were not expecting more than two years.[21] This comment was repeated in the Defence Committee by John

[19] Dalton Diaries, 18 Feb. 1946.
[20] DO (46) 12th, 15 Apr. 1946, CAB 131/1.
[21] Jay to Attlee, 30 Mar. 1946, PREM 8/609.

Strachey, the Parliamentary Under-Secretary of State for Air, who said that unless some hope could be held out that conscript service was coming down to a year or a year and a half there would be a markedly adverse reaction both in Parliament and in the country.[22] The acquiescence of the Liberal Party and sections of the Labour Party who were opposed to the longer-term continuation might turn into opposition. The Conservatives could make political capital out of the issue as they were doing over the demobilization scheme. These political arguments reinforced the economic case.

Bevin's response was, first, to spell out the serious foreign policy implications in the Foreign Office memorandum described above. Second, as Chairman of the Manpower Committee and acting on the Defence Committee's request, he examined Alanbrooke's suggestion to change the link between the periods of service for men already in the forces and those for men who would be called up under the scheme. The idea was that men called up before 1 January 1947 should be released 'in accordance with the age and length of service release scheme without any overriding limit of service but subject to the condition that all men conscripted before that date should be released before men conscripted for a fixed period after that date'.[23]

The three schemes were now revised on this assumption. A fourth proposal (Scheme D) was added, based on a fixed term of service of two years but with the same rate of release as Scheme A. By changing the link between men called up before 1 January 1947 and men called up after that date the problems posed by the rate of run-down in 1947 could be largely overcome. The number of men retained would be more or less as in the original Scheme A. This just about satisfied the Chiefs of Staff. It changed little from the Board of Trade's point of view. It also meant that some men would be serving for more than four and a half years compared with only two years for the newcomers. It had been accepted that there would have to be disparities and Bevin argued that in any case the numbers of men with four years' service actually serving with men called up for only two years would be relatively small. But it also meant increasing the existing disparities

---

[22] DO (46) 12th, 15 Apr. 1946, CAB 131/1.
[23] CP (46) 194, 10 May 1946. This replaced CP (46) 121.

between the same release groups in different services. Men would be serving longest in the army and certain sections of the RAF.

The value of Scheme D was that it not only came close to meeting the Chiefs of Staff's stated requirements, but also dealt with the principal political problem. This, Bevin now admitted, was threatening the longer-term acceptability of conscription: 'Any longer period is likely to meet with strong opposition and might prejudice the acceptance of the principle of compulsory military service under a permanent scheme.'[24] It did not, however, even begin to deal with the economic consequences of having a million men in the forces in 1947. 'Bearing in mind that 1947 is a crucial year economically,' Jay warned Attlee, 'I should be on balance inclined to favour the revised Scheme C.'[25]

However, Scheme D was viewed as a compromise and Attlee, getting his military briefs from Ismay and by now well aware of the foreign policy implications that Bevin had made clear, swung behind the new proposal. The Prime Minister was far from satisfied with the army's use of manpower and demanded that the War Office provide a detailed breakdown of, and make reductions in, the forces stationed in the United Kingdom engaged on nucleus training and in administrative organizations. The Defence Committee requested in addition that the service departments consider the pooling of common services. Dominion contributions were also to be sought.

On the question of apprentices it was decided that the Ministry of Labour would defer at least some apprentices from January 1947. But this was made conditional upon the recruitment of women, for which the Prime Minister pressed. The question of the permanent establishment of female forces was being considered separately. The case for that had been becoming clear for some time and indeed the decision to found permanent women's services was taken in time for it to be announced in the White Paper published in May 1946.[26]

The economic case against Scheme D remained as before: it still entailed over a million men in the armed forces in 1947. Yet even before account was taken of the apprentices it meant a shortage of some 39,000 men at mid-1947 rising to 73,000 by the end of that

[24] Ibid.
[25] Jay to Attlee, 16 May 1946, PREM 8/609.
[26] Cmd. 6831, *Call-up to the Forces in 1947 and 1948*, May 1946.

year. It was, moreover, accepted that the estimates were based on what the Manpower Working Party described as 'extremely optimistic' assumptions about the number of regular- and short-service volunteers. Any deferments of apprentices for 1947 were therefore considered by the Defence Committee to be contingent on the yield from female recruiting (estimated at 12,000–15,000 by the end of 1947) together with the reduction in army home administration, the pooling of common services (e.g. the medical and chaplaincy services), and any Dominion help, although the last of these was recognized as too nebulous to be of immediate assistance. The War Office on the other hand did not see these reductions as a *quid pro quo* for the apprentices but as filling the gap in their stated requirements. The Cabinet was however unmoved. Scheme D was discussed on 20 May 1946 and approved on 27 May, when the deferment of apprentices was also agreed.

The scheme for continuing the call-up was published as a White Paper at the end of May and announced in a statement to the House of Commons on 30 May by the Minister of Labour, George Isaacs. As has been shown it was a compromise, fashioned out of an irreconcilable conflict between economic and foreign policy needs. Yet this was not readily apparent to those excluded from the Whitehall deliberations. The government was hardly likely to advertise the fact that it was supplying the Chiefs of Staff with fewer men than they said were needed. Nor was it prepared to admit that its estimates were based on 'very optimistic' assumptions about regular recruiting. Equally, it was not going to announce that having a million men in the forces might seriously jeopardize the prospect of economic recovery.

Without the necessary information—especially the details of military requirements for foreign policy—any debate would be characterized by generalities, speculation, and inaccuracy. Yet even that much debate did not happen at this stage. The White Paper merely described the lengths of service for which men called up in 1947 and 1948 would be conscripted. It gave no indication of the implications for the size of the forces. More importantly, the consequences of extending the age and service release scheme to those already in the forces (i.e. making them serve longer) were not set out.

Sensing that the proposals had not created significant disquiet Morrison, the Leader of the House, was able to ignore demands for a debate on the White Paper.[27] As the scheme outlined was concerned with the continuation of conscription under existing (wartime) legislation, he was able to argue that it was no more than a piece of administrative action. If the opposition wished to press for a debate it could set aside a supply day. However, the Conservatives were not unduly alarmed at the White Paper and made it clear that they supported the continuation of conscription.

The Parliamentary reaction was muted, partly because of the opposition's quiescence and partly because of a failure to grasp the possible implications of linking the periods of service for those already liable and those becoming liable for conscription. The government did state that all men serving in the forces at 31 December 1946 would be released before the end of 1948, before any of the men called up from 1947. Yet extending the age and service scheme to those in the forces meant that they would serve longer. It also paved the way for the slowing of the rate of release which was announced in November and which fuelled criticism of and opposition to the government's long-term conscription policy.

The real opposition could come only from Labour and Liberal MPs, who did not have recourse to a supply day. They were unable to persuade the government of the need for a debate. The initial demands for this came from Rhys Davies and from the two ILP members Campbell Stephen and John McGovern. The latter put down a strongly worded motion in which they called upon the government to end compulsory military service. They argued that this had been imposed upon the British people to defeat Hitler but that its continuation would represent a 'betrayal of the living and the dead'.[28] If the government was in any doubt about public opinion they should put the matter to a referendum.

These reactions were only to be expected and did not pose any great problems for the government. Only a minority of irreconcilable opponents were involved. Potentially more significant was an early day motion (EDM) initially dated 25 June 1946 and eventually signed by ninety-three MPs (eighty-eight of them Labour). This stated:

[27] *HC deb.*, vol. 423, 6 Jun. 1946, cols. 2164–5.
[28] *HC deb.*, vol. 423, 30 May 1946, cols. 1342–3.

That this house while welcoming the decision of His Majesty's Government as set forth in Cmd 6831 gradually to reduce the period of compulsory service in the fighting forces is of the opinion that Military Conscription in peacetime is alien to the traditions of this country and should come to an end as soon as is practicable.[29]

This was significant, especially as nearly a third of the Labour MPs who signed the EDM were not involved in the back-bench revolts of November 1946 or April 1947.[30] Yet the motion was explicit in its support for the government on the short-term question.

The government had thus succeeded in avoiding a political fight on the continuation of the call-up. The two-year period of service for men called up from 1947 (falling to eighteen months by December 1948) was accepted by the Liberal Party and in important sections of the PLP. The question of whether either of the two-and-a-half- or three-year periods would have been acceptable is difficult to judge. Given that MPs were unable to examine or challenge the detailed assumptions involved (particularly with regard to the provision of military backing for foreign policy commitments) it is unlikely that the opposition would have voted against the government. Yet the longer the period of service proposed the more likely a Parliamentary debate would have been. Had there been a debate there is no doubt that the divisions in the PLP would have become visible; and if the period of service had been longer there is equally little doubt that the strength of opposition would have been greater.

Yet this would still not have been particularly significant unless, as in the EDM, the debate and the divisions had focused on the issue of conscription in the long term. The motion was considered at a meeting of the PLP on 3 July when William Whiteley, the Chief Whip, reminded the party that in February it had been agreed that a decision on National Service would be deferred until August.[31] He warned that 'the independent action of members in Tabling Motions such as these was contrary to the spirit and understanding which existed'—a reference to the suspension of the Standing Orders of the PLP. Dalton also appears to have helped

[29] Notice of Motions, 25, 26; and 27 Jun. 1946. EDM 53/45.
[30] Calculated from the Notice of Motions, *HC deb.*, vol. 430, 18 Nov. 1946, cols. 639–44, and *HC deb.*, vol. 435, 1 Apr. 1947, cols. 1961–6.
[31] Whiteley to Attlee, summary of discussions on conscription, 28 Mar. 1947, Papers of Earl Attlee (Bodleian Library, Oxford), dep. 51.

persuade the party to drop the matter until later in the year. The issue was clearly seen by most MPs, including many of those who otherwise rejected conscription in principle, to be separate from the long-term question. The government had succeeded in its political objective. Similar success on the long-term issue would be a great deal more difficult.

Appendix

TABLE 3.A1.   Possible Call-up Schemes Outlined by Manpower Working Party: Periods of Service

Period of entry	Length of service, years		
	Scheme A	Scheme B	Scheme C
Pre-July 1946	<3	<2½	<2
Jul.–Dec. 1946	3	2½	2
Jan.–June 1947	2¾–3	2¼–2½	2
Jul.–Dec. 1947	2½–2¾	2–2¼	2
Jan.–June 1948	2¼–2½	1¾–2	1¾–2
Jul.–Dec. 1948	2–2¼	1½–1¾	1½–1¾
Jan.–June 1949	1¾–2	1½[a]	1½
Jul.–Dec. 1949	1½–1¾		
1950	1½[a]		

[a] and onwards.

Source: CP (46) 121, 22 Mar. 1946.

TABLE 3.A2.   Effect of Possible Call-up Schemes on Service
Strengths

	1947 mid	end	1948 mid	end	1949 mid	end	1950 mid	end
Scheme A								
Strength ('000)	1,082	1,003	1,000	1,000	990	865	865	825
Effect of deferring call-up of apprentices in 1947 ('000)	−31	−63	−63	−63	−32	*a*	+63	+63
Scheme B								
Strength ('000)	1,052	944	934	946	907	753	720	764
Effect of deferring call-up of apprentices in 1947 ('000)	−31	−63	−63	−63	−32	+63	+63	+32
Scheme C								
Strength ('000)	1,018	875	881	842	817	747	720	764
Effect of deferring call-up of apprentices in 1947 ('000)	−31	−63	−63	−63	*a*	+63	+63	+32
Scheme D								
Strength ('000)	1,086	1,006	950	842	817	747		

a No change.

Source: CP (46) 194, 1 May 1946.

4

The Military Argument for Conscription

THE question of when the Cold War began is inextricably involved with the question of why it happened and who was
responsible. For American 'post-revisionist' historians such as
John Gaddis the critical year was 1946, when the goal of a working relationship with Stalin finally gave way to the policy of
containment and the manichean rhetoric of the Truman doctrine.[1]
In Britain, long-term military planning proceeded on assumptions
which had yet to be agreed with the government and which were
at variance with the Prime Minister's views, both on Britain's role
in the Middle East and on the prospect of a *modus vivendi* with the
Soviet Union.[2] However poor East–West relations had become in
1946, they clearly did not prevent Attlee from questioning what
were to become central tenets of British national security policy.

As work was beginning on the long-term issue of conscription
and the Chiefs of Staff continued their study on the long-term size
and shape of the armed forces, the opening exchanges were taking
place in a critical battle fought largely between the Prime Minister
and the service chiefs over British strategy in the Middle East. Attlee
had become acutely aware of the financial liability of a large overseas deficit and this was a key element in his attempt to disengage
from the area. If Britain decided on withdrawal the consequences

---

[1] John L. Gaddis, *The United States and the Origins of the Cold War, 1941–7* (New
York: Columbia University Press, 1971).

[2] For discussions of British defence policy in the Middle East, see Alan Bullock,
Ernest Bevin: Foreign Secretary (Oxford University Press, 1985); David Devereaux,
The Formulation of British Defence Policy in the Middle East 1948–56 (Macmillan,
1990); Ritchie Ovendale, *The English-speaking Alliance: Britain, the United States, the
Dominions and the Cold War 1945–51* (Allen & Unwin 1985), and *Britain, the United
States, and the End of the Palestine Mandate, 1942–1948* (Royal Historical Society,
1989); and Roger Louis, *The British Empire in the Middle East 1945–61* (Oxford
University Press, 1984). For a reappraisal of Attlee's views, see Raymond Smith
and John Zametica, 'The Cold Warrior: Clement Attlee Reconsidered, 1945–7'
International Affairs, 61 (1985), 237–52.

for British defence policy would be considerable.[3] For Dalton the idea had considerable merit: it would put 'a wide glacis of desert and Arabs between ourselves and the Russians'.[4] With India making its exit from the Empire the strategic need for the Mediterranean as the essential route for Imperial communications was called into question.

Attlee's arguments for withdrawal from the Middle East were set out in a paper calling for a reconsideration of the Mediterranean strategy 'in the light of our resources and of modern conditions of warfare'.[5] The thrust of the argument was that Britain's position had been built in the era of sea power. Given that fleets were no longer interdependent with air forces the political changes that rendered base facilities doubtful threatened the viability of the whole strategy. The position of India was changing and the Prime Minister wondered whether it would remain in the Commonwealth. He rejected the idea of defending British oil interests in South Persia and Iraq as 'we are not in a position to defend this area from a determined land attack from the North'.

Attlee's move was a critical initiative in post-war defence policy. Yet his efforts came to nought in the face of the implacable opposition of the Chiefs of Staff. His 'defeatist'[6] paper exasperated and eventually provoked the service chiefs into the threat of resignation. Equally important, Bevin was adamant that Britain's position in the Mediterranean was not just of military significance but was vital to the idea of being a great power. 'If we move out of the Mediterranean, Russia will move in,' he argued. Nevertheless, the Foreign Secretary was initially 'strongly in favour' of the Mombasa proposal 'of relocating the main Middle East base in Kenya rather than Egypt'.[7]

The Middle East strategy in war and peace developed as a crucial element in Britain's security policy during and after the years of the Attlee administration. The Chiefs of Staff regarded the defence of the Middle East as second only to the defence of the United Kingdom in their priorities, in part because they viewed

[3] For discussions of these issues see Philip Darby, *British Defence Policy East of Suez 1947–68* (Oxford University Press, 1973).

[4] Diaries of Hugh Dalton (London School of Economics), 22 Mar. 1946.

[5] DO (46) 27, 2 Mar. 1946, CAB 131/2.

[6] Brooke diaries, 5 Apr. 1946, Papers of Lord Alanbrooke (Liddell Hart Centre for Military Archives, King's College, London), 5/12.

[7] DO (46) 27, 2 Mar. 1946, CAB 131/2, annex.

it as the basis for offensive air action against the Soviet Union. When the events of 1946–7 (Indian independence, the reference of the Palestinian issue to the UN, the failure to reach agreement with Egypt over the Canal base) began to undermine the foundations of that defence, there was no reappraisal of the strategy —despite the claims of the Chiefs of Staff in March 1947 that 'we would not have the ability to fight in and hold the Middle East'.[8]

If British troops were not needed in peacetime the final post-war army could be reduced by at least one division and the envisaged strategic reserve of two divisions redeployed elsewhere. Reductions would also be possible in the navy and air force. If the Middle East did not have to be reinforced at the beginning of a major war then the argument that conscription was necessary to provide trained forces ready for embarkation on mobilization would be unambiguously reduced to a commitment to Europe. That in itself did not mean that conscription would be unnecessary. And unless there were other reductions in anticipated long-term overseas commitments, National Service would still be necessary to provide embodied forces in peacetime. Withdrawal from the Middle East (in peace and war) was a necessary but not sufficient condition for the abolition of conscription.

The military case for conscription had been rehearsed in the APW Committee. The substance of that case had not significantly changed, though the situation had been affected by the imminence of Indian independence. The form in which the argument was put to ministers was modified by the autumn of 1946.[9] The case for conscription now rested on two related but separate arguments. The first was that until there were sufficient regulars to provide the necessary embodied forces National Service would be needed to fulfil peacetime commitments. This was an argument for conscription in the long term though not necessarily for permanent compulsion. The commitments included occupational responsibilities (especially Germany), post-Imperial liabilities (particularly Palestine), and permanent overseas garrisons. The eventual aim was to achieve a level of regular recruiting that would provide

---

[8] DO (47) 23, 7 Mar. 1947, CAB 131/4.

[9] Major-General Sir Ian Jacob (Military Assistant Secretary to the Cabinet) to A. J. Newling, 13 Oct. 1945, DEFE 7/146. At this time Jacob could 'see no possibility of ministers committing themselves beyond' the next five years and he did 'not think it would be right to try and make them do so'.

for the permanent overseas responsibilities. It was assumed that once normal peacetime conditions were achieved the forces' regular strength—especially that of the army, which would be shouldering most of the burden in manpower terms—would correspond to the irreducible overseas roles.

In this context the need for conscripts was contingent on two different factors: regular recruiting/re-engagements and the scale and duration of military commitments. As will be seen, neither of these two elements was to allow for an end to compulsory military service. Regular recruiting for both the RAF and the army was to remain well short of what had been expected. As for overseas responsibilities, it has been shown that commitments in Greece, Venezia Guilia, and Austria were already lasting longer than had been anticipated; no long-term solution was apparent in the German and Palestinian contexts; and new commitments were to arrive—in Malaya, Hong Kong, and Korea—as the Cold War developed.

Conscription was thus inextricably linked with the pursuit of foreign policy. This was not only because it appeared to be the only means of providing the armed forces that would enable Bevin to 'speak the language of power politics'. It was also because the existence of conscription was a symbol of Britain's will to act and maintain its position and interests. This somewhat visceral rationale had long been accepted in the Foreign Office and played a significant part in determining Churchill's attitude throughout the period of his opposition.[10] Bevin did not dissent from this. His concern lay with the need for Britain to be seen to be backing foreign policy with military force. That meant two things: first, large numbers of men, and secondly, a mobile striking force which would give Britain 'a very necessary psychological argument in defending and asserting British interests'.[11] In theory National Service could meet both these requirements. But, as will be seen, a series of restraints—most importantly financial and manpower ceilings—severely hampered the development of balanced military forces, able to perform these two different peacetime tasks. When the need to prepare for war was added the problems increased considerably.

[10] Churchill to Martel, 14 Apr. 1951, Papers of Sir Gifford Martel. (Imperial War Museum, London).
[11] Bevin to Montgomery, 18 Oct. 1947, WO 216/239.

An effective critique of the case for National Service thus required one or both of two elements: that regular forces could be provided to perform all the overseas tasks, and/or that foreign policy had to be adjusted according to what could be provided. The two most celebrated military critics of conscription—Liddell Hart and Martel—together with a variety of serious-minded political opponents, were in no doubt on at least the first of these issues. It was increasingly accepted inside and outside the services that conscription was an impediment to regular recruiting. Despite the earlier optimism in the Air Ministry, experience began to suggest that the morale of the regular forces was affected by their responsibilities for training National Service airmen.

More important was the view, which gained currency rapidly both in and out of Whitehall, that conscription was bought at the expense of reasonable conditions for the regulars. Shortages of housing, particularly of married accommodation, together with perceived inadequacies in service pay may have inhibited recruiting and re-engagements. When the decision was taken in 1947 to pay conscripts at the same basic rate as the regulars, this was seen as exacerbating the problem of resource allocation. The initial cost of paying conscripts the same rates as the regulars was put at £30 million.[12] It also reduced the financial inducement for men to take up regular and particularly short service engagements.

Yet the shortage of housing was to remain one of the critical unsolved social problems of the immediate post-war years, and the question of service pay was, for the government, inevitably embroiled in its overall incomes policy. Moreover, as was recognized in the War Office and the Air Ministry, there were inherent limits on regular recruiting. Bevin's view that unemployment had been the chief recruiting officer for the pre-war services was widely accepted. Nevertheless it should be noted that the post-war regular strength—even with both conscription and full employment—was higher than before the war. However dissatisfied the services professed to be with the pay code agreed by the government in 1946,[13] it provided for the highest rates of pay that the services had known (although in an argument between Alexander and Montgomery in September 1948 the Chief of the

[12] Memorandum for Leslie Rowan (Attlee's PS), Nov. 1946, Papers of Earl Attlee (Bodleian Library, Oxford), dep. 45.
[13] The Post-war Code of Pay was announced in Dec. 1945, Cmd. 6715.

Imperial General Staff informed the Minister of Defence that 'the Army regarded the Pay Code as a first class bollock'[14]). Britain had gone through six years of war. In the short term at least it was only to be expected that 'war weariness' among the men (and their families) would limit recruiting and re-engagement.

Even if the money saved from training, accommodating, and equipping conscripts could be diverted into providing better conditions for the regulars, it is difficult to see how an army much in excess of 200,000 could have been provided. Subsequent experience with the 'professional army' of the post-conscription era suggests that such a target was over-ambitious. Given the sort of budgetary restraints in place and the nature of the politics of defence budgeting, it is far from certain that resources could simply have been transferred from provision for conscripts to provision for regulars.

The critics of conscription at the time saw little difficulty in providing for an adequate level of regular recruiting. Liddell Hart, for example, argued that a 250,000-strong army could be provided if there were sufficient inducements for regular recruiting.[15] In October, when the Defence Committee was asked to decide on the issue of permanent conscription, it was also confronted with the existing state of the regular forces. At that stage, and despite a national recruiting campaign personally supported by Attlee and Bevin, the regular strength of the forces was described as 'desperate' by the Chiefs of Staff.[16] The army was 93,000 men short of its target strength for 1 January 1947. There were 284,000 regulars when there should have been 377,000. The War Office was planning on a strength of over 400,000 in 1948–9 and the run-down to that point was contingent on reductions in, and terminations of, existing commitments that were already being recognized as optimistic.

Given that the short-term continuation of conscription was a numerical necessity, the problem arose of handling the change-over to an all-regular force. Assuming the transition to all-regular forces required the prior build-up of an adequate regular strength, then it would be necessary to attract the additional regulars while

[14] Montgomery diaries, 1–30 Sept. 1948, Note by CIGS, Papers of Viscount Montgomery of Alamein (Imperial War Museum, London), BLM 186/6.

[15] 'The Army We Need', in John Bull, 12 Jun. 1948, Martel papers. Martel argued that 200,000 would be sufficient: see An Outspoken Soldier (Sifton Praed, 1949), 342–7.   [16] DO (46) 119, 11 Oct. 1946, CAB 131/3.

at the same time holding on to the conscripts. From the critics' point of view this was not a problem—given additional resources and sufficient regulars. It was at worst a short-term investment that would yield long-term benefits. Yet even if an all-regular force were cheaper in the long run, it would not be so in the short term. As will be seen, the defence budget entailed a constant and in many ways unresolved struggle between the services and the Treasury. Whatever the political advantages of ending National Service, it is difficult to envisage the government providing additional resources for the services. Any increase in short-term costs would in these circumstances have had to have been borne within the defence budget. Given the constraints on defence expenditure, particularly after the convertibility crisis in 1947, any cuts in defence for this reason would have been bitterly contested.

It is difficult to escape the conclusion that the critics' estimates of realizable regular strength represented little more than wishful thinking. Yet in fairness, it should be noted that Liddell Hart's figure of 250,000 was comparable to the earlier War Office view that 275,000 men could be recruited—a total that made no allowance for Gurkhas or women, nor for the anticipated effect on army morale caused by the burden of training conscripts. Yet even if Liddell Hart's figure could be secured (and if, moreover, a similar level could be achieved by the RAF) it was still clear that the forces envisaged by the critics were well short of what the Chiefs of Staff said was necessary.

Those criticisms therefore had to incorporate a radical revision of the military basis of foreign policy. The critique advanced by Liddell Hart in particular paid considerable attention to this problem. He repeatedly stressed the comparison with the pre-war scale of commitments and argued that the disparity was to be attributed to unchecked excesses of military bureaucracy, particularly in the United Kingdom. He also advocated wholesale withdrawal from the Middle East and indeed wrote directly to Attlee in 1946 at the time when the Prime Minister was engaging the Chiefs of Staff on that very issue.[17]

The former argument was heard in many quarters. The charge of

[17] Memorandum dated 20 Mar. 1946, sent to Attlee 10 May 1946, Attlee papers, dep. 36. Liddell Hart also wrote to Morrison who forwarded the paper to the Prime Minister with approval. For an analysis of Liddell Hart's thinking see John Mearsheimer, *Liddell Hart and the Weight of History* (Brassey's, 1988).

manpower inefficiency was frequently levelled at the government by concerned and/or dissentient elements in its own Parliamentary ranks and, not surprisingly, by the opposition. Numerical comparisons with the pre-war army certainly supported the Liddell Hart view. So too did the numerous instances of the military's waste of manpower recorded in the press and by MPs. The reports of the Service Manpower Committees (especially that appointed for the army) showed an embarrassingly inefficient use of men.

It was evident that the complexity of new weapons systems meant that more men were necessary to operate them and provide the administrative and logistic support than had been the case before the war.[18] The 'teeth to tail' (more appropriately 'teeth to gums') ratio had shrunk considerably since before the war. Furthermore, comparisons between pre- and post-war commitments were less than accurate in assessing bureaucracy or waste. For example, the political and military situation in Palestine had deteriorated and the 100,000 men that the British were to commit proved incapable of achieving their objectives.

The major overseas responsibility was Germany and it was clear this would remain. Few of the critics suggested major troop withdrawals from Europe. Liddell Hart argued that the army on the Rhine should be conceived of in comparison to the pre-war forces based in the United Kingdom.[19] No one seriously envisaged abandoning the occupational commitment, and without doing so the army would remain dependent on conscription, unless all other overseas roles were discarded. One 'drastic and unconventional' idea was put forward by Richard Wood, Alexander's private secretary, who, recognizing that Germany was the 'kernel of the problem', suggested that the burden of occupation duties be shifted to the RAF—'inconvenient and temporarily crippling though it may be'.[20] The idea appears to have made little impact on the Minister of Defence.

The critics of manpower inefficiency had a strong case, although translating greater efficiency into fewer numbers was not

[18] See Appendix 5.
[19] Liddell Hart, Notes on the Question of the 'Commitments' and Strength of the British Army, 17 Mar. 1947, Papers of Sir Basil Liddell Hart 11/1949/11, (Liddell Hart Centre for Military Archives, King's College, London).
[20] Memorandum by Wood for Alexander, 5 Jun. 1947. Papers of Viscount Alexander (Churchill College, Cambridge), 5/11.

easy. The government was anxious to reduce the scale and size of the military burden by cutting the administrative side, especially that of the army in the UK. The Defence Committee had continued to press for reductions in army administration despite bland service assurances that the forces were the minimum required.

Yet at the height of the balance of payments crisis in 1947 Bevin was to admit privately that 'the reason for maintaining a permanent military formation of 700,000 [in the United Kingdom] . . . even with the difficulties of transition . . . passes my comprehension'.[21] Despite subsequent savings—through cuts, economies, and amalgamations—it is evident that the government was unable to come to terms with the problem.[22] To some extent this is hardly surprising. The period immediately after the war was a time of considerable flux. Not only were the services trying to adjust to potentially revolutionary changes in military technology (particularly in air warfare), they were also preoccupied with demobilizing with a minimum of dislocation and a maximum of fairness; all this while attempting both to fulfil post-war obligations and to retain the structure and personnel necessary to provide for the final post-war forces. On top of this Attlee was in the process of restructuring the higher organization of defence policy decision-making with a new Ministry of Defence and a new Minister of Defence.

Yet these factors in themselves did not satisfactorily explain why the forces remained so swollen. It is apparent that there was reluctance—at least in the War Office—to admit to the seriousness of the problem. When in December 1946 it was suggested that there should be a general investigation of army manpower along the lines of the RAF's Manpower Economy Committee the Army Council agreed with the Permanent Under Secretary at the War Office, Sir Eric Speed, who argued against the involvement of outside experts with little knowledge of service life.[23] The Royal Electrical and Mechanical Engineers and Ordnance departments were already under examination and Speed claimed that this was equivalent to the RAF's study.

[21] Bevin to Attlee, 15 Aug. 1947, PREM 8/833.
[22] This was made clear by the Army Manpower Committee Report in 1949 (WO 216/300) and its sub-committee on the Army Working Day Investigation (the Wood Report) in 1948 (WO 216/316).
[23] AC/M (46) 10, 13 Dec. 1946, WO 163/63.

This decision was eventually overridden by the government. In March 1947, under pressure from the PLP and in an attempt to defuse opposition to the National Service bill, the government established both Army and Admiralty Manpower Economy Committees which included civilian experts (including trade unionists) as well as service representatives. The establishment of these committees also helped to deflect opposition criticisms of manpower efficiency and Churchill's request for a select committee inquiry which the government rejected. However, these studies inevitably took time to gather information and report.

Strong ministerial pressure was clearly essential if the short- and long-term problem of the military's use of manpower was to be solved. With the Ministry of Defence not yet established this required strong and imaginative service ministers (particularly at the War Office). These were conspicuous by their absence. The Secretary of State for War in 1945–6, Jack Lawson, remained at the War Office for just over a year before ill-health forced his retirement. Frederick Bellenger held the same post for a similar period before being sacked. To expect very much of a new minister in such a short time is perhaps less than fair. Neither had significant ministerial experience (though Bellenger enjoyed an apprentice year as Financial Secretary to the War Office). Yet it is evident that they were not the men to impose reforms on the army. According to Alanbrooke, Lawson

was a serious puzzle. He was one of the most charming of men. A religious man of high principles and of great charm but completely ignorant of all military matters. He had not got the faintest idea what his job required of him and as far as I could see it was impossible to make him realise it. I feared it quite beyond my powers to brief him on various items for discussion on Cabinet agendas. As far as I could see he never read any of the papers that were circulated to him and I doubt if he would have been any the wiser if he had read them.[24]

Lawson did at least command a certain respect: Ismay and Montgomery also recorded their high opinion of his personal integrity.[25]

Bellenger was less fortunate. He arrived at the War Office with

[24] Brooke, Notes on My Life, 28 Aug. 1945, Alanbrooke papers, 5/10.
[25] Ismay to General Burrows, 17 Aug. 1945. Ismay IV/Bur/9 Montgomery to Grigg, 9 Aug. 1945, Papers of Sir P. J. Grigg (Churchill College, Cambridge).

the reputation of a 'stunt journalist'.[26] His cultivated image as the 'soldier's friend' did little to endear him to the 'brass hats' whom he had attacked and the new CIGS, Montgomery, apparently snubbed him when they first met.[27] Perhaps influenced by this reaction, and despite assurances to Liddell Hart that he intended to do something about manpower efficiency,[28] he made little headway. At an admittedly early stage in his new post Montgomery confided to Sir James Grigg, the wartime Secretary of State: 'The new Secretary of State is behaving very well so far. He leaves me alone, signs everything put to him and is clearly anxious to please.'[29] Yet even as Financial Secretary he had been acquiescent in the face of the military. In the Army Council, when Lawson raised the question of press reports about manpower wastage, Bellenger had argued that his recent tour of the army in Germany had convinced him that the troops were fully extended.[30] When Shinwell had been at the War Office for some time he spoke 'scathingly' of his predecessors and confessed that 'as far as he could see they had hardly ever drawn the files on any problem and he could not imagine what they did with their time'.[31]

Ministerial pressure for reform made little impact. The lack of military initiative was also apparent. The principal reason for this lay in the nature of the problems. For the army, demobilization and the increasingly worrying issue of the role of the final post-war army were the main priorities. In organizational terms the General Staff and especially Montgomery concentrated their attention on the idea of what he was to call the 'New Model' or Citizen Army.[32] The emphasis would be on using National Service to provide large numbers of trained reserves ready on mobilization. The principle of the Citizen Army predated any detailed appreciation of the strategic purpose to which it would be put. For Montgomery it was most important to have adequate numbers of trained men. In contrast to the RAF, the purpose of training

[26] Liddell Hart, Notes for History, 28 May 1948, Liddell Hart papers, 11/1948/14.   [27] Ibid.
[28] Bellenger to Liddell Hart, 30 Nov. 1946, Liddell Hart papers, 1/61.
[29] Montgomery to Grigg, 31 Oct. 1946, Grigg papers, 11/1.
[30] AC/M (45) 2, 12 Oct. 1945, WO 163/63.
[31] Liddell Hart, Notes for History, 22 Apr. 1948, Liddell Hart papers, 11/1948/9.
[32] Bernard Montgomery, *The Memoirs of Field Marshal The Viscount Montgomery of Alamein* (Collins, 1958), 418.

reserves was not to provide for specific manpower targets. It was to provide for reserves in general.

This distinction may have had some impact on attitudes. Certainly comparison with the RAF, where experiments in operational research and manpower efficiency studies were pioneered, is revealing.[33] The dynamism and realism of the air force are apparent—a feature perhaps attributable not least to the influence of Air Marshal Sir John Slessor, the Air Member for Personnel. When Liddell Hart was asked by Shinwell to compile a list of generals capable of providing similar reforming spirit he could produce only a handful of retired officers.

While Montgomery was accepted as being probably the best available (a view not shared by Martel or Major-General J. F. C. 'Boney' Fuller, the military writer and exponent of armoured warfare), he had not had any experience in the War Office. The same was to be true of his successor, Field Marshal Sir Bill Slim. General Sir Richard O'Connor was to be a disappointment as Sir Ronald Adams' replacement in the crucial position of Adjutant-General, and was in turn replaced by General Sir James Steele in 1948. None of these men was willing to attempt the sort of re-organization that the likes of Liddell Hart deemed necessary. Other priorities directed their energies in different directions. For Montgomery conscription was to become the foundation of the army, in effect a training organization for the production of reserves. The sorts of reductions, economies, and reorganization that Liddell Hart envisaged would have taken the CIGS and the War Office in a wholly different direction and one in which they had little interest in travelling.

However, even assuming that the critics of the War Office had a strong case, the position of the government was not an easy one. To support the critics meant challenging the considered opinions of their professional military advisers, whose view was that the demands of foreign policy, technological change, and political uncertainty required an unprecedented scale of armed forces. The economic cost of this was considerable and Attlee and his colleagues repeatedly pressed for economies and reductions—a constant pruning that occasionally gave way to arbitrary hacking, particularly in the wake of the balance of payments crisis.

[33] Slessor to Noel-Baker, 2 Apr. 1947, AIR 8/800.

Hindsight suggests (as the opposition did at the time) that those cuts should have come earlier; dramatic and perhaps arbitrary cuts were the only way to bring the forces under control. This argument is not without force. But in government at the time, Bevin, however much he might be privately exasperated at military bureaucracy, needed the troops. As was to become evident, arbitrary and dramatic cuts were followed by shortages of trained troops; and when the Cold War began and new commitments arose any long-term notions about the reorganization of the forces had to be set against the short-term need to have troops in the field. The waste of manpower was both bad for morale and a political embarrassment to the government. Yet the problem was how to translate improvements in efficiency into direct and immediate cuts. Reductions in administration and in the home army were not effective substitutes for ending overseas commitments.

Another possible solution was to find other sources of manpower, either domestically or from abroad. In May 1946 the government had decided that the women's services would be constituted on a permanent basis. Yet even though women were to replace men on a one-to-one basis it was anticipated that a total strength of only 13,000–17,000 would be raised.[34] This was recognized as a valuable contribution but limited in scale. Likewise the use of civilians in administrative roles was recognized as a valuable supplement. The Defence and Services group of the PLP was to urge greater use of them; but although the forces were not predisposed against employing civilians it was evident that they could be used only in a restricted number of roles.

Potentially of much greater value was overseas manpower. Securing the aid of the Dominions was seen as vitally important both by ministers and by the military. This was especially true with regard to the Middle East. Almost every discussion of manpower needs included exhortations to secure such help; but agreement from the Dominions on the provision of that support did not materialise and the Chiefs of Staff remained unwilling to develop plans that were dependent on the political decisions of friendly but independent states.

[34] DO (46) 63, 8 May 1946, CAB 131/2, discusssed at DO (46) 16th, 17 May 1946, CAB 131/1.

The latter problem could be overcome in part by the use of Colonial manpower—in theory a large reservoir of potential support. But the War Office and the Colonial Office were reluctant to use Colonial troops outside their own territories. Where these forces were valuable was in freeing the British of responsibility for internal security, particularly in wartime. Attlee was to press the military to make greater use of Colonial manpower, although it was not until 1950 that a detailed evaluation of the use of Imperial troops was made, and even then little change resulted.[35] The Gurkhas provided the best example and one of a number of precedents. Yet although the War Office was keen to make use of the Nepalese troops, it deliberately delayed a decision on a permanent Gurkha establishment until 1947 in order to prevent the government from using this as a pretext for reducing the number of British regulars in the final post-war army.[36] In October 1947, when Gurkhas and women units had been accepted, the army argued that they should be supplementary to, rather than instead of, male British regulars. Colonial troops could have provided a substitute form of manpower if the government had disregarded the War and Colonial Offices' reluctance to deploy them in peacetime outside their own countries. However, as the British Exchequer would have had to meet the cost of this, the financial saving would not have been as significant as that from reductions in British manpower. The government did continue to press the War Office but the army remained extremely reluctant to accept the idea of Colonial troops performing tasks which it believed the British Army should undertake—a view reinforced by its experience of Colonial troops in administrative roles in the Middle East. No serious consideration was given to using Colonial troops in Western Europe. One further possible source of overseas manpower was a French-style Foreign Legion. In early 1946 this was seriously considered at the behest of the Prime Minister.[37] There was little support and effective service opposition.

[35] JP (50) 170, 28 Dec. 1950, discussed at COS (51) 1, 2 Jan. 1951, DEFE 4/39.
[36] Executive Committee of the Army Council, ECAC (47) 51, 11 Mar. 1947, WO 163/78.
[37] For the service responses see: Admiralty: DO (46) 26, 27 Feb. 1946; Air Ministry: DO (46) 28, 23 Feb. 1946; War Office: DO (46) 29, 1 Mar. 1946, CAB 131/2. These were discussed at DO (46) 7th, 6 Mar. 1946, CAB 131/1.

The preceding analysis has been concerned to show that unless the government was prepared to discard assumptions about the conduct of foreign policy there was little practical alternative to the view that National Service was unavoidable if the numbers of forces necessary for the pursuit of that foreign policy were to be supplied. To dispense with National Service would have meant, inevitably, a contraction of British commitments. If National Service were abolished this would mean a precipitous abandonment of occupational and other commitments. Even if conscription were only phased out, then British strategy in peace and war would still have had to be radically reorientated. For the government the former was unacceptable. Britain's international obligations were the priority, even though in the spring of 1947 the financial burden led Attlee and Bevin to seek American support in Greece and Turkey, which unwittingly became the genesis of the Truman doctrine. Only after the severest economic crisis in August 1947, when Attlee's personal position was in jeopardy, were those priorities subordinated to domestic objectives.

This leads to a consideration of the other principal reason why permanent conscription was necessary: to provide trained men at the outbreak of a major war. That aim was inextricably linked with British military strategy in war. Yet the relationship between National Service and military strategy was not straightforward. This point should be emphasized. In the Great War conscription had been introduced to provide troops for the war in Europe; when in October 1946 the decision was taken to continue conscription, no inter-service agreement had yet been reached on a common long-term strategic doctrine, around which the services would plan their forces. When this did emerge in mid-1947 it did not involve the commitment of a British army to the defence of Western Europe. The Chiefs of Staff argued:

In the past we have relied on building up an alliance of European countries to unite with us from the very beginning in resisting aggression. There is now, however, no combination of European Powers capable of standing up to Russia on land, nor do we think that the probable military capabilities of an association of European States at present justify us in relying upon such an association for our defence. Nevertheless, any time which we can gain to improve our defences would be of such value that every effort should be made to organise an association of Western

European Powers, which would at least delay the enemy's advance across Europe.[38]

To a large extent each of the services, drawing upon its recent experiences, set about the development of its own doctrines with its own concomitant force structures. For the RAF the atomic bomb was an instantaneous justification for the doctrine of strategic bombing, even though, as Clark and Wheeler point out, 'What is interesting about early British nuclear plans is not the legacy of area bombing . . . but the rapidity of the move towards counter-military targeting notions, which in an important sense, represented the rejection of that war-time inheritance.'[39] Yet, although in both the RAF and the government generally this capability was quickly recognized as the principal element in a strategy that would deter the Soviet Union from embarking on a major war, this was not seen to obviate the need for conventional defences. Fighter Command and anti-aircraft (AA) defences were also required.

Whereas the RAF was concerned to win the Battle of Britain and the Battle of Berlin, the navy's aim was to repeat its success in the Battles of the Atlantic and the Mediterranean, as well as to maintain British peacetime interests and prestige throughout the globe. For the army the question of strategy was more problematic, as it raised what before the war had been the critical issue of Britain's military and political relationship with Europe: the continental commitment. In the War Office, however, this issue was subsumed under the less precise question of how to prepare an army that would be capable of mobilizing effectively at the outset of a war. The question of where it should fight was not critically examined, especially after Montgomery took over as CIGS, the answer being increasingly taken for granted. By 1946 whom they would be fighting was also increasingly taken for granted. In 1945 Alanbrooke recorded his view that war with the Soviet Union was unthinkable, though in May Churchill insisted on contingency plans for war with the Soviet Union being drawn up.[40] After the

[38] DO (44) 47, Future Defence Policy, 21 May 1947, para. 12. Document retained but reprinted in J. Lewis, *Changing Direction: British Military Planning for Post-war Strategic Defence 1942–7* (Sherwood Press, 1988), 370–87.
[39] Ian Clark and Nicholas Wheeler, *The British Origins of Nuclear Strategy 1945–55* (Oxford University Press, 1989) 92–3.
[40] Brooke diaries, 31 May 1945, Alanbrooke papers, 5/11.

war military contingency planning suffused by habit, experience, and perception of Soviet expansionism quickly led the military to turn its professional eyes on the Soviet Union. War with America was discounted and planning assumptions for the Soviet threat proceeded within the service departments. In April 1946, when Attlee was pressing for reconsideration of the Middle East strategy, the Chiefs of Staff's appreciation was based on the contingency of a war against the Soviet Union with the United States as Britain's ally.[41]

National Service was necessary to provide the reserves of trained manpower that could be mobilized at the outset of war, although as there was no agreement on the long-term size and shape of the forces, a decision on the scale of this provision had yet to be reached. The need for trained reserves was important for the RAF and the army. For the latter this was the crucial lesson that the War Office and particularly Montgomery had learned from their experiences of 1939 and their memory of 1914. It reflected disillusionment with the efficacy of the voluntary Territorial Army of the British Expeditionary Force and a belief that there would in a future war be no similar period of grace in a 'phoney war'. Modern war demanded quick reaction.

In theory this did not necessarily entail an army designed for the continent. It was possible that such a force could be used either for the defence of the Middle East or (less plausibly) for the defence of the United Kingdom. Indeed, until 1949 the Chiefs of Staff remained committed to sending the first four TA divisions mobilized in war to the defence of the Middle East. The threat of an invasion of Britain was always recognized as a remote contingency, although in early 1948 the army was temporarily forced back on this prospect to justify a large part of its existence; air and sea power nevertheless remained the effective defence against invasion. The idea that National Service would be useful for Civil Defence was not overlooked. When the Defence Committee discussed conscription, Chuter Ede, the Home Secretary, raised the issue of manpower for Civil Defence,[42] and it was recognized that the provision of a trained body of troops would be invaluable. This was later endorsed when Civil Defence planners incorporated

[41] DO (46) 47, 2 Apr. 1946, CAB 131/2.
[42] DO (46) 27th, 16 Oct., CAB 131/1.

mobile army forces into their schemes. Yet the army did not use Civil Defence as a principal justification for conscription, and indeed was anxious not to have to undertake too many Civil Defence responsibilities.

Traditionally conscription had been designed to send an army to the continent. The other services were, however, strongly opposed to such a commitment. The Chief of the Air Staff Lord Tedder and his colleagues were in agreement on the need to avoid this. Air Vice-Marshal Slessor summed up the argument in a letter to Tedder early in 1947:

Even that [a peacetime army of 320,000] I think is more than we can afford and is based on the 'Continental idea'. I think it is essential that our peacetime army should be reduced to that required for Anti-Aircraft defence, a small mobile field force and overseas garrisons as necessary without any idea of creating in war another colossus which will absorb as it did last time, near 60% of the national effort.[43]

The argument against the continental Army was rooted in the unavoidable inter-service competition for resources; Slessor also inveighed against an 'obsolete pattern navy including a large fleet of battleships and aircraft carriers'.

It was this competition for resources that had begun to change attitudes towards conscription within the Admiralty. It will be recalled that in 1945 the navy had accepted the principle of conscription and agreed to take some 27,000 conscripts on the condition that financial allowance was made for them, and for the 'second fleet' that would be used for training. By late 1946 this grandiose idea had evaporated. Moreover, inter-service competition for resources within the defence budget was, in Admiralty eyes, leaving less room for a large army. Opinion was now divided within the navy towards conscription, though in October the Board of Admiralty felt that with limited resources for defence expenditure conscript reserves would be at the expense of the equipment budget or the regular content.[44] In these circumstances conscription would not, on balance, be of advantage to the navy, though if the government proceeded with National Service, the navy would need to take its share of conscripts. In that event, it

---

[43] Slessor to Tedder, 27 Jan. 1947, AIR 8/799.
[44] Board of Admiralty minutes, 14 Oct. 1946, ADM 167/126.

was now felt that a period of eighteen months might be a better investment for the navy than twelve months.

The navy did not have the same sort of manpower problems as the other services and did not require National Servicemen to man the fleet, although it was prepared to accept conscripts to be trained as reserves. So complacent was the navy that the Admiralty took the view that a recruiting campaign at this time would be 'premature and doomed to failure' and that men 'bounced into the services' would not form the essential firm foundation on which to build Britain's post-war forces.[45] This was an anachronistic perspective that was alarming in its failure to understand the manpower problems of the other services. According to Montgomery's account, when the issue of conscription was discussed in the Chiefs of Staff Committee it provoked 'much argument', with Admiral Sir John Cunningham, the First Sea Lord, arguing that it would be 'a millstone round the neck of the armed forces'.[46] This was an argument against a large army *per se*, not just against a continental army.

There was opposition in the RAF to a continental commitment, but despite the perceived link between conscription and the army's role, the Air Ministry nevertheless supported the War Office on the principle of National Service. This was for two reasons. First, from its own service interests, it recognized that the scale of the air force it envisaged could not be manned by regular recruits alone. Despite the belief that the RAF would prove inherently attractive, a large number of ground and administrative personnel would be required, and it was assumed from the outset that regular recruiting would be unable to provide these. This assumption was reinforced as regular recruiting fell below expectation.

The RAF needed National Service for the same reason of inescapable arithmetic as the army. And like the army it needed the trained reserves of manpower necessary to expand the force on the outbreak of war. From the perspectives of strategic offence and home defence, it was vital to reinforce the front line and bring the reserve and auxiliary air forces into readiness at the earliest possible opportunity. National Service, preferably with a reserve liability, was needed for this purpose. As Slessor told Tedder in January 1947:

[45] COS (46) 45th, 22 Mar. 1946, CAB 79/46.
[46] Montgomery, *Memoirs*, 477.

We might be able to get on without conscription in the Service in peace
—in fact, in some ways it would be an advantage in that we wouldn't
have to employ so many regulars training him. But I do not believe we
can ever raise reserves, especially aircrew reserves on the scale and state of
training required for a modern air force without compulsory military
service.[47]

This was a view which he retained during his time as Commandant of the Imperial Defence College and with which he returned
to the Air Ministry as the Chief of the Air Staff from January
1950. Indeed, the RAF's need for trained men at the start of a
major war was in many ways greater than that of the army, particularly as since 1945 many of its essential functions in war (e.g.
early warning and operations room watches) had been transferred
to the auxiliary forces. Critics of conscription such as Liddell Hart
and Martel generally paid little attention to the RAF's position in
terms of either regular recruiting or the provision of trained men
to secure its effective strength.

The second reason why the RAF supported conscription was
that it recognized the army's need for embodied forces necessary
to meet occupational and longer-term overseas commitments. On
a number of occasions Slessor was to note that the RAF's support
was based on an acceptance of this key part of the army's case.[48]
This recognition may also have reflected the RAF's involvement
in, and awareness of, occupational obligations. Also, the trained
reserves that the army required would be needed to man the anti-
aircraft defences, which the Air Ministry regarded as essential. When
the War Office referred to AA defence needing some 290,000 men
it was self-evident that no such number could be procured except
by conscription.[49] The need to man these defences had been one of
the crucial reasons why conscription had been introduced in 1939.
In 1946 surface-to-air missiles were yet to be developed. Until a
concept of nuclear deterrence had obviated the need for effective
defence against manned bombers anti-aircraft guns would be needed.
This assumed that they would be effective against high-altitude
bombing, which in the autumn of 1947 was questioned in the Chiefs
of Staff Committee when Tedder and Cunningham launched a
major attack on the size and role of the peacetime army.[50]

[47]   Slessor to Tedder, 27 Jan. 1947, AIR 8/799.
[48]   Ibid.; also Slessor to Martel, 24 Jun. 1949, Martel papers.
[49]   AC/M (46) 5, 4 Jun. 1946, WO 163/63.   [50] See ch. 7.

AA defence remained a powerful argument in the army's favour (particularly when the threat posed by Soviet medium-range bombers was analysed), even when feeling in the RAF moved against conscription. In 1948 Slessor still believed that while it 'might just be possible' to get around the problem of acquiring sufficient regulars, he could not see how the problem of manning the AA defences could be solved without conscription.[51]

The relationship between conscription and a strategy for war was thus less than straightforward. National Service was designed to provide an army that was capable of fighting at the earliest possible stage in a major war. *Where* the army would fight did not necessarily determine its size or structure. It is clear that in 1946–7 the army was being prepared in a strategic vacuum. It was being created as an instrument of military force whose specific purpose had yet to be decided. That the people who were forging that weapon were in little doubt as to where, and against whom, it was to be used, did not alter that fact. However, this raised problems for the development of British defence policy.

At the time that conscription was accepted in October 1946, it was anticipated that the final post-war army would amount to some six regular and eight to ten TA divisions.[52] Almost all of the latter were to be infantry divisions. These would clearly be incapable of taking on the Red army on their own. Even with an emphasis on strategic nuclear bombardment, from the military perspective it only made sense to commit the British Army to Europe or the Middle East within a framework of collective security. This clearly raised a number of enormous political and military assumptions.

The defence of Western Europe against the Soviet Union at this time required a large French army. This was a necessary but not sufficient military condition of collective security. In military terms it was increasingly evident that German and/or American ground forces would also be necessary, and in 1946 the political problems raised by either prospect were enormous and intractable. As far as Europe was concerned, then, the value of a British conscript army was contingent on a number of political and military conditions. Yet it was inevitably predicated on a specific set

of assumptions about those conditions. It was assumed that a
commitment to defend Western Europe had to take the form that
it had in 1939. Air power and/or a standing army of regular
and/or armoured divisions were implicitly discounted as sufficient
contributions. This raised familiar arguments about limited liability and about the political need for military guarantees, particularly to the French. A continental army would help to be a 'land
check' designed to shield Western Europe (and thereby the United
Kingdom) while the sword of strategic bombardment struck at the
vitals of the Soviet Union.

For the army this was not necessarily a problem. For the other
services, given their own ambitious plans and their perception of
an increasingly limited defence budget, it was as though the army
had learned nothing and forgotten nothing. But even on its own
criteria the War Office's case for conscription was inadequate in a
number of respects which could indeed be seen as weakening the
idea not just of a continental role but of any major overseas ven-
ture in the initial phase of a major war. The justification for conscription was to provide armed forces and particularly an army at the
outset of a major war. Given that within five years this system would
be able to produce over a million trained men who could be readily
mobilized and embarked, there would be no repeat of 1914 or 1939.
The British Army would go to war as one army rather than two.
There would be one well-trained and well-equipped force, not a
group of ill-equipped professionals, reinforced by enthusiastic but
largely amateurish territorials, who would have to hang on until
the bulk of the main conscript army arrived after the delay caused
by its training. There were two problems with this.

The first was that on the most optimistic of calculations it
would be at least three months before the first of the TA divisions
would be ready. If modern warfare really did put a premium on
preparedness and/or if the Soviet Union kept a significant number
of divisions in being, there was a great deal of doubt about
whether the 'cavalry' would get there in time. In 1949 the Chiefs
of Staff grudgingly told the government that some commitment
was necessary for West European defence and that this required a
guarantee to send two of the first four TA divisions to Europe in
the event of attack.[53] When making this request the service chiefs

---

[53] See ch. 9.

pointed out that as it was probable that the defence on the Rhine would collapse fairly rapidly, it might well be unnecessary to disembark them at all. Although this was a question of short-term plans for the defence of Western Europe it also applied to the long-term issue. The time that the 'New Model Army' would take to reach the battlefield was recognized as being too long by Liddell Hart, who claimed that a conscript army was 'slow to mobilise and in a democratic country there is a natural inclination to delay its mobilisation'.[54]

The second problem was also recognized by the military critics, and especially by Giffard Martel, for whom it formed the basis of his opposition to conscription. This was that the nature of the army that Britain would be sending would be less than adequate for modern war. The lessons that Liddell Hart and Martel had learned from the Second World War were very different from those learned by Montgomery and the War Office. For the critics the war had shown the need for mobile and armoured forces of the sort which the Germans had used to such devastating effect in their blitzkrieg tactics. For Martel the twenty armoured divisions that the Germans had used to spearhead their attack on the Soviet Union were immeasurably more effective as a defence against a Soviet attack than a mass army composed of conscript infantry. If Britain could supply four or five such divisions, permanently emplaced in West Germany, then a firm foundation for European defence could be established.

For Liddell Hart these were familiar issues. The experience of the war and German armoured warfare, especially in Western Europe and Russia, did not so much enable him to learn new lessons as to validate his pre-war ideas. For him as for Martel there was a direct relationship between the structure and the tactical outlook of the army. The idea that the new Territorial Army could provide effective mobile and armoured units was dismissed, a view largely shared by official thinking since only one of the eight TA divisions was to be armoured and this was going to be in the 'second wave' of mobilization. The adoption of conscription was seen as a preference for the French militia of 1940 rather than the German Panzer divisions that overran them.

---

[54] 'The Question of Conscription', 4 Mar. 1947, published in *World Review*, 2 (1947), Liddell Hart papers, 10/1947/4a.

Linked to the criticism of tactical outlook was Liddell Hart's attack on the teeth to tail ratio and the size of the British division. He argued that by radically restructuring the latter on the pattern suggested by German or even Soviet experience, more divisions, each with firepower equivalent to existing units, could be provided. These ideas were to find little favour in the army, not least among the men responsible for the armoured regiments. The Commandant of the Royal Armoured Corps, General Roberts, displayed a marked lack of enthusiasm at the prospect of pitting armoured divisions equipped with the relatively light 'Cruiser' tanks against the heavy Stalin tanks of the Soviet armoured brigades.[55] This raised the question of how the British armour was to be organized, and whether the heavy Centurion tanks were to be arranged in independent brigades or integrated into the armoured divisions proper. Martel advocated the deployment of independent heavy tank brigades and urged that the lighter, quicker 'Cruiser' divisions be used in blitzkrieg-like fashion against the vulnerable rearward and supply units of the enemy.[56] This had been a recipe for tactical success on the Eastern Front when the Germans were on the defensive, and had also appeared to compensate for the inferiority of most German tanks in the early years of the war.

Yet this did not accord with British military experience. The British Army had won its laurels in essentially linear positional battles. Perhaps most importantly, Montgomery's own victories had been in positional warfare, which, especially in Normandy, had involved a gruelling struggle of attrition between the British and German armour (admittedly aimed at freeing the Americans for the decisive mobile attacks). The experience of Arnhem had shown the difficulties of attempting daring mobile thrusts when the enemy was not thrown tactically or psychologically off balance, as blitzkrieg theories expected and required. Martel privately told Churchill that while Montgomery was 'the greatest soldier' at positional warfare and 'had to his credit the magnificent victories' of El Alamein and Normandy,[57] he was in consequence 'carried away with similar ideas'. But even in those successes, so Martel claimed, he had never really understood mobility: 'He could have put Rommel in the bag after El Alamein and when we

[55] Martel, exchange of letters with Roberts, Feb. 1951, Martel papers.
[56] Martel to Churchill, 21 Aug. 1950, Martel papers.   [57] Ibid.

broke out from Normandy no plans were made to maintain the mobility of the armoured divisions.' Fuller had less praise for Montgomery. He believed Monty to be suitable for Hollywood —'never the War Office'.[58]

Whatever the merits of Martel's views it is not surprising that the army, especially under Montgomery, acted on the basis of experience. The dissemination of German military practice on the Russian front into Western military and intellectual circles had hardly begun. If blitzkrieg was synonymous with German armoured warfare, then there were various counter-examples (The Ardennes offensive in 1944, the Battle of Kursk in 1943) to suggest that the approach was far from infallible. The Germans had lost the war and the British had won. Furthermore, the radical approach of the critics took little account of the political problems that mobile defence raised in West Germany.

None of this is meant to suggest that the critics were correct in seeing conscription as inevitably bound up with the psychology or indeed tactics of 'positional' warfare. As the Germans themselves had shown, compulsory military service and armoured warfare were compatible.

These sorts of issues were rarely examined by the politicians, and no systematic and coherent criticism of the War Office's view appeared at a ministerial level. The general ineffectiveness of Lawson and Bellenger has already been noted. Whatever Shinwell's abilities (and his stock rose considerably while he was at the War Office), challenging military orthodoxy was a formidable task. The way that the army would fight in a major war was determined by the General Staff, not the Army Council. Shinwell, indeed, complained that he was excluded from the critical areas of 'strategic' policy-making.[59] The idea that politicians should be involved in matters of operational concern was not accepted. The role of the Secretary of State for War was restricted to carefully delineated areas of policy outside the issues of purely 'military concern'.

Departmental ministers were inhibited in influencing areas of policy. More importantly, they were unwilling to try, principally because they did not share the military critics' perception and

[58] Fuller to Martel, 9 Oct. 1945, Martel papers.
[59] AC/M (48) 3, 20 Apr. 1948, WO 163/63.

preferred the advice of their professional advisers. This was also true of ministers as a whole. The Defence Committee did not discuss these questions. When it examined strategic issues it invariably did so at a more general level. Opportunities for ministerial discussion were provided by the Staff Conferences with the Chiefs of Staff, which involved the Minister of Defence and/or the Prime Minister (and sometimes the Foreign Secretary). Yet the Chiefs of Staff were invariably keen to preserve a united front in the presence of ministers, and no attempt was made to challenge the army's assumptions, at least until after the National Service Act had been passed.

The principal reason for this was that conscription did not entail a single strategy. When conscription was decided upon, no agreement on strategy had been reached among the services, let alone by the government. It was not seen to be necessary to reach decisions on these matters of even greater importance and complexity. It can be argued that this represented a failure on the part of the government, either because conscription entailed the sort of army that was inappropriate (as Liddell Hart argued) or because the strategies that each of the services was developing on the basis of conscription meant an overcommitment and/or misallocation of resources. When the services did reach an agreement of sorts in mid-1947, it demonstrated that the scale of forces they anticipated was far beyond what the government could afford. These issues will be returned to in later chapters.

In adopting National Service on a long-term basis, there is no doubt that policy predated strategy—in one sense means predated ends. Those means did not determine the ends, not least because the RAF needed National Service. Nevertheless, within an increasingly constrained defence budget the policy of universal military conscription exercised an important influence on the allocation of resources. The extent of that influence was to vary according to the size of the budget and the inter-service allocation between the forces. National Service also reflected the strategic perspectives of the army. In the eyes of the army leadership the commitment to Europe in war required military conscription. The army had other needs for conscription in peace as well as war. Yet at least until a firm commitment was made to the defence of Western Europe, a conscript army at the outbreak of war did not represent the most effective strategy within an increasingly constrained defence budget. Even when that commitment was made there were still those, especially in the RAF, who argued that a conscript army was a misappropriation of resources. Just as conscription did not determine strategy, neither would the abolition of conscription have determined the precise structure and doctrine of the forces. It would, however, have been viewed as curtailing a British commitment to the continent, unless it was linked to a permanent standing army in Western Europe within a system of collective defence. As that was opposed by the government until well after the North Atlantic Treaty Organization (NATO) was established, the abolition of conscription would have been seen as an indication that Britain was not prepared to send its army to Europe.

These issues were clearly complex and required a level of understanding and an interest in defence that most Members of Parliament, particularly Labour MPs, might not be expected to possess. Nevertheless, there was a significant number who were neither ignorant nor unwilling to look critically at defence issues. This was particularly true of the PLP. Despite (or perhaps because of) its pre-war traumas with defence issues, a number of informed and radical young thinkers had emerged whose interest and whose numbers had been reinforced by the war. By 1945 there was a significant group of Labour MPs who had served in the forces and who were keen to make use of their experience: Lieutenant-Colonel Wigg, Captain Bing, Major Wyatt, Lieutenant Callaghan, Wing-Commander Millington, Major Bruce, Major Freeman. Several of these, along with the likes of Major Healey (then International Secretary of the party) and Mr Crossman, were to play important roles in subsequent debates on nuclear weapons and British defence policy. During the period of (Major) Attlee's government a number of these men were prominent in the Defence and Services Group of the PLP and in Labour Party debates on defence in general. Of interest is the high proportion of former serving officers who were in the Keep Left group and who had emerged from wartime service with insight, knowledge, and profound dissatisfaction with what they had found.

Despite the presence of these informed and energetic ex-officers, the debates on conscription in the House of Commons did not provide a thoroughgoing critique of the military case for being able to fight at the beginning of a war in general, or in Europe. The basic reason for this was quite simple—a shared perception that the lessons of 1939 should not be ignored. There were other reasons. In the first place, information available to MPs about defence issues was kept to a minimum. In August 1948 Liddell Hart was to complain to Montgomery that 'the basic facts and figures have never been so carefully hidden from friendly critics as they are now'.[60] Although more information gradually became available, the government was to follow the advice of the military deputy secretary to the Cabinet, Major-General Hollis, who in July 1947 urged the Minister of Defence to engage in 'more or less meaningless verbiage' to avoid admitting that the forces were not in a position to 'undertake major operations against a first class power'.[61]

Furthermore, many of the crucial technical and military issues had not emerged in 1946–7. In terms of manpower policy, no decision had yet been reached on the permanent post-war strength of the RAF. It was not until 1950 that there was any public discussion of how the Royal Armoured Corps was to be equipped and organized.[62] For Martel this latter question was central to his critique of conscription, yet in 1946–7 it had not emerged on to either the military or the political agenda. Indeed, few of the military arguments against conscription were heard until after the National Service Act had been introduced. Liddell Hart did take up the issue in early 1947. Martel said he was not clear in his own mind: he 'became convinced that conscription was a thoroughly bad thing' only after he had been persuaded by Liddell Hart in April 1947.[63]

The strategic issues were touched upon only in abstractions. The question of whether Britain should have a permanent standing army in Europe or one designed to be sent there at the beginning of a war was central to British defence policy and the long-term question of conscription. When announcing the National Service Act, Attlee said that 'the development of modern warfare has made this country more vulnerable. We are now part of the continent. We can be reached by attack from the continent.'[64]

---

[60] Liddell Hart, Notes for Montgomery, 31 Aug. 1948, Liddell Hart papers, 1/519/38a.

[61] Hollis to Alexander, 7 Jul. 1947, DEFE 4/5.

[62] See articles by Martel in the *Daily Mail*, 31 Aug. 1950, *Star*, 7 Sept. 1950, and *Evening Standard*, 28 Mar. 1951.   [63] Our Defence Forces, i, Martel papers.

[64] *HC deb.*, vol. 430, 12 Nov. 1946, col. 40.

The implications of this appeared to be straightforward and indeed echoed Bevin's arguments in 1945. Yet when the left-wing Labour MP Konni Zilliacus suggested that conscription was therefore intended to fight the Russians,[65] this was indignantly denied and the *Daily Herald* retorted that there was 'no case for impugning the government's fidelity in its work for peace'.[66]

Moreover, Attlee himself remained opposed to the commitment of the army to the defence of Western Europe. In one sense conscription *was* intended to fight the Russians. But it was also intended to provide the forces in peacetime necessary for the government to pursue its foreign policy. In parliamentary terms, ministers were not keen to admit the former or emphasize the latter. This meant that discussion of particularly the long-term issue of Britain's defence policy was conducted in abstract terms. Concern with preparedness for war became a psychological objective divorced from its strategic purpose. In so far as this reflected the government's position it was to create considerable problems when the implications for the allocation of resources were fully understood.

The military case for conscription rested on two different bases: the need for embodied forces in peacetime and the need for trained reserves ready on mobilization. It should be noted that there was little truth in the accusation that the military wanted conscription as an end in itself. It was recognized that National Service would improve the physical well-being of young men through regular meals and physical exercise, and it was claimed that military values such as discipline were intrinsically desirable. But these were no more than rhetorical glosses which were frequently voiced also by ministers, notably Alexander.[67] The case for conscription within Whitehall rested on purely military requirements.

There were arguments and support for conscription on non-military grounds. Major-General Lord Mottistone, Secretary of State for War in Asquith's government, for example, argued that National Service was a 'civic and patriotic duty' designed 'to safeguard the Christian way of life'.[68] Instead of drills he suggested that men should be taught 'woodcraft, knowledge of internal combustion engines, how to build a boat or a raft and if possible

[65] *HC deb.*, vol. 435, 31 Mar. 1947, col. 1775.
[66] *Daily Herald*, 1 Apr. 1947.
[67] See ch. 7.   [68] *Sunday Times*, 20 May 1945.

ride, drive and care for a horse'. Mottistone believed that 'We need it for defence and for health in body and mind as well'. General Martel himself wrote in 1945:

As regards conscription we all saw that a large proportion of the young men of this country benefited very greatly from the good food and physical exercise which they received when they were called up. They increased rapidly in weight and strength and general fitness. They also acquired a grand team spirit and became conscious of their duty of service for their country. These are great attributes.[69]

Montgomery was one of the main architects of conscription and he did argue that 'the army must be woven into the social fabric of the nation'.[70] The political implications of a 'trained and disciplined nation' or of the view that 'anything which weakens the national character weakens the army' were not lost on left-wing and other critics. Yet whatever Montgomery's views of the benefits of military life, these were not the grounds on which he argued for National Service within Whitehall. Similar conclusions can be reached about Bevin's views of the social obligations of citizenship, which were originally aired in the Coalition government and appeared to point to permanent conscription. Yet for Bevin the real case for conscription lay both in providing the troops required by his foreign policy and, it should be emphasized, in producing a military system which, at least in 1947, he compared favourably with that designed by Haldane.[71]

The military arguments against conscription took different forms, and emerged as the problems of the defence budget and the experience of the services developed. In the autumn of 1946, when the government was required to take the decisions, the military objections were muted and the only significant opposition emerged on non-military lines.

[69] Giffard Martel, *The Problem of Security* (Michael Joseph, 1945) 75.
[70] Speech in Portsmouth, 26 Jul. 1946, Attlee papers, dep. 40.
[71] Bevin to Attlee, 15 Aug. 1947, PREM 8/833.

5

The 1947 National Service Act

HUGH Dalton described 1946 as the *annus mirabilis* of Labour's fortunes.[1] The party's dramatic programme of social reform was proceeding apace, buttressed by bold, self-confident, and seemingly successful economic and fiscal policies. In international affairs 1946 was a decisive year. In February, George Kennan composed his 'Long Telegram'. In March, Winston Churchill delivered his 'Iron Curtain' speech. American government attitudes towards the Soviet Union began to change.[2] The dispute over Soviet claims in Azerbaijan was resolved when Washington stood firm. British–Soviet diplomatic relations also deteriorated. There was little progress over Germany. The hope that the UN would portend a new world order was vanishing.

The summer of 1946 was in many ways the Attlee government's 'High Tide'.[3] By then it was also becoming clear that the tide was turning. Domestic and international problems loomed on the horizon. Under the terms of the United States loan, sterling was due to become convertible in the summer of 1947. Relations with the Soviet Union were deteriorating, while the United States was still withdrawing its forces from Europe. In Palestine Jewish terrorism was sapping the will of the British to maintain the Mandate as well as rekindling American hostility toward British imperialism. Even the weather was to turn against the government. The winter of 1946–7 was the worst in memory and, compounded by ministerial incompetence, led to a crippling fuel crisis in early 1947.[4]

---

[1] Hugh Dalton, *Memoirs*, iii: *High Tide and After 1945–60*, (Muller, 1962), part II.

[2] See J. L. Gaddis, *The United States and the Origins of the Cold War, 1941–7* (New York: Columbia University Press, 1971), chs. 4 ff.

[3] Dalton, *High Tide and After*.

[4] For an account of the fuel crisis see P. M. Williams, *Hugh Gaitskell* (Cape, 1979), ch. 6.

The adoption of a scheme of compulsory military service was therefore of major importance to the British economy and to British foreign policy. As the various schemes for the continuation of the call-up were being devised it became apparent that not only the services but the educational and industrial authorities needed to know whether National Service would be adopted as a long-term policy. Under pressure from Education minister Ellen Wilkinson, in February Attlee told the Defence Committee that it was necessary to study a number of complicated problems, such as exemptions, before a decision about a permanent scheme of National Service was possible. As a result the Manpower Committee established a working group to provide material on a permanent scheme of conscription.[5] That study lasted until well into the summer, by which time Montgomery had taken over as CIGS. In September he returned from a tour of the United States determined to get a decision on the long-term issue of conscription.[6]

In October the CIGS gained the agreement of the Chiefs of Staff Committee and confronted Attlee. By that stage the working party had only just completed its report. Bevin, the chairman of the Cabinet Manpower Committee, was abroad so Attlee had the report taken directly to the Defence Committee, bypassing the Manpower Committee. It is possible that Montgomery persuaded Attlee to act in this way. On the other hand, Attlee's action predated the COS Committee meeting to which Montgomery refers.[7] Nevertheless, the Ministry of Labour assumed that the National Service Act would not be necessary until the 1947–8 parliamentary session and there is little doubt that but for the Prime Minister's action a decision would not have been taken in time for its inclusion in the King's Speech on 6 November 1946.

The report's leapfrogging the Manpower Committee meant that a number of important details did not receive ministerial scrutiny. Cripps was to complain that there had not been enough time to consider specific implications, particularly concerning the

---

[5] DO (46) 5th, 15 Feb. 1946, CAB 131/1; Minute of a Meeting to Discuss Preparation of a Paper for the Manpower Committee on Permanent Arrangements for Providing Manpower for the Forces, 25 Mar. 1946, DEFE 7/146.

[6] Bernard Montgomery, *The Memoirs of Field Marshal The Viscount Montgomery of Alamein* (Cassell, 1958), ch. 30.

[7] Attlee to Bevin, Min M. 330/46, 1 Oct. 1946, CAB 21/2069.

proposed length of service.[8] A number of crucial questions about
the size of the intake and the duration of National Service were
not worked out until the following spring.

The scheme that was devised by the working party drew upon
all the experience that had been accumulated before, during, and
after the war. In most, though not all, respects the National
Service Act represented continuity with recent practice. The
central feature of the scheme was its universality. In 1945 Bevin
had been adamant that conscription was acceptable only if it were
applied to all young men. The General Council of the TUC had
been equally insistent that only a universal scheme was fair and
only a fair scheme was acceptable. Fairness and equality were
synonymous. There would be no exemptions on the basis of privi-
lege. For those who argued that National Service was an obligation of citizenship, it was only right that all citizens should
shoulder their responsibilities.

In October 1946 no one in the Defence Committee, the Cabinet, or the PLP was seriously prepared to argue against the principle of universality. Nor was this substantially challenged by the
military. Despite a naval preference for some form of selective
service it was accepted that a universal liability was an essential
political prerequisite for its introduction. The Chiefs of Staff's
priorities lay in getting the principle of conscription accepted and
then securing the longest possible period of service. It was not
until the financial and manpower ceilings had begun to impact
that military and political arguments for selective service and for
other methods of controlling the intake of National Servicemen
began to receive serious consideration.

The universal nature of the scheme is a useful focal point for
examining various features of the National Service Act, largely
because it was not as universal as it appeared. In the first place
there were the students and apprentices. These were to be entitled
to defer their military service until they had completed their
studies or apprenticeships. This raised no real problems. All those
who deferred their service were still required to discharge their
military obligations eventually. Moreover, there was virtually
total agreement that this was essential for the economic and social
good of the country. The facility of deferment was the natural

[8] DO (46) 27th, 16 Oct. 1946, CAB 131/1.

continuation of the provisions which had been fought through earlier in the year; politically it was not only expected but positively welcomed by the opposition and in the labour movement.

Students and apprentices were to be called up eventually, but this was not true of a number of industrial occupations. Coalminers were exempted. So, for the time being, were agricultural workers and men in the Merchant Navy. During the war there had been a whole range of occupations which were considered essential to the war effort and in which men had not been conscripted for military service. Similarly, in a future war men who were now to be trained in the services would be needed in essential industries. This suggested that there was a prima-facie case for extending the list of exemptions. However, as the purpose of National Service was not just to provide trained men in war but also to create embodied forces in peacetime, the argument was not accepted.

The handful of industries that were selected for exemption did not provide any real problems for the government as they were seen as necessary exceptions. Although the criterion of 'an essential industry' was highly problematic there were few who doubted that feeding the nation was essential. As for coalmining, this was not only vital to the nation's economic survival, but the job of the coalminer was every bit as arduous and potentially lethal as that of the serviceman. As these specific exemptions were continuous with past practice and as they conformed to existing expectations they did not create any political disquiet.

In addition a number of other groups were excluded: conscientious objectors (COs); the medically unfit; women; and Ulstermen. Under the 1939 Military Training Act and then during the war men (and from 1941 women) who could convince the necessary tribunals of their status as COs had been exempted from combat service or military service in general or, in a minority of cases, work that might assist the war effort. The Labour Party was strewn with vociferous and long-standing pacifists. Indeed, the Cabinet contained three former conscientious objectors— Morrison, Creech Jones (the Colonial Secretary), and Pethwick Lawrence (the Secretary of State for India), and would have probably had a fourth if Bevan had not been declared medically unfit.[9]

⁹ Foot, *Bevan*, i: 33–5.

Even among those who had not been pacifists the memories of the degradations and humiliations of some of the COs in the Great War were still poignant.[10]

Provision for conscientious objection was insisted upon when Labour ministers considered conscription. On the other hand, as Attlee told the Defence Committee, these men would be required to undertake some form of compulsory service in fairness to those called up. This would be more limited in scale than during the war, partly because the numbers involved would be smaller. Forestry and land reclamation were mentioned as the main areas of employment. During the war COs who had been granted conditional exemptions mainly served on the land and from 1941 on Civil Defence work. Within the armed forces they served in the Royal Army Medical Corps and from 1940 in the Non-Combatant Corps. It was anticipated that there would be about 400 COs a year.[11] Provision for COs aroused little unease. It was an extension of a wartime system that had been designed with the experience learned from the mistakes of the Great War and which was generally viewed as having worked as humanely and fairly as was administratively possible.

Ulstermen also were not conscripted. Again, this reflected past experience. In 1918 Lloyd George's proposals to extend conscription to Northern Ireland had provoked vigorous opposition from the Catholic community. In April 1939 Lord Craigavon's government in Stormont publicly called for the application of the Military Training Act to the province.[12] De Valera denounced the suggestion. Chamberlain had no interest in provoking trouble in the province at this time and personally asked Craigavon not to press the issue. The Northern Ireland leader backed down and despite further Unionist pressure in May 1941 the British government did not extend conscription to Ulster during the war.[13]

In 1946 the exclusion of Ulstermen again met with the displeasure of Ulster's Protestant leaders. While there was considerable sympathy within sections of the labour movement towards the Roman Catholics and indeed towards republican nationalism, this does not in itself explain why the British government ignored

[10] For an account of this see John Rae, *Conscience and Politics* (Oxford University Press, 1970).   [11] CP (46) 403, 29 Oct. 1946, CAB 129/13.
[12] Robert Fisk, *In Time of War: Ireland, Ulster and the Price of Neutrality 1939–45* (Paladin, 1985), 92–7.   [13] Ibid. 509–25.

Stormont's wishes. There was no consultation with Stormont before the decision was taken by the British Cabinet and Sir Basil Brooke, the Prime Minister of Ulster, was informed only a matter of days before the public announcement in the King's Speech. This was despite Brooke's attempts to persuade Westminster to consult beforehand. In April 1945 he wrote to Morrison, then Home Secretary, urging that should the 'Imperial government' adopt some form of compulsory military training Northern Ireland should not be excluded;[14] and in November 1945 he urged the Home Secretary to hold prior discussions with his government should such a scheme be imminent.

When informed of the decision Brooke, together with his Home Secretary Edmond Warnock and three of their Cabinet colleagues, visited London to meet Chuter Ede and Alexander to urge that conscription should be applied in Ulster. While they felt that National Service would not in itself be popular they nevertheless believed that the citizens of Northern Ireland should 'be given the opportunity of playing their part in building up the armed forces requirements and of sharing the burdens and responsibilities of their fellow citizens'.[15] These were sentiments that Brooke and his colleagues were to repeat in the parliamentary debates, but to no avail.

Privately, the Ulster Unionists claimed to be confident that they could overcome any difficulties arising from the inevitable republican opposition and they quoted the Inspector General of Constabulary who had 'expressed his confidence in being able to handle any situation that might arise'.[16] However, as Warnock noted in a memorandum hastily prepared for the Westminster government: 'There is no doubt any proposal to apply a Military Service Act to Northern Ireland will be a signal for a very active—not to say violent—anti-conscription campaign. We have had two previous experiences [1918 and 1939] and the pattern of agitation can be drawn with fair accuracy.'[17] He recognized that 'there will be opposition, much of it sincere and all of it vigorous or violent from the Roman Catholic community in Northern Ireland and beyond'.

[14] Brooke to Attlee, 6 Nov. 1946, PREM 8/280.   [15] Ibid.
[16] Chuter Ede to Attlee, 11 Nov. 1946, PREM 8/280.
[17] Memorandum by Warnock, Nov. 1946, PREM 8/280. In 1940 Warnock had been vociferous in his criticisms of Unionist leaders for failing to get conscription extended to the province. See Fisk, *In Time of War*, 282–3.

When pressed by Alexander and Chuter Ede, the Unionists conceded that there might be shootings and that the military might have to intervene in the Catholic quarters of Belfast. Not surprisingly these admissions did little to alter the attitude of the British government. Neither then, nor in January 1949 when the issue of conscription briefly arose in the context of the Eire Bill, did the prospect of internal disorder (possibly extending to Liverpool and Glasgow) or external 'agitation' (especially from the Irish Americans) offer any inducement for the British to reconsider their position. In 1939 De Valera had bitterly attacked the attempt to introduce conscription in the North, describing it as 'an act of aggression'.[18] A similar attempt in 1946 would have undoubtedly jeopardized relations between London and Dublin.

The exclusion of the province did not create political problems on the mainland. For the services the issue was an essentially political question and it was assumed from the outset that Ulster would be excluded. The problems of training rebellious republicans did not encourage the military to press for their conscription (during the war the vital strategic need to keep Eire at least neutral had been the overriding reason). As time went on, and as manpower and financial ceilings led to reductions in the intake of National Servicemen, there was less and less military sense in extending liability. Moreover, with the persistence of overseas commitments the precarious situation of the British Army's strategic reserve provided a strong military incentive against any action that would require reinforcements for internal security purposes.

Politically, the exclusion of Ulster did not create problems since Churchill accepted the wisdom of the government's decision. Indicative of both the low saliency of Ulster affairs in British politics and the fact that Ulster's exclusion was not deemed significant on the mainland was a pair of articles in the *Manchester Guardian* in 1949 which examined the size of the National Service intake.[19] The purpose was to show the extent of the exemptions and deferments; yet no mention was made of Ulster. In Labour Party and trade union debates the issue did not arise. The attitude of the opposition was equally important. In May 1947 Anthony Eden, speaking from the opposition benches, expressed his sympathy for

---

[18] Fisk, *In Time of War*, 93.   [19] *Manchester Guardian*, 3 Oct. 1949.

the Unionists but spoke in support of the government when the Ulster MPs proposed an amendment to include the province.[20] When the amendment was pressed to a division the opposition abstained, although some thirty-four Conservative MPs supported their Ulster colleagues.[21]

Women were not conscripted. Although there was some support for their inclusion among women's groups, the government decided against the idea. The National Council for Women supported inclusion on straightforward egalitarian grounds.[22] In Parliament most women Labour MPs did not publicly support conscription for women although Barbara Ayrton Gould, who was also a member of the NEC, was an exception.[23] Most female Labour MPs who played any role in the debates on defence were of pacifist inclination and appeared to share their male colleagues' views that women as mothers possessed a greater natural predisposition against war and the preparation for war.

The government's reluctance to conscript women was hardly surprising. It could be argued that given the rights of citizenship and/or the demands of equality women should undertake at least an equivalent form of National Service. Furthermore, there was the self-evident argument that in war the nation's fortunes required the mobilization of all available 'manpower'. On the other hand, so far as equality was concerned the argument hinged upon a particular view of rights. It could be argued that as women did not enjoy equal opportunities or benefits they should not be expected to undertake the more burdensome obligations.

More importantly, wartime experience had shown a very strong popular feeling against the idea.[24] Any argument about egalitarianism had to be tempered by more powerful prevailing social norms and by a sense of the publicly and politically acceptable. The introduction of conscription in peacetime for men was a radical departure from British traditions and something of a shock to post-war expectations. Such a radically egalitarian notion as the

[20] *HC deb.*, vol. 437, 6 May 1947, cols. 305–7.
[21] *HC deb.*, vol. 437, 21 May 1947, cols. 2429–32.
[22] CP (46) 380, 21 Oct. 1946, CAB 129/13.
[23] *HC deb.*, vol. 435, 31 Mar. 1947, cols. 1727–31.
[24] See Alan Bullock, *The Life and Times of Ernest Bevin*, ii: *1940–5* (Heinemann, 1967), 122, 138–9, 255. Bullock describes the wartime conscription of women as 'one of the boldest acts of policy ever carried out by a democratic government' and 'Bevin's greatest achievement as Minister of Labour' (255).

conscription of women would have risked undermining the popular and political acceptability of the National Service scheme as a whole. The opposition would have been able to support the general proposals while making enormous political gain on an issue which they themselves would never have seriously considered. Indeed it is doubtful if the measure would have got through the House of Commons as Conservatives would have been joined by a significant number of Labour MPs in voting against the government.

Within the government there was some sentiment in favour of the conscription of women. Bevin had argued in the APW Committee in favour, claiming that as certain service jobs could 'only be done by women' serious consideration should be given to their conscription.[25] These sentiments were supported by Sir John Anderson at the time[26] and by *The Economist* in November 1946.[27] The one occasion in the post-war government when the idea was considered was in January 1947 when Dalton drew up radical proposals which he claimed were desperately needed for the economy.[28] They included the conscription of women on the same basis as in war, leaving them the option of industrial/agricultural or military service. Although the proposals were supported by Cripps and the other economic ministers, Attlee and Bevin rejected them in what Dalton described as a mood of 'easy going muddle headed irresponsibility'.[29]

It was not until May 1946 that a decision had been reached to maintain permanent women's services. Provision for the conscription of women remained until January 1947, but few were called up after 1944. While the value of female regulars was recognized, they were nevertheless seen only as a supplement. Although women were taking on a number of active service roles, and although they were expected to accept as much responsibility as their male counterparts, they were only intended to augment male strength. This was despite the fact that in many areas they replaced men on a one-to-one ratio. It was to be over thirty years before women in the British services carried arms, and the idea of female combat troops received no consideration whatsoever

[25] APW (45) 7th, 22 Mar. 1945, CAB 87/69.   [26] Ibid.
[27] *The Economist*, 23 Nov. 1946.
[28] Diaries of Hugh Dalton (London School of Economics), 17 Jan. 1947.
[29] Ibid.

in the 1940s. No other European or Western society had ever conscripted women, except on occasions in times of direst emergency. Even the Communist Party of Great Britain remained opposed to conscripting women at the time when it supported the principle of military conscription itself.[30]

A fifth category of exemption was the medically unfit. As far as military service was concerned this was only to be expected. The forces did not want men who were physically or mentally incapable of effectively discharging their duties. Fixing the medical standards was of course an inherently arbitrary affair and became bound up with the question of how many men were needed by the services or could be afforded by the government. As manpower and financial ceilings came under increasing pressure adjusting medical standards became a convenient administrative means of reducing the conscript intake. Yet in 1946 the government was reluctant to be seen to be discriminating against the medically fit and did not raise standards. Some 87 per cent of men were expected to be passed fit for military service, slightly more than during the war.[31]

The system of medical examinations was in any case under review and a new scheme drawing upon the lessons of wartime experience was to be introduced, initially in the army, subsequently in the other services. This more comprehensive medical examination was known as the Pulheems system and was adopted by the army for regulars and conscripts in 1948.[32] Even this did not remove one particular problem for the army. Although the Pulheems system took greater account of psychological and mental abilities it did not disqualify men below a certain level of mental ability, who were consigned to the Pioneer Corps. As time passed these men were increasingly seen as a waste of ever more scarce resources.

The Pulheems system did provide the categories and means of classification which could be used to prevent men who were 'unfit' often in only technical senses from slipping through the net.

[30] *Towards a People's Army* (Communist Party, Jun. 1946).

[31] Sir Norman Brook, brief for Attlee, 30 Oct. 1946, PREM 8/610.

[32] For an account of the Pulheems system see R. T. Fletcher, 'Pulheems: A New System of Medical Classification'. *British Medical Journal*, 1949, i. 83–8. PULHEEMS stood for: P physical capacity; U upper limbs; L locomotion; H hearing; EE eyesight; M mental capacity; S stability (emotional).

Nevertheless it was initially anticipated that those in Grades I and II of the old system would be accepted into the forces. The political need for what the military regarded as a relatively low standard was attributable to the declared aim of universality. It is interesting, however, that there was no attempt to make those who were not fully fit nevertheless perform some form of service in military or non-military occupations, although Isaacs did recommend that men in Grade III should be conscripted as they had not been during the war.[33] There was a sort of precedent in the provision for conscientious objectors. Although the Pulheems system was to provide greater flexibility in classifying different sorts of disability any attempt to make military 'rejects' undertake a form of National Service would have meant developing a range of non-military tasks that would have required additional expenditure. Within the services it would have also been administratively complicated and the service ministries were opposed to placing the less medically fit in more sedentary occupations.

These various features of the National Service scheme reflected the British experience of compulsory military service and in 1946–7 this was evident in a political consensus on the form of conscription. The categories of deferment and exemption aroused no real controversy. It was only later that the need to reduce the size of the National Service intake raised such questions as selective service in a serious way.

The question which generated the most heated debate, both in government and in Parliament, was the length of service. The principle of conscription created a great deal less fuss, especially at a ministerial level. On 23 October 1946 after the Defence Committee had reached its decision but before the Cabinet had done so, Dalton noted in his diary that, 'The view of ministers—

[33] CP (46) 403, 29 Oct. 1946, CAB 129/13. The wartime scheme was based on four categories: Grade I—men who, subject only to such minor disabilities as can be remedied or adequately compensated by artificial means, attain the formal normal standard of health and strength and are capable of enduring physical exertion suitable to their age; Grade II—those who, while suffering from disabilities disqualifying them for Grade I, do not suffer from progressive organic disease, have fair hearing and vision, are of moderate muscular development, and are able to undergo a considerable amount of physical exertion not involving severe strain; Grade III—those who present such marked physical disabilities or evidence of past disease that they are not fit for the amount of exertion required for Grade II; Grade IV—those who suffer from progressive organic disease or are for other reasons permanently incapable of the kind or degree of exertion required for Grade III.

with no dissentient so far—is that we must continue compulsory military service for an indefinite period and that one and a half years is an inescapable minimum'.[34] In so far as this suggests that there was no ministerial opposition to the eighteen months' period it is less than accurate, as Cripps certainly argued against that in the Defence Committee. Nevertheless there was no ministerial opposition to the principle of conscription.

This is particularly interesting because a number of ministers had, at one time or another since 1945, voiced their opposition to that principle—notably Bevan, Shinwell, Bellenger, Noel-Baker, and Wilkinson. As noted above, the Cabinet also contained three former conscientious objectors in Morrison, Creech Jones, and Pethwick Lawrence, although this was less significant as they had all changed their views since the Great War. None of those who opposed conscription in the past did so now. They had all spent at least two years in government and were at least acquiescent, and in some cases enthusiastic, supporters of the main assumptions of Bevin's foreign policy which required military forces that only conscription could provide. The military and foreign policy arguments therefore went unchallenged.

In Defence Committee on 16 October 1946 Bevin surveyed the world situation and noted that:

In Europe Russia had already acquired absolute control of a number of satellite states and was making vigorous efforts through communist propaganda to bring other states such as France, Italy, the Scandinavian countries and others under her domination . . . He was convinced that if we were not prepared to accept certain risks and show by our example that we are determined to fight this menace then all Europe would fall under Russian influence.[35]

This in itself did not necessarily entail the commitment of an army in war. Nor was it inevitably a long-term policy. Indeed, in the next breath Bevin held out the hope that by 1950 the political situation might have clarified—implying that conscription might by then no longer be necessary. The risks that Bevin spoke of were only short-term. What he wanted in Europe and indeed elsewhere was the psychological backing for Britain's foreign policy that military force would give him. Preparation for war was a

[34] Dalton Diaries, 23 Oct. 1946.
[35] DO (46) 27th, 16 Oct. 1946, CAB 131/1.

secondary consideration, just as the ability to wage a general strike might be in relation to normal industrial activity. Yet just as normal industrial activity required powerful and cohesive unions capable of industrial action, so diplomacy required military forces.

Those military forces were required for a worldwide role. As it was clear to the Foreign Secretary that the Soviet Union 'sought by every means to bring about the dissolution of the British Empire' it was therefore

imperative that a plan should be prepared for the zonal defence of the Empire and its communications in which the Dominions should assume their full share of responsibility. He felt confident if this country gave a lead it could rally the Dominions to our support and our determination to defend the Empire would be our greatest contribution to the peace of the world.

In addition, British conscription would have a salutary effect on the United States which, Bevin argued, was beginning to show that it had a clear objective in foreign policy.

These were powerful arguments, even though they were unduly optimistic about the Dominions and about the effects of British actions on the policies of foreign governments. To question the need for military forces required a sustained and radical critique of Bevin's foreign policy. Within the framework of that foreign policy the only effective alternative to the acceptance of conscription lay in the hope that regular recruiting could provide sufficient troops, and Bevan did raise the question of whether regular recruiting might be sufficient. As the service departments were able to show, regular recruiting would not be enough.

The services' tentative estimates of their needs were as shown in Table 5.1. The army needed 320,000 full-time trained troops. It was anticipated that regular recruiting could provide only 220,000–275,000—figures that were to prove optimistic. Indeed, at the same Defence Committee meeting on 16 October ministers were informed that the recruiting campaign launched earlier in the year had been a failure. The estimate of the regular deficit for 1 January 1947 amounted to 93,000 men and the services maintained that this was even more serious than the figure suggested as shortages in skilled trades and non-commissioned officers (NCOs) were particularly bad. The positions of the RAF and the army were described as 'desperate'.

TABLE 5.1.   Services' Estimates of Manpower Needs, October
1946

	Full-time trained force	Reserves/expansion for war
Royal Navy	162,000	210,000
Army	320,000	930,000[a]
Royal Air Force	299,000	155,000[b]

[a] Including 600,000 TA.
[b] Including RAAF.

Source: CP (46) 380, 21 Oct. 1946, CAB 129/13.

The case for conscription was put by the Chiefs of Staff, backed
by Bevin, and supported by Attlee. The case for National Service
rested on the two arguments described in Chapter 4. What discussion there was concentrated on the foreign policy dimension.
The issue of providing trained reserves available on mobilization
appears to have received no serious attention.

Nevertheless there was conflict. This centred on the period of
military service, as it had done earlier in the year and as it was to
do in Parliament in the following spring. The debate was over the
choice between periods of eighteen and twelve months' full-time
service. Although the services had made it clear that they wanted a
two-year period they recognized that the government would not
accept this. They therefore argued for the eighteen-month period,
which they were adamant was the minimum acceptable. In early
1945 the Admiralty had stated that unless there was a three- or
four-year period of service there was no point having more than
twelve months. The RAF had been in a similar position although
it had always generally favoured eighteen months. Neither service
had described this as essential. In October 1946 they nevertheless
closed ranks behind the army and supported Montgomery who
'could not over emphasise the importance to the army of adopting
the one and a half year period'.[36] The army would be 60,000 men
short in operational units if the twelve-month period was chosen.

[36] DO (46) 28th, 17 Oct. 1946, CAB 131/1.

Without eighteen months he 'doubted very much whether the army could fulfil its commitments'.

There was no suggestion that the services should be allowed different periods of service, as was the practice in many countries. However, in February 1947 the Cabinet did agree, under pressure from the RAF, to allow the individual services to transfer men to the reserve before their period of full-time service was complete.[37] This allowed for greater administrative flexibility in controlling manpower levels, although it meant that some men in the RAF would not serve the full eighteen months. As the numbers and amounts of time involved were small this was not seen to undermine equal treatment between the services.

In October 1946 the opposition in the Defence Committee was led by Cripps. The objection to the longer period was based on the damage that it would do to the economy. Although the committee was supplied with estimates of the impact of conscription on the economy which were highly speculative, it was nevertheless apparent that the loss of productive manpower would have a considerable and harmful effect on the economy. The Defence Committee was informed that

a survey of prospective extra demands and extra supplies of manpower in 1952 shows that the position may be very tight. If output per head is only the same in 1952 as in 1939 the manpower absorbed by the planned size of the armed forces plus that needed to meet the other claims . . . would leave between 150,000 and 700,000 fewer men and women to produce consumer goods and services for the home market. To be able simultaneously to achieve the armed forces programme and meet the other claims on additional manpower and regain 1939 standards of home consumer supplies will involve raising output per man by some 3–4% more than what will be required anyway to offset reductions in working hours which have yet to be agreed.[38]

It was apparent from this that the loss of manpower from industry was only one economic variable and there was no immediate way of predicting how some of the others, such as increase in output per man/hour, would compensate for that loss.

On different assumptions different manpower deficits could be estimated. There were also other methods of characterizing the cost of the deficit. Ministers were informed that

[37] CM (47) 20, 11 Feb. 1947, CAB 128/9.
[38] DO (46) 117, 13 Oct. 1946, CAB 131/2.

if those absorbed by production of forces' supplies and by supplying services of all kinds are excluded, the numbers in production of civilian goods are likely to be about 11 to 12 million in 1952 so that this ½ million (the number of additional men in uniform) would be likely to add about 4–5% to goods produced. It is this 4 or 5% which is the real cost of having an army of 500,000 more than 1939.[39]

The economic cost of half a million young men in the services represented a loss of £200 million a year from industrial production and about 22 per cent of the expected level of exports in 1946–7 (£100 million).[40] In addition there was the cost of the industrial dislocation caused by the movement of men in and out of industry.

The size of the armed forces envisaged in the National Service scheme thus threatened both to denude industry of the manpower it needed and to undermine the government's economic and social priorities. The government's housing programme, for example, required an increase in building labour from a million to a million and a quarter. The export drive would need an estimated extra 800,000 workers to secure the necessary 75 per cent increase required to balance Britain's trade. Both of these objectives were crucial for the government. In particular, the threat to the export drive aroused the greatest concern.

Earlier in the year the Board of Trade had played a major role in opposing the more expansive schemes for the call-up for 1947 and 1948. With Cripps now returned from India they could be certain that the economic side of the case would be pressed hard. Cripps warned that

if exports were not increased over the 1939 figure by the prescribed target 70% [sic] the alternative was either to reduce imports by 40% or to make a corresponding reduction in the consumer goods for the home market . . . furthermore failure to increase exports would jeopardise the balance of international payments with perhaps disastrous consequences.[41]

He pointed out that the economic appreciation had been hurriedly put together. Yet it was still evident that the longer period meant an even greater drain on the economy and he found it difficult to say whether the country could afford the eighteen-month period. This was supported by Isaacs, who drew attention to the overall manpower deficiency estimated at between 400,000 and 830,000.

[39] Ibid.   [40] CP (46) 380, 21 Oct. 1946, CAB 129/13.
[41] DO (46) 28th, 17 Oct. 1946, CAB 131/1.

That could be reduced by some 100,000 if the twelve-month period was adopted.

However, these arguments proved insufficient. According to his own account, Montgomery 'attacked and routed' the President of the Board of Trade.[42] A hundred thousand men was clearly a large deficit, but not proportionately large in the manpower budget as a whole. Dalton was to record a later occasion when Attlee and his colleagues reacted with apparent complacency in the face of the manpower shortages. In January 1947 the deficit was written off by reference to increases in productivity. A similar argument was used at this time when it was pointed out that an adjustment in the level of unemployment from 600,000 to 500,000 could accommodate the additional burden.

Cripps clearly needed a great deal of support. With Attlee's ear turned towards Montgomery, and Bevin resolutely backing the longer period, he was already outmanœuvred. The absence of Morrison from the Defence Committee did not help his cause: in Cabinet Morrison was to express support for the general warning on the economy and in 1949 he proposed the phasing out of National Service. By the time the issue reached the Cabinet in 1946 it had been effectively decided. The crucial support that Cripps needed had to come from the Treasury in the Defence Committee. Given Dalton's battles over the defence budget and particularly in January 1947 his attitude to the size of the industrial manpower deficit, the Chancellor's support for Cripps was conspicuous by its absence.

The Manpower Working party had considered that it was impracticable to assess the financial cost of National Service as it was contingent on too many other factors. The services were still a long way from agreement on the size and shape of the permanent post-war forces. While this reluctance was understandable, there was perhaps less justification for not providing comparative costings of the twelve- and eighteen-month periods.

Dalton's preliminary calculations were based on a strength of 968,000 embodied servicemen together with a munition labour force of 600,000. This would entail expenditure of the order of £700–750 million a year (excluding terminal charges—release benefits, contracts, land requisition). As events were to show, this

[42] Montgomery, *Memoirs*, 477.

estimate was optimistic. When Cripps became Chancellor he was preoccupied with trying to get even smaller forces within a larger budget. Although the £700–750 million was appreciably higher than the admittedly speculative figure of £500–550 million arrived at by the Coalition government, Dalton was prepared to accept it. He explained that while it would entail a heavy burden on the taxpayer it would not present such serious difficulties as those in the economic/manpower field. The cost to the nation would nevertheless be seen in the reduced size of the cuts in taxation.

Dalton was convinced of the case for conscription and for the longer period of service. Although he was well aware of the need to cut the defence budget, to reduce the burden of the overseas deficit, and to provide essential manpower for industrial recovery he clearly felt that these problems could be tackled within a framework fixed by the eighteen-month period of service. One of the same Defence Committee meetings in fact saw a serious argument with the War Office over its proposals to slow the rate of releases to allow the army to meet its commitments in early 1947.[43] With the Venezia Guilian and, more significantly, Palestinian commitments continuing, Attlee subsequently decided to back the War Office. This was despite the impact on men who had already served for over four years and despite a hostile reaction within the PLP.

Dalton did not spend much time thinking about the problems of defence.[44] He had nevertheless separated in his own mind the issue of National Service from the size and shape of the forces as a whole. Like Attlee (but unlike Bevin) he was to reflect critically on Labour's opposition to the 1939 Military Training Act. He had long believed that military force was necessary to back British foreign policy. Without his support Cripps's opposition stood little chance.

The Defence Committee decided on the principle of National Service on 16 October 1946 and met the following day to agree the length of full-time service, reserve liability, and other details. The Cabinet considered the proposal as a whole on 24 October.[45] It is evident that the real debate on the length of service, and therefore the main decision, took place in the Cabinet committee.

[43] DO (46) 28th, 17 Oct. 1946, CAB 131/1.
[44] Dalton to Liddell Hart, 7 Jul. 1961, Papers of Sir Basil Liddell Hart (Liddell Hart Centre for Military Archives, King's College, London), 1/218/35.
[45] CM (46) 90, 24 Oct. 1946, CAB 128/6.

Cripps did not repeat his objections to the eighteen-month period in Cabinet. He nevertheless made it clear that conscription would impose a heavy burden on the economy.

There was one element of the new National Service scheme that was without precedent. Conscripts would be liable for reserve service and to undertake refresher training after they had completed their period of full-time service. The reserve liability would last for a period of five and a half years, thus making for a total period of seven years. Reserve service was designed to ensure that men called up in the event of war were as well trained and conversant with any recent technical or tactical changes as possible. It was indeed essential to the idea of Montgomery's Citizen Army. Montgomery argued that the decision to adopt a sixty-day period of refresher training (spread over the six years) in preference to a 120-day period was more important than the government's volte-face over the length of full-time training.[46]

The question of reserve liability did not lead to any ministerial discussion of the military case for providing trained reserves at the outset of a future war. The question was discussed solely in terms of the need to balance the requirements of the services against the demands of industry. Here the economic ministries had some success, with the Defence Committee deciding on a sixty-day aggregate part-time liability, in the face of strong opposition from Montgomery.[47]

The issue had already arisen in July 1946 when the Defence Committee discussed a War Office proposal for the re-creation of the Territorial Army.[48] It was envisaged that the future content of the TA would be about 60 per cent National Servicemen (of a total of 600,000). Until those conscripts began to become available the territorials would be a skeleton force composed of volunteers and a small regular cadre of some 12,000 men.

The War Office was keen to impose the reserve liability on men called up from 1 January 1948, under the transitional scheme. This proposal was supported by the Air Ministry even though it had not yet decided whether its conscript entries would require refresher training. The Admiralty, on the other hand, did not contemplate having the necessary training staffs and had no desire

[46] Montgomery, Notes on the Post-war Army, 6 Feb. 1948, WO 216/248.
[47] DO (46) 32nd, 8 Nov. 1946, CAB 131/1.
[48] DO (46) 88, 8 Jul. 1946, CAB 131/3.

to see a reserve liability imposed until the scheme for compulsory military service was introduced.

Even with the imposition of a reserve liability for men called up from 1 January 1948 the TA would be in 'limbo' for some three years until it received the bulk of its strength. This, it was believed, would have a deleterious influence on morale and hence on recruiting. Moreover, the 180,000 men who were to be called up in 1948 would be lost to the forces once they had finished their full-time service. On the other hand, any emergency could be handled by the recall of the 'Z reserves' — men who had served during and after the war.

There were, however, strong political arguments against imposing reserve service on the men called up in 1948. The imposition of this liability had not been mentioned in the White Paper on the transitional scheme and the government would therefore be open to the charge of a breach of faith.[49] Isaacs in particular felt that the government would find it impossible to justify imposing reserve liability on men whose obligation had already been fixed merely to bring closer by six months the date when the reserves would become available. The build-up of the TA was a long-term objective designed to provide a national army on the outbreak of war. Given that the Chiefs of Staff had adopted 1957 as the date for planning purposes when the armed forces should be ready to go to war,[50] the case for immediately reconstituting the TA in this manner was not particularly strong. When conscription was extended in 1948 and 1950 the preparedness of the TA was further delayed. The Defence Committee had little hesitation in following the Minister of Labour's line.

The length of refresher training was not decided in October 1946. This was because the details had not yet been worked out within the service departments. Montgomery told the Defence Committee that a new approach to training the territorials would be necessary as the 'old system of drills' was now out of date. It was the army that led the Chiefs of Staff to propose an annual maximum of twenty-one days' training, although Montgomery said that it would be unnecessary to call men back for at least one and possibly two years after their embodied service.

[49] Cmd. 6831, *Call-up to the Forces in 1947 and 1948*, May 1946.
[50] For discussion of this see Ian Clark and Nicholas Wheeler, *The British Origins of Nuclear Strategy 1945–55* (Oxford University Press, 1989).

The other services did not need a similar system. In October the navy was thinking in terms of calling up entrants for only three to four weeks in the whole of the five-and-a-half-year period. They hoped that many of these would in fact serve for longer by volunteering for additional refresher training. The RAF believed that it would be necessary to call up aircrew every year, but only for fourteen days. As for ground crew, this would vary according to the trade in question, but it was anticipated that recall would only be necessary every three years or so. The imposition of the aggregate sixty-day reserve liability was agreed in November by the Defence Committee. This represented the maximum period that men would be required to serve. Neither the navy nor the RAF intended that most of its reserves would serve that number of days.

In economic terms reserve service was viewed as a further burden upon the economy. According to Cripps it would involve the loss of a million men from productive labour, as 'no doubt', he added sourly, they would 'insist on having their holidays in addition'.[51]

There was one other important issue which had to be settled: the duration of the National Service Act. It will be remembered that the service chiefs had pressed for a decision on a permanent scheme in 1945. So, too, in October 1946 they were insistent that conscription was here to stay. This was essential to enable them to plan for the long-term development of the forces. Military planning within the service departments was already proceeding on the assumption that the forces would need to be ready for war by 1957. Bevin backed the Chiefs of Staff over permanent conscription despite having told the Defence Committee that the situation might change by 1950 should the United Nations Organization prove to be effective. But his colleagues and, most importantly, Attlee were less sympathetic.

The Chiefs of Staff had, after all, not yet agreed on the size and shape of the armed forces. Until that happened, and moreover until the financial implications were fully understood, there was a strong case for the government not to commit itself irrevocably. Attlee was well aware of the need to limit the defence budget. The drastic reductions of 1947 in the financial and manpower ceilings

[51] DO (46) 28th, 17 Oct. 1946, CAB 131/1.

did raise the issue of whether conscription was the best long-term policy. Also, in military terms it was evident that technology was changing quickly. The decision to manufacture a British atomic bomb was taken by January 1947. In October 1946 it was virtually impossible to predict how this and other developments in military technology would alter the nature of modern war. The strategic implications of these changes and the developments in international relations were perceived within a framework fixed by past military practice. Yet it is clear that given the likely allocation of resources that framework would be inadequate and harsh choices about British strategy would be necessary. Attlee was increasingly aware of these changes, as was evident during his attempt to reorientate British strategy away from the Middle East. As will be seen, he was also unwilling to commit the army to the defence of Western Europe.

These considerations may have played some part in Attlee's reluctance to accept permanent conscription. But there was a more immediate political judgement involved. Anything which suggested that at some point National Service might no longer be necessary would help defuse Labour Party opposition. When Isaacs proposed the idea of a time limit on the National Service Act to Cabinet he explicitly stated that it was designed to forestall amendment to the bill from opponents. The decision was taken in February 1947 when backbench Labour opposition was running high.[52] The scheme would run for five years, after which the approval of Parliament would be necessary for any continuation. It was claimed that as the state of the world might have changed by then a review of conscription could allow a reduction in, or indeed an end to, National Service. A further political consideration (although not one which would have been much in ministers' minds in 1946) was that the refusal to commit Labour to a permanent scheme would allow for opposition if or when Labour lost office in the future. This was not enough for some MPs who attempted at the committee stage of the bill to have the date of the review brought forward to 1951. This was defeated by 261 votes to 36.[53]

In February 1947 the government decided to operate the scheme

---

[52] CM (47) 20, 11 Feb. 1947, CAB 128/9.
[53] *HC deb.*, vol. 427, 8 May 1947, cols. 909–49.

until 1954, after which it would continue 'only by Order in Council made in the Address presented by His Majesty to each House of Parliament'.[54] Planning would proceed on the assumption that conscription would remain. In the preparation of the 1948 National Service Consolidation Act the clause about the parliamentary vote was excluded. This was spotted by the veteran anti-conscriptionist Rhys Davies and the civil servants involved claimed a mistake had been made. After due apology the original intention was reinstated in the legislation.[55] The form of the Order in Council nevertheless meant that a positive parliamentary decision to discontinue conscription would be necessary.

The existence of the time limit was reluctantly accepted by the service departments, although not without concern. Sir James Barnes, the Permanent Secretary at the Air Ministry, noted: 'I am afraid that even with a ruling that planning should proceed on the assumption that National Service will continue until such time as there is a positive decision to discontinue it we should in practice find ourselves seriously hampered as the date for a review approached.'[56] This concern was shared by the War Office. The services wanted to secure the most explicit ruling possible. What Attlee decided was that the departmental directors of manpower would be issued with a directive instructing them to plan on the assumption that conscription would remain in force. This proved to be satisfactory for planning purposes. When in later years there was some discussion of phasing out National Service this had no effect on the preparations for defence. The imposition of a time limit was significant only in so far as it suggested an element of doubt about the government's long-term design. As argued above, there were reasonable grounds for such doubts. This was to become apparent within government particularly after the balance of payments crisis in 1947. It was a different set of doubts that was to have more immediate repercussions when opposition within the PLP erupted, and as will be seen it was that reaction that was to have the most dramatic impact on government policy.

[54] CM (47) 20, 11 Feb. 1947, CAB 128/9.
[55] Rhys Davies wrote to the Attorney General on 14 Oct. to draw his attention to the matter: CAB 124/594.
[56] Barnes to Noel-Baker, Jan. 1947, AIR 8/799.

6

The Politics of the National Service Act

THE decision that for the first time since the Napoleonic wars Britain would have military conscription in peacetime was announced to the House of Commons in the King's Speech on 6 November 1946, explained on the twelfth and debated on the eighteenth. The second reading took place in March 1947. These occasions resulted in significant backbench revolts in the PLP. The second rebellion led directly and immediately to a change in government policy on the period of full-time military service which was reduced from eighteen to twelve months. Michael Foot claimed that this was a major triumph for parliamentary democracy.[1] Robert McKenzie was to describe it as 'perhaps the most striking single illustration of the effectiveness of back-bench opposition to government policy during the lifetime of the 1945 and 1950 governments'.[2] To account for these revolts, and for the government's reaction to them, it is necessary to look at the history and diversity of Labour objections to conscription and to the situation that existed in government and in the PLP from the autumn of 1946 to the spring of 1947.[3]

Opposition to conscription in the labour movement illustrates the truism that the Labour Party has always been a coalition of different groups and different perspectives at their happiest, or at least most united, in opposition. In analysing the revolts it is important to bear in mind that the dissidents in November were opposed to the principle of conscription, while those who rebelled in March and April included opponents both of the principle and of the particular length of service that the government had chosen.

Opposition to compulsory military service was founded on different arguments and expressed in different sections of the party.

---

[1] *Daily Herald*, 9 Apr. 1947.

[2] Robert McKenzie, *British Political Parties* (Heinemann, 1955), 451–2.

[3] For an analysis of the revolts see Hugh Berrington, *Backbench Opinion in the House of Commons 1945–55* (Pergamon, 1973), 72–8.

Pacifists, non-conformists, trade unionists, liberals, and even the occasional military thinker all had their own reasons for opposition. This was the case within Labour and also elsewhere—the Liberal and Independent Labour parties were to remain resolutely opposed to military conscription. As already noted, military writers such as Liddell Hart and Giffard Martel were strongly opposed to National Service.

In analysing the threads of opposition it is worth noting that the various arguments were not automatically advanced by the corresponding sections of the party. The view that conscription represented an intolerable burden on the economy was used by Liberals and others—Liddell Hart was to talk of 'the economic draught of the military draft'.[4] Fear of industrial conscription was voiced by non-conformists and pacifists. Perhaps most interestingly, pacifists were among those who attempted to criticize conscription on military grounds. The process of conflating a series of theoretically different arguments into a single position is of course the stuff of politics and certainly the stuff of opposition politics. When moving the November amendment against the government, the pacifist MP Victor Yates used five different arguments, dismissing conscription as militarily unsound, economically wasteful, likely to stimulate rather than deter international conflict, unhealthy in a democracy, and a suppression of 'inalienable rights in all matters which affect human prerogatives'.[5] Yet it is important to recognize that identifiably different sections of the party were against the principle of conscription.

Some of that opposition was rooted in the bitter (and often personal) experience of the Great War. The fear that industrial conscription would follow military service aroused memories and folk memories of the exploitation and loss of trade union rights that had taken place under Lloyd George's wartime government. This had been a powerful factor governing the attitude of the unions in 1939 when the labour movement had united against Chamberlain's limited and temporary measure of compulsory military training. It had even exercised an influence on Bevin who, as Minister of Labour, had otherwise been fully committed to getting Labour to back British rearmament, and who was

---

[4] *Free Man or State Slave?* (No Conscription Council, Jun. 1946), Liddell Hart papers, 10/1947/6 (Liddell Hart Centre for Military Archives, King's College, London). [5] *HC deb.*, vol. 430, 18 Nov. 1946, cols. 595–8.

eventually responsible for mobilizing Britain to an extent unprecedented in the nation's history.

Under Bevin compulsory military service had been followed by the conscription and direction of labour, including the conscription of women from 1941. The government was well aware of party feeling and Attlee and Bevin had repeatedly made clear that any form of peacetime industrial conscription was ruled out. On the other hand it is interesting to note that the severe shortages of manpower in the coalmining industry did lead the National Union of Mineworkers to press for National Servicemen in the coalfields. In 1947 the National Union of Mineworkers wanted the government to extend the existing scheme of releasing men from the forces who had experience in the mines to include anyone in the forces who preferred coalmining to military service.[6] The government refused and accepted the other unions' insistence on an end to compulsion in industry. Despite this and other government assurances, inveterate opponents still claimed that industrial conscription would follow. But for most trade unionists and Labour MPs the existence of a Labour government which they trusted was a sufficient guarantee. Equally, the miners' advocacy of conscription in the pits would have never happened if the mines had still been in private ownership under a Conservative government. Most party members—even those opposed to military service—would have accepted Dalton's dismissal of the argument as 'a catchphrase of long ago'.[7] The other and more significant element in the attitude of the trade unionist MPs was concern with the amount of time men would serve and the impact this would have on the economy. This will be examined later.

The use of troops in industrial disputes had touched upon a raw Labour nerve in the past. At the committee stage of the bill Walter Ayles and Ian Mikardo moved an amendment to prevent the use of National Servicemen in industrial actions. This was defeated by 208 votes to 22, with nineteen Labour members voting against the whip including three, most notably Robert Mellish, who otherwise supported the government on conscription.[8] (Among those

---

[6] National Union of Mineworkers, Report of Executive Committee to Conference (May 1948) 201–2. The miners' leaders raised the issue in a meeting with Attlee and senior members of the Cabinet in Jul. 1947: FO 800/493.

[7] *HC deb.*, vol. 430, 18 Nov. 1946, cols. 632–40.

[8] *HC deb.*, vol. 437, 7 May 1947, cols. 617–20.

who supported the government were Zilliacus and John Platts-Mills.) It was clear that this sort of issue did not raise the same problems for the labour conscience when Labour was in power. Nevertheless, troops were used in industrial disputes in January 1947 and July 1949.[9]

Non-conformist objection often overlapped with industrial fears. The basis of non-conformist opposition was rooted in the traditional antagonism felt towards the state, authority in general, and military authority in particular. This theme had played and continued to play an important role in the Liberal Party's opposition. By 1946 the heirs of the radical liberal tradition were to be found mainly in the Labour Party. Prominent in both parties were Welsh MPs, particularly in the Liberal Party as Wales was one of their few remaining areas of electoral strength. The only Conservative to express any opposition to conscription was Colonel Price-White, the MP for Caernarvon Boroughs, who insisted on voting as his constituents would have wished. This non-conformism was not necessarily pacifist, as was illustrated by Bevan's statement in 1917 to Ebbw Vale magistrates: 'I am not and never have been a conscientious objector. I will fight, but I will choose my own enemy and my own battlefield, and I won't have you do it for me.'[10] Yet as that speech well illustrated, it had often been linked to a political form of pacifism.

It was true that compelling young men to enter the armed forces was generally viewed as a bad thing. Only a small number of people, most of them on the right of the Conservative Party, saw compulsory service as intrinsically valuable. A large number of people felt that it would be of some benefit and that conscription was an unfortunate necessity that might nevertheless be used to social or educational advantage, a view Alexander clearly shared. Compulsion was nevertheless regarded as alien to the British tradition even by those who accepted the need for it. Liddell Hart, who saw the military objections as of overwhelming force in the issue of conscription, represented the choice between being a 'Free Man or State Slave'.[11]

---

[9] K. Harris, *Attlee* (Weidenfeld & Nicolson, 1982), 332, 432–3. Interestingly, Aneurin Bevan strongly supported the use of troops in the dock strikes in 1949. See Kenneth Morgan, *Labour in Power, 1945–51* (Oxford University Press), 79.

[10] M. M. Foot, *Aneurin Bevan*, i: *1897–1945*, 34.

[11] No Conscription Council, *Free Man or State Slave?* June 1946, Liddell Hart papers, 10/1947/6.

In an article written in March 1947 in which he carefully examined
the advantages and disadvantages of National Service, he stated that

the most fundamental conclusion of all was that conscription immensely
increases the power of the state over the individual. It has been of great
service to dictators as means of enslaving people to their own purposes.
Liberty loving peoples are foolish if they help to preserve such a system
as a natural and proper custom. For conscription has been the cancer of
civilisation.[12]

The reference to dictators was not lost on the Labour MPs. Hitler
was only occasionally invoked but Napoleon and the Prussians
were frequently mentioned.

The Co-operative Party had a long history of opposition to
conscription—a particular irony as its most senior parliamentary
figure was A. V. Alexander. The tradition was reflected in the
behaviour of its MPs, although the majority remained loyal to the
Labour whip. Of its twenty-three members (three of whom were
ministers), eleven supported the government on both the first and
second readings; six opposed the first reading; and eight rebelled
in April 1947; while of those who abstained, Edith Wills had
signed the EDM in 1946 and Norman Dodds voted in favour of an
amendment to terminate the act in 1951 rather than 1954.[13]

Pacifists and pacifism had emerged from the war few in number
and with little influence. Pacifism in its political and religious
forms remained a residual but reasonably tolerated feature in the
post-war world. Hitler, Nazism, and by 1945 the evidence of
genocide, presented a greater moral dilemma for would-be pacifists, Christian or otherwise, than had been the case in previous
wars. Those who kept to their beliefs were, by 1945, small in
number but more resolute in conviction. Yet in general it was
easier to reject conscription in peacetime on these grounds. In 1946
the issue of military conscription and indeed of war itself was
considered in something of a political vacuum. The Cold War had
not yet begun. Military service in peacetime did not present the
same dilemmas as during the Second World War. There were
none of the moral problems that arose from living on food which

[12] Liddell Hart, 'The Question of Conscription'. Liddell Hart's later writing
contained less hyperbole and focused more closely on the military arguments. See
his *Defence of the West* (Cassell, 1950).
[13] *HC deb.*, vol. 437, 8 May 1947, cols. 911–38.

had been fought through a U-boat blockade. On the other hand, the moral problems associated with the fight against facism were no longer evident. This was reflected in the fact that at its annual general meeting in April 1947 the Peace Pledge Union called on people to refuse to obey the National Service Act, whereas previously they had always abided by the law.[14]

Christian pacifist objectors had not changed their position. Prominent among these were the Quakers. Their view, expressed in their 1945 annual statement, was that:

The training of men to kill each other is a violation of the sacredness of personality for it is a crime against that of God in every man. It requires an inhumanity and a blind obedience that is a negation of responsible service to our fellow men. It demands much that in private life is recognised as anti-social and criminal.[15]

Most of these sentiments would have been shared by other Christian pacifists, though their principal objection would have been less concerned with the violation of personality and more with the straightforward contradiction of their God's command.

Political pacifists were invariably on the left of the PLP and included a number of people who had had personal experience of conscientious objection in the Great War.[16] At this stage the non-religious pacifist view was an essentially abstract argument based on the belief that military force would encourage rather than discourage international conflict. This was therefore a rejection of the Foreign Office argument that conscription was symbolically and mathematically necessary for Britain's foreign policy (with which most of the pacifists disagreed in any case). For non-pacifists, for the government, and for many on the left the rise of Hitler and the experience of the 1930s suggested that the pacifists had learned nothing and forgotten nothing. As the Cold War emerged many on the pacifist left frequently expressed sympathy for the Soviet Union and antipathy towards the United States, the

---

[14] *Daily Herald*, 9 Apr. 1947. Martin Ceadel recounts how opposition was later modified: see his *Pacifism in Britain 1914–45* (Oxford University Press, 1980), 313–14.

[15] Statement by the Religious Society of Friends, 19 May 1945, published in *Three Views on Conscription* (Religious Society of Friends, Jun. 1945), Papers of Earl Attlee (Bodleian Library, Oxford), dep. 31.

[16] John Battley and Sydney Silverman were among the unrepentant opponents.

latter shared by many in other sections of the left.[17] This was an early political expression of what later revisionist theories about the origins of the Cold War were to provide, but which in some cases went beyond sympathy or empathy into essentially pro-communist positions.

Whether the pacifists were right, either in their assumption about the dysfunctional value of military force or about the impact of British and American policy on the Soviet Union, raises fundamental questions about the Cold War. These cannot be answered adequately here. What is clear is that for the government and the Labour Party as a whole, the lesson of 1939 was that force was necessary to deter aggression. The optimistic rhetoric of left understanding left quickly gave way to the perception of the Soviet Union as ideologically and imperially set on expansion. Perception was reinforced by, and in turn reinforced, experience. In terms of Soviet expansion, the Cold War was to demonstrate to most MPs in the Labour Party that military force was indispensable for Britain's security.

Nevertheless, within the Labour Party pacifist beliefs were held in respect. Moreover, for the pacifists to rebel openly was not a political catastrophe. Three-line whips were issued and while it was normal practice for conscience-stricken individuals (including non-pacifists) to abstain rather than vote against the whip, rebellion at this point did not mean a crisis for the party given the nature of the issue. However, in March, when a larger and more representative section of the party publicly revolted, the situation was a lot more serious.

Given the strength of feeling that had been generated in the past, it was evident from the outset that National Service would not be accepted by the labour movement without a struggle, and in certain sections would not be accepted at all. In the years immediately after the war, the issue of peacetime conscription was entangled in the process of demobilization. As the government had yet to reach a decision on long-term military policy it was not unreasonable for Attlee and his colleagues to want discussion in the party deferred, until both defence policy and the international situation in general had become clearer.

[17] For the development of these opinions see M. R. Gordon, *Conflict and Consensus in Labour's Foreign Policy 1914–65* (Stanford: Stanford University Press, 1969), chs. 4–8.

Attlee was successful in avoiding discussion of conscription in the PLP in 1945–6. On 18 December 1945, the Liaison Committee was presented with a motion that came before the PLP on 6 February 1946. It stated:

That this House is of the opinion that the atomic bomb has radically altered the significance of large armies; and in view of the limitation of National Sovereignty implicit in the United Nations Organisation believes the present provides a favourable opportunity for the abolition of all forms of military conscription throughout the world and urges His Majesty's Government to take every possible step to secure international agreement by United Nations to this end.[18]

This was moved by Victor Yates and Leah Manning. It had initially been put down by the Revd. Reginald Sorenson and was supported by over a hundred Labour members. In itself the motion was not critical of the government. Moreover, as it explicitly aimed for worldwide abandonment of military conscription achieved through international negotiation, it did not necessarily entail any unilateral decision by the British government.

The view that atomic bombs had rendered conscript armies obsolete was of particular interest, and reflected the profound reaction that the destruction of Hiroshima and Nagasaki had caused. The idea that these weapons had made war unthinkable appears to have been widespread. Serious thought about the military implications was a considerable way off. Although the Labour Party contained a number of people who made a significant contribution to subsequent debates on defence and strategy, this was well in the future. For every potential military intellectual that the party could muster, there were a score or more who reacted instinctively.

For a number of Labour MPs the relationship between the atom bomb and the abolition of conscript armies involved a reaction against both. This became clear in the parliamentary speeches of left-wing and pacifist MPs. Yet in moral and military terms, there were profound problems with this link. If conscription were to be abolished because of the existence of weapons of mass destruction, it followed that these weapons should exist. If they were to displace a conscript army in a nation's defence policy, then that defence policy would be based on the use, or threat of use, of

[18] Whiteley to Attlee, 28 Mar. 1947, Attlee papers, dep. 51.

those weapons. This posture of 'massive retaliation' was precisely the strategic rationale given in 1957, when the Macmillan government used explicit reliance on Britain's strategic nuclear capability to bring National Service to an end. Aside from the military problems created by this choice, the moral basis of such a policy posed great problems for pacifists and anti-militarists.

The idea that the Soviet Union might come to possess the bomb when Britain would have abandoned it raised an issue that was to reappear in the debates on nuclear weapons in the 1950s and 1980s. The decision to develop a British atomic capability predated the formation of the NATO organization. Even supposing a Soviet nuclear monopoly would have been acceptable, the abolition of British conscription in 1946–7 would have been seen as effective unilateral disarmament (conventional and nuclear). It was presupposed by left-wing advocates of abolition that an international political solution would obviate the need for an effective defence policy, a presupposition that the government never shared.

These problems did not occupy the time of MPs like Rhys Davies and Victor Yates. They wanted an end to conscription. They also wanted an end to weapons of devastating destructive power which, at first glance, did appear to remove the need for conventional armies. If Britain was attacked with atomic bombs, then Britain would be destroyed. What pacifists and others wanted to see was the international control of atomic weapons so that they would never be used. This international control would go hand in hand with the collective security of the UN. The stark question about whether collective security itself should be based on the atomic threat was invariably avoided. Similarly, mass armies might be abolished 'because of' the bomb, but the bomb should never be used.

It is easy to criticize with hindsight, particularly with the analytical categories that have subsequently emerged in thinking about nuclear weapons. If Bertrand Russell could argue for preventive nuclear war against the Soviet Union if Stalin did not agree to American proposals for the international control of atomic energy then it is not surprising that Labour MPs reacted as they did.[19] Nevertheless, a logic by which the inherent wrongs of

---

[19] Margaret Gowing, *Independence and Deterrence: Britain and Atomic Energy, 1945–52*, ii: *Policy Execution* (Macmillan, 1974), 497–8.

military service were held to be comparable to, or indeed worse than, the threat to employ weapons of mass destruction (including chemical and biological weapons) was deeply flawed. However, as much as pacifist and other left-wing MPs might quote Liddell Hart on the military advantages of regular armies, they remained unwilling to think through the arguments in defence terms. (Although Liddell Hart himself argued that the atomic bomb and rocket technology had made conscript forces obsolete.[20]) There was no attempt to examine such mundane matters as how the RAF was to be manned. Even for those who were opposed to a British strategic bombing capability, it was much more difficult to argue against a strong air defence, so long as nuclear weapons could only be delivered by aircraft.

The question of how to prevent a future war was the crux of the issue. Pacifists and some non-pacifists rejected the government's answer, which was to prepare for, in order to deter, future war. They believed that as there was no defence against weapons of mass destruction then there was no point having defence. The government, on the other hand, believed both that defending Britain was still possible and that the devastation of modern war required an ability to deter that war by offensive means.

None of this is to suggest that the choice had to be between nuclear weapons and military conscription, although in the political debates of the 1950s many of Labour's military thinkers opted for one or the other, as indeed the Macmillan government was to do. Both the Attlee government and its pacifist critics shared the view that it was not necessary to make such a choice. What this suggests is that the link between nuclear weapons and conscription that was evident in the PLP motion showed that, for many MPs, issues of defence policy were subsumed under generally optimistic views about the international order. The validity of that position must rest on judgements about the nature and development of the post-war international order. Yet as far as defence policy was concerned, the link between the issues was essentially flawed and one which the government was unprepared to accept, even when couched in the rhetoric of multilateralism and international negotiation.

These issues were clearly complex and controversial. Attlee did

---

[20] Liddell Hart, 'The Question of Conscription'.

not want to discuss the issue of the atomic bomb, the decision on which had yet to be taken and which he was at pains to keep secret. The issue of conscription was also inherently controversial, although Attlee did answer specific questions on this at the party meeting. In February 1946 the difficulty in predicting how the world would develop was enormous. The government had yet to consider the continuation of the call-up even for the transitional period. As the Prime Minister himself was not properly briefed on the issues there was an overwhelming case for deferring a decision by the party.

Those who argued that the party should decide at this time did not see the issues as complex, but as matters of principle. What is apparent is that Attlee succeeded in preventing the parliamentary party making up its mind before the government took the real decision. Attlee was under pressure to agree to permanent conscription and much of the necessary information required was not yet ready. Nevertheless, the decision in October 1946 was taken by the government and then communicated to the PLP only a matter of hours before it was announced on 6 November.[21] Although Attlee met with senior trade union leaders and with the NEC before the announcement these consultations were of an *ex post facto* sort aimed at winning over the relevant sections of the movement to a decision already taken.

Attlee's reluctance to have conscription considered by the party is evident. In May 1946 the government published its White Paper on the Call-up to the Forces in 1947 and 1948. As mentioned in Chapter 3, this was accepted by the party but had been followed by a warning on the long-term issue, when an Early Day Motion calling for an end to conscription had been signed by eighty-eight Labour MPs. The EDM was 'minor criticism of government policy'.[22] It merely stated that conscription was alien to British tradition and that it should come to an end 'as soon as is practicable', a sentiment which many in the Cabinet would have shared.

It nevertheless indicated that opinion in the PLP was still ill-disposed towards National Service. The list of MPs who signed the EDM (and the earlier December 1945 motion discussed above) shows that the number of people who voted against the government

---

[21] The NEC accepted the government's decision on 30 Oct. (Labour Party files).
[22] Robert Jackson, *Rebels and Whips* (Macmillan, 1968), 58.

in the rebellions (particularly in November) did not adequately reflect the strength of feeling within the PLP. Analysis of those who signed the EDM shows how widespread the feeling within the party was. Of those eighty-eight, twenty-two voted with the government on the first reading; twenty-two (mostly the same) obeyed the whips on the second reading. This was not necessarily illogical. It was perfectly consistent to believe that conscription should come to an end as soon as possible, but to accept that that was not yet practicable.

Furthermore, signing an EDM was not the same as defying a three-line whip. For at least some of the people concerned, party loyalty was as vital a consideration as the political issue in question. It was not unacceptable for someone like Viscount Corvedale (who was Parliamentary Private Secretary (PPS) to Lawson and then to Bellenger) to sign a motion; it was less acceptable for PPSs to rebel openly and expect to keep their jobs (though this did occur). Moreover, some of the most vociferous critics of the government in what was to become the Keep Left group supported the government in both divisions, though very few of them signed the EDM.

The EDM expressed opposition to the principle of conscription. The Keep Lefters opposed only the proposed length of service; indeed, Crossman in particular went out of his way to argue for the principle of National Service. This suggests one or both of two things: that within the PLP there was even stronger feeling against conscription than is evidenced by the size of the rebellions, and/or that there may have been some movement in favour of accepting the principle of conscription.

The first proposition is certainly true. Even given the emotions that were aroused on the issue, party discipline and loyalty to the leadership were strong. This reflects the crucial role played by the leaders of the party in establishing support by minimizing open dissent. Thus Bevin succeeded with the unions in 1945, on at least the short-term issue, while in Parliament Attlee's role was crucial. The Prime Minister was also supported by Dalton, who appears to have placated the party meeting in July and helped to gain the deferment of a debate within the PLP.

The second proposition, that opinion moved towards the positive acceptance of conscription, is therefore less likely. However, in one section of the party—the intellectual non-pacifist left—there is some evidence of movement behind the principle of National Service which was not based on party loyalty. Certainly George Wigg's position changed from opposition in June 1946 to positive support by 1947. But Wigg was atypical in defence matters; he was, for example, one of a very small number of people who remained committed to National Service even after the bipartisan consensus had moved away from it in the late 1950s.

Yet there was a current of opinion, dating from mid-1946 to 1948 in the political and intellectual circles of the non-pacifist left, that saw Britain's political role as that of a third force in world affairs.[23] The idea of an 'armed but neutralist' Britain (or Europe) clearly called for military force. Conscription could be seen as the symbol and means of providing that force. Crossman and Wigg put this view in a joint article in the *New Statesman*. Conscription was a 'political necessity for a Socialist Britain conscious of its duty to Europe'.[24] In one sense this was a more systematic formulation of a long-standing view of those on the left, whose objection to wars and the preparation for war had been rooted in the political nature of the conflict in question, but who did not object to the provision of military force in the abstract. Increasing awareness of the military implications of third force ideas may well have played a part in moving some MPs behind the principle of conscription.

Nevertheless, the non-pacifist element in which the Keep Left group was rooted was to play an important part in the backbench revolt in April which led to the government's decision to alter the period of service. Writing of the second reading rebellion, one historian has asserted that the 'conscription revolt was in effect the first initiative of Keep Left'—although since he also states that 'previous revolts had not been pressed to a vote' (which ignores the November rebellion) this somewhat underestimates the breadth of opposition and the peculiar nature of the issue.[25] When chastising the government for its lack of nerve, Churchill was to accuse them of retreating before a 'breed of degenerate intellectuals'[26] —a clear reference to Crossman *et al.* In fact, few of the Keep Lefters voted against the government. Of the fifteen signatories

---

[23] Gordon, *Conflict and Consensus*, chs. 4–7.
[24] *New Statesman*, 29 Mar. 1947.
[25] Mark Jenkins, *Bevanism: Labour's High Tide* (Spokesman, 1979), 44.
[26] *HC deb.*, vol. 437, 6 May 1947, col. 457.

of the group's pamphlet, only Mikardo and Millington voted against the government on either reading of the bill. Almost all the others voted with the government on both occasions. Nevertheless, it was clear that their presence in the 'Aye' lobby in April was contingent on the government's changing its mind, as Crossman made clear in the debate. According to Crossman it was James Callaghan, who was associated with, though not a member of, Keep Left and more importantly was chairman of the PLP's Defence and Services Group, who was 'chiefly responsible for conspiring to reduce the term of military service from eighteen to twelve months'.[27] Crossman himself appears to have been directly approached by Attlee to see what he wanted. To understand why Attlee took such trouble and why it was not just the non-pacifist left but many normally loyal and dependable MPs who were involved in the rebellions, it is necessary to look more closely at the opposition to the eighteen-month period of service within the PLP.

For those who were opposed to conscription in principle the debates on the National Service Act were an opportunity to express their beliefs. For those who accepted the principle, there were nevertheless two important objections to the eighteen-month period: unhappiness at Bevin's foreign policy, and the realization that the longer period of service would mean an even more damaging loss of productive manpower from industry. When the issue of the principle of conscription became entangled with questions of foreign policy and manpower, 'it threatened to destroy the internal cohesion of the Labour Party'.[28]

In November increasing unhappiness within the PLP had led fifty-seven MPs from what Dalton called 'a wide and sensible section of the party' to sign an amendment to the King's Speech, criticizing the government's conduct of foreign policy.[29] This was debated on 18 November, just before the military conscription issue. The government took this criticism very seriously and Attlee himself persuaded the leaders of the rebellion—particularly Crossman—not to press the issue to a division. When the ILP divided the House notwithstanding, although none of the dissentients voted against the government, between seventy and a

---

[27] Janet Morgan, *The Backbench Diaries of Richard Crossman* (Hamish Hamilton, 1981), 88.   [28] Jackson, *Rebels and Whips*, 58.
[29] Diaries of Hugh Dalton (London School of Economics), 29 Oct. 1946.

hundred members abstained.[30] The amendment created considerable conflict within the Labour Party and indeed completely
overshadowed the revolt on the first reading of the National
Service Bill. Given the nature of the subjects at issue, this was
hardly surprising. Ironically it meant that the greater crisis resulted
over the abstentions on foreign policy rather than the revolt on
conscription.

As shown in previous chapters, the eighteen-month period
was essential for the government's foreign policy. To propose a
twelve-month period was to express support for the principle of
conscription and for the means but not the ends of military power.
This must have been in the minds of many of the rebels. In so far
as it meant that foreign policy would be constrained by this political limit imposed on defence, it suggested that the military tail
would wag the foreign policy dog. Yet this was a charge that
Crossman was concerned to deny as it raised all the old issues with
which, in his view, the party had failed to come to terms in the
1930s and which he himself had attacked in 1939. Nevertheless, he
argued: 'I cannot accept the principle which is not accepted by any
European democratic country at all that conscript soldiers should
be used for garrison work overseas.'[31]

It would be a mistake to view the revolt on conscription as
a straightforward revolt on foreign policy. As most if not all of
the foreign policy rebels abstained on the foreign policy amendment, this can be illustrated by the fact that a significant number of
MPs supported the government on foreign policy but did not on
conscription—thirty-one voted against the Crossman amendment,
but for the critical amendments on either the first or second reading of the National Service Bill. If that list is extended to those
who had signed the EDM in June–July 1946 another twenty-one
MPs can be found who were opposed to conscription but obeyed
the whips on foreign policy.

Such figures are meant to convey only that the issues could be
considered as separate. This is not to suggest that they were not
interwoven. Many of the pacifists and a great many of the other
dissentients viewed them as inseparable and looked at conscription
as the domestic cost of Bevin's foreign policy. *The Economist*, for

---

[30] Jackson (Rebels and Whips, 57) says 70. J. M. Burns puts the figure at 100:
'The Parliamentary Labour Party in Great Britain', *American Political Science Review*,
44 (1950), 863.   [31] *HC deb.*, vol. 435, 1 Apr. 1947, col. 1869.

example, regarded the eighteen-month period as necessary for the Middle East policy.[32] Since the paper rejected the idea of remaining in the theatre, so it argued against the longer period of service. Interestingly, the same editorial did not argue against eighteen months on economic grounds: the domestic considerations were examined solely in terms of the impact on individuals and their careers.

Elsewhere outside the Labour Party the issues were treated separately. The Liberal Party backed much of Bevin's policy but remained resolutely against conscription. On the other hand, at least initially, the Communist Party was in favour of conscription while critical of Bevin's foreign policy, and this meant that some of the neo-communist 'fellow travellers' were ambivalent in the early dissent.[33] As relations with the Soviet Union deteriorated, so the CP line against conscription hardened accordingly. The government itself was anxious to emphasize that conscription was not just a matter of foreign policy and that the principal reason was to provide the trained reserves ready on mobilization; an emphasis and a distinction in general that Crossman himself made clear: 'If the government's foreign policy is wrong I think we should need conscription all the more.'[34] Nevertheless, the longer period of service was essential for the government's foreign policy, as Montgomery had stressed in the Defence Committee. As will be seen, reduction of the period of service to twelve months was to entail acceptance of potentially dramatic changes in foreign policy.

The economic implications of the longer period were well appreciated in general terms both inside, and outside the Labour Party, and the debate in government had largely focused on this issue. As a *Times* leader commented in November, 'It is consideration of this relation between policy and resources that inspires the sounder part of the present doubts about the conscription programme which are not confined to labour dissentients but are shared by many economists.'[35] Objections to the cost to the Exchequer and the loss of productive manpower from industry were concerns of a wide section of PLP opinion. The Keep Left MP, Ian Mikardo, claimed that this was the sole reason for his

[32] *The Economist*, 23 Nov. 1946.   [33] *Towards a People's Army*.
[34] *HC deb.*, vol. 430, 18 Nov. 1946, col. 528.   [35] *The Times*, 16 Nov. 1946.

opposition. For those with other objections the economic costs and the implications for national recovery and Labour's social reforms added a powerful argument to their case. The period of service provided a point at which the different tributaries of opposition came together. The confluence took place on the second reading in March.

The leadership of the party had long recognized that conscription would be difficult for Labour. Yet up until the revolt in March the scale and nature of the opposition had not been sufficient to dissuade the government from pressing for the longer period. On 6 November 1946 the PLP had voted to accept the proposals by 126 votes to 54.[36] On the first reading of the bill forty-five rebels had voted against the government in the House with some ninety abstaining.[37] It was clear from the debate that there was ample evidence that dissatisfaction went beyond those who had dissented in the vote. By March 1947 that feeling had grown and took the form of a much larger-scale revolt. On 29 March seventy-five MPs signed a motion rejecting the bill. Of these, thirty-three had abstained in November and fifteen later abstained on the second reading.[38]

There was a 'stormy meeting' of the PLP on 30 March 1947, when Attlee made a last-ditch attempt to bring sufficient sections of his party back into line.[39] But the appeals that had worked with the foreign policy amendment in November made little impact now. On 31 March the debate began. On 1 April the amendment was pressed. Seventy-two Labour MPs voted against the government. Over seventy more abstained, twenty of them publicly. Only 242 members of the PLP obeyed the three-line whip, and this included over a hundred ministers of various sorts and indeed the Keep Left MPs who supported the government only on the condition that the eighteen-month period would go. There were also some MPs who were opposed to conscription, but who voted as the whips instructed.

To explain why opinion in the PLP appears to have strengthened so much against the National Service Bill, it is necessary to look at a number of developments during the winter. The most important

[36] Burns, 'The Parliamentary Labour Party', 865.
[37] Philip Norton, *Dissension in the House of Commons 1945–74* (Macmillan, 1975), 15.   [38] Note in Morrison's file: CAB 124/594.
[39] Burns, 'The Parliamentary Labour Party', 860.

was the condition of the economy, plagued by the worst winter of the century and a severe fuel crisis. This provided the background for the publication of the *Economic Survey* in January, which had shown the appalling manpower situation facing industry.[40] Within government this had led Dalton to propose a series of stark and dramatic measures to reduce that deficit which were dismissed out of hand by his senior Cabinet colleagues.

The Chancellor had also been engaged in a struggle over the size of the existing defence budget. He had sought a 10 per cent cut which was bitterly resisted by the services. As a compromise he and Alexander agreed a 5 per cent reduction, which cut the budget by some £40 million.[41] These battles (over manpower and the budget) 'spilled over' into the back benches on the conscription issue.[42] There is no evidence to connect Dalton or indeed Cripps with the rebellion, and it should not be forgotten that in October Dalton's support for both the principle of conscription and the eighteen-month period was significant and unequivocal. Yet the issues and, most important, the problem of manpower, were there for all to see after the publication of the *Economic Survey*. The link between industry's manpower problems and conscription was to feature in the pamphlet *Keep Left*, published in April.

The military's appetite for manpower was increasingly alarming. The problem was exacerbated when the government announced the retardation of the rate of releases which the army had sought since the spring of 1946. The size of the forces was increased from an anticipated 1,200,000 to 1,385,000 at 31 December 1946. This in itself was a compromise—the Chiefs of Staff wanted the troops for a longer period to provide army manpower in Austria, Venezia Guilia, and Palestine. Reaction within the PLP was highly unfavourable. The Defence and Services Group passed a resolution condemning the decision and arguing for an increase in the rate of release, including the immediate demobilization of all men who had served for four years.[43] In late 1945 it had been party and more-over union pressure which had played an important role in getting the demobilization scheme speeded up. The reversal of that trend caused considerable resentment. It fuelled the accusations of man-power inefficiency that were rife in the popular press, and which

---

[40] Cmd. 7046 *Economic Survey for 1947*.   [41] Dalton Diaries, 27 Jan. 1947.
[42] C. J. Bartlett, *The Long Retreat* (Macmillan, 1972), 22.
[43] MP (46) 39, 22 Dec. 1946, ADM 116/5652.

featured in letters to MPs from ex-servicemen, families of men currently serving, and indeed from servicemen themselves. Will Nally expressed a widespread feeling when he stated that back-bench MPs were much better informed of servicemen's grievances than ministers.[44] This issue of the rate of demobilization was linked in the Keep Left pamphlet to conscription and to the loss of productive labour. Resentment on the decision extended throughout the party.

Pressure to reverse that decision and indeed to accelerate the previous rate of release was applied through the Defence and Services Group, which was chaired by Callaghan and had a Keep Left vice-chairman in Geoffrey Bing. The group also pressed for a wider range of reforms in the armed forces, which raised the more general question of Labour's view of the military. A set of radical proposals was sent to the Prime Minister on 25 November,[45] having been outlined in a letter published in the *New Statesman* on the twenty-third.[46] The government's unwillingness to take action on these proposals may well have been a contributory factor in hardening opposition to conscription. On 17 December Bing warned Alexander that 'unless the party was satisfied that such changes in the democratisation of the forces were in fact being made a number of those members who had supported the government on conscription would be unable to vote for the National Service Act'.[47] Democratization of the armed forces was one of the original conditions laid down by the TUC for its acceptance of conscription and one of the objectives proclaimed by Bevin at the party conference in 1945.

Before the war the harsh and 'undemocratic' nature of the services had been a focus for Labour criticism. In February 1938 Attlee himself had written of the 'problem of adapting the army to the requirements of an educated democracy' and argued that

if the citizens of a democratic community are to be asked to serve in the army they must be satisfied that the army will be used for the defence of

[44] Minute of a meeting held on 17 Dec. between Alexander and the Defence and Services Group, 19 Dec. 1946, PREM 8/600.
[45] Callaghan to Attlee, 25 Nov. 1946, PREM 8/600.
[46] *New Statesman*, 23 Nov. 1946.
[47] Minute of meeting between Alexander and Defence and Services Group, 19 Dec. 1946, PREM 8/600.

democracy both at home and abroad and that it will be so organised that self-respecting and intelligent men will be able to find satisfaction in that service.[48]

Many such 'self-respecting and intelligent men' had served during the war and returned to become Labour MPs. It was evident from the strength of their criticisms that there were many areas of service life where they had clearly not found much satisfaction.

There were of course members of the Labour Party for whom almost no reform of the forces could have substantially changed their attitude. Tom Scollan spoke for a number of left-wing MPs when he stated 'that it is an evil thing to hand over the youth of the country to the militarist people to be trained in the army'.[49] The equation of militarism and the military was a popular theme in such circles.

The view that the military was in some way corrupting the youth of the nation was not confined to the pacifist left. Many liberals believed that compulsory military service would under- mine the values of a free people.[50] A variant on these themes was found in Liddell Hart's charge that a large conscript army would give the generals and the military as a whole deleterious influence on government policy. It would distort civil–military relations in the fields of policy-making and resource allocation.[51] This was a view not without foundation. Although it was not generally known at the time, the Chiefs of Staff's threat of resignation had played a crucial role in ensuring that Britain would stay in the Middle East. The scale of the defence effort gives at least prima- facie support to the view that Britain was spending too much and attempting too much. Whether that was avoidable or not (and indeed whether it was true) raises fundamental questions about British foreign policy in the Cold War and the transition from Empire. This sophisticated critique was often reduced to accusa- tions of less complex motives: the generals wanted conscription to give themselves more jobs and greater power.

---

[48] Introduction to L. Clive, *The People's Army* (Gollancz, 1938).

[49] *HC deb.*, vol. 430, 18 Nov. 1946, col. 605.

[50] Lord Moran (Churchill's wartime physician) was concerned at the pro- spect of conscription given the incidence of venereal disease in the armed forces: Moran to Rowan, 18 Nov. 1946, Attlee papers, dep. 46.

[51] Liddell Hart, 'The Question of Conscription'.

Against the view that military service was synonymous with militarism the government was able to argue that conscription was a potentially far more democratic system of recruitment in so far as it was based on a fundamentally egalitarian principle of equal service. Bevin's view of the relationship between the new-found rights of the citizen in the welfare state and the resulting social obligations has been noted. Ministers and their supporters (and indeed the opposition) were keen to argue that National Service represented a far more egalitarian military system than a professional army. Writing in the *Daily Herald*, the Keep Left MP Michael Foot was to declare that Britain 'should not abandon military power . . . not put her trust in a small highly paid, highly privileged military force which would be more anti-democratic than any conscript army'.[52]

The discovered preference for the egalitarianism of a conscript army represented the sort of intellectual somersault that Chamberlain had performed in 1939. In March of that year conscription was repugnantly alien to British tradition. By April it had become the fairest method of sharing the national burden. Yet in arguing thus, the supporters of the Attlee government did assume that military service under a Labour government would be as different as Labour leaders promised.

In one respect it already was. In early 1946, the new pay code was announced. Although this was not received without some disappointment in the forces, it did provide the best rate of pay that the services had ever known, and was the foundation for a rate of regular recruiting that, though well below what was required, was nevertheless an improvement on pre-war regular strength.

Yet this was clearly not enough for Labour MPs, who wanted fundamental changes in the conditions of service life. Bing, replying directly to Scollan, argued that 'many of the evils' which had been spoken of 'are not evils of conscription but evils of the army as it is at present organised'.[53] It was in reform of that organization that the Defence and Service Group sought to extract concessions.

The government was already pledged to democratize the armed forces and indeed a number of reforms had already been put

---

[52] *Daily Herald*, 1 Apr. 1947.
[53] *HC deb.*, vol. 430, 18 Nov. 1946, col. 607.

in hand.[54] The courts-martial procedure, which had long been criticized by Labour, was put under review (though that was not to produce any change until 1950). Compulsory church parades— an issue on which the Army Council had been unable to agree— had now been abandoned, along with other 'unnecessary' parades. Vocational training had improved as the services became more technical. The system of entry for naval officers at Dartmouth College was under review. More attention was being paid to clothing, to the men's families, and to the general 'humanization' of service life. Consideration was even being given to the collective representation of grievances.

Much of this reflected the experience of war. Moreover, anything which made the services attractive would boost regular recruiting. Hence some of the proposals put forward were not without support in the services. After all, they were coming from men who had recent and considerable experience of what they were talking about (a somewhat untypical phenomenon in political life). The list of reforms under way (or under examination) may appear quite impressive or it may appear bland and cosmetic, but it did not impress Labour critics. As Dalton admitted on 18 November, the forces were not yet truly democratic and other action would be necessary to make them so.[55]

The proposals put forward by Callaghan and his colleagues were wide-ranging and extended from economy of manpower to the recruitment of officers. They wanted a working party established on the lines of the public-sector working parties, which would be composed of service representatives and people from civilian life with military experience, who would urgently consider the recommended reforms. It was only by such 'an imaginative step' not wholly dissimilar to the Haldane Committee that 'public confidence in the government's determination to carry through reforms' would be gained and 'the public anxiety and cynicism of those who served in the ranks' would be allayed.[56] Anxiety, cynicism, and experience were very much in evidence in the parliamentary group. When the unfortunate Alexander was despatched to placate MPs, he faced a critical and unsympathetic

[54] Notes for Prime Minister, 16 Nov. 1946, DEFE 7/147.
[55] *HC deb.*, vol. 430, 18 Nov. 1946, col. 636.
[56] Callaghan to Attlee, 25 Nov. 1946, PREM 8/600.

audience composed of men with considerable recent experience.[57] He did not have an easy time.[58]

Increased efficiency and the establishment of 'scientific methods of operational research' were pressed as vital for the army. After the announcement of the slowing down of the rate of release in November, the group argued for an independent working party to investigate these areas. The government yielded on this point and in the face of War Office opposition established Manpower Economy Committees for the army and the navy. A second success was scored over the form of entry to Dartmouth Naval College. The MPs were opposed to any system which they saw as socially exclusive. They wanted a higher age of entry to the college to widen the social base of recruits. The Admiralty was in any case in the process of recommending a modification of the scheme, reform was agreed, and the Labour MPs congratulated themselves on having achieved some change as the age of entry was raised from fourteen to sixteen.[59] A third area where the services and the MPs found common cause was with the use of civilian manpower, which the forces were prepared to accept, although not on the scale envisaged by the MPs.

But in most of the other areas there was little significant change. Of particular concern was the socially exclusive nature of the officer class. For Labour, democratization was in part based on egalitarianism of an inevitably meritocratic sort. Positions of authority should be gained by ability. Attention thus focused on the Guards regiments and the 'hidden means tests' and other special arrangements for officers by which prestige regiments were 'reserved for the wealthy classes'.[60] These arrangements

[57] The membership of the group included: Major Asterley Jones, Captain Bing, Major Bramall, Lieutenant Callaghan, Mr Crossman, Mr Driberg, Mr Hughes, Lt.-Col. Lipton, Mr Nally, Commander Pursey, Lt.-Col. Sharp, Captain Swingler, Major Vernon, Lt.-Col. Wigg, Major Wyatt. In addition to the military service indicated by their ranks, Will Nally had been a gunner in the Royal Artillery and Richard Crossman had served in the Psychological Warfare Executive. The original Chairman of the Group was General Sir F. Mason-Mcfarlane, who gave way to Callaghan in early 1946 because of ill-health.

[58] Minute of meeting between Alexander and Defence and Services Group, 19 Dec. 1946, PREM 8/600.

[59] It was Callaghan, as Parliamentary Secretary at the Admiralty, who administered this change, which the navy quickly found to be unsatisfactory. See Anthony Seldon, *Churchill's Indian Summer* (Hodder & Stoughton, 1981), 315.

[60] Minute of meeting between Alexander and Defence and Services Group, 19 Dec. 1946, PREM 8/600.

should be abolished. It was nevertheless accepted that 'certain kinds of school and education' provided 'officer types'—a tacit acceptance of the problematic nature of the 'abilities' of potential officers. There was an implicit recognition that removing negative financial inhibitions would not in itself facilitate the social transformation that a 'meritocratically' selected officer corps would involve.

The services showed no enthusiasm for such proposals, even though the shortage of officers was already a severe problem. The army resolutely defended its regimental traditions. Anything which undermined the *élan* and morale of the officer corps was seen as a threat to regular recruiting and regular re-engagement. There was a great deal of worry at the time at the prospect of a Corps of Infantry that would replace the regimental structure. Such reforms were firmly and successfully opposed. In the RAF even someone like Slessor, who combined a piercing intellect with a first-hand knowledge of the RAF's manpower problems, was to speak of the importance of compensating Flying Officers for the loss of their horses and their hunting.[61] Although the RAF was not as socially unrepresentative as the army, the exclusive nature of British officers as a whole remained evident, although perhaps no more exclusive than other elements of the British elite. The Guards remained secure. The army argued that as living in London entailed additional expenses the private incomes of individual officers were necessary. As the Treasury would be unwilling to pay 'London weighting' the War Office was able to provide economic camouflage for a traditionalist argument.

Conditions of service and welfare were obvious concerns and not surprisingly some of them were shared by the services. It was argued that marriage allowances should be paid to all married men (not just those over a certain age). The Navy Army Air Force Institute (NAAFI) and its pricing policy should be overhauled. Uniform and kit should be improved. Most of this did not meet with opposition from the military, except that they were reluctant to accommodate the cost of reform from within their budget. They were less favourably disposed to the idea that NCOs and other ranks should have their own messes, as this was seen as an 'equalization downwards'.

[61] See ch. 9.

It was suggested that there should be more effective procedures for individual and, more controversially, collective representation of grievances. While there had been something along the latter lines in the navy's welfare committees, anything which hinted of trade unionism was bitterly opposed by the services. Anything which appeared to threaten traditional patterns of military authority met with implacable resistance.

The idea that military life might provide a vehicle for social change was not received with much favour in the services. However, one set of proposals did reflect that sort of hope in the area of education.[62] A People's University in the armed forces was proposed, although the idea was not explained in detail. In part this reflected the perceived success of the wartime provision for general education, including the Army Current Affairs (ACA) discussion groups which some Conservatives believed were responsible for persuading servicemen to vote Labour in 1945.[63] The Defence and Services Group's ideas were not wholly at variance with existing thinking at the War Office where, under the guidance of the Adjutant-General, Sir Ronald Adam, the army was preparing to provide for both voluntary individual education and compulsory 'citizenship' classes based on wartime experience.[64] Ironically, the contraction of the period of full-time service substantially reduced the scope of these designs.

The success of the Defence and Service Group was recognized to be limited. The government did promise a review of the parliamentary acts governing service regulation. However, this general assurance was accompanied by a specific rejection of the idea of a Standing Advisory Parliamentary Committee to ensure continuous oversight of service conditions, on the ground that this would undermine ministerial responsibility. Furthermore, the MPs had no success in reversing the decision on the rate of release. Bing's warning to Alexander that failure to make concessions would jeopardize support in the second reading suggests that the government's reaction (or lack of it) may have strengthened dissent. The

[62] Wigg in particular looked to the educational potential of conscription: *HC deb.*, vol. 430, 18 Nov. 1946, cols. 625–7.

[63] Morgan, *Labour in Power*, 21–3.

[64] Papers for Armistice and Post-war Planning Committee on Post-war Army Education, the Future of the Army Education Corps and Militia Education, papers of General Sir Ronald Adam, VI, Aug. 1945 (Liddell Hart Centre for Military Archives, King's College, London).

reformers were not confined to the conscription rebels. Moreover, most of those in the group and in the PLP who objected to conscription had other grounds for their attitude. For both those who objected in principle and those who were against the longer period of service, it is difficult to envisage reforms which would have changed their behaviour even if they had been acceptable to the services.

Nevertheless, although many of these proposals came to nought, Attlee was not so politically insensitive or indeed so personally unsympathetic as to ignore demands for reform. He had already taken some steps and was to take others during the winter in an attempt to defuse opposition, although he refused to discuss the question of conscription itself with the backbenchers. In October, when Lawson had retired through ill-health, Bellenger the Finance Member had been promoted and the War Office found itself with a Secretary of State who had earlier cultivated the reputation of being the 'soldier's friend'. Also in October the review of the courts-martial procedure was announced.

More important, in a move calculated to placate Labour opposition, the government decided that National Servicemen would receive the same pay as regulars. This had long been identified as a potentially difficult political issue with the services, and particularly the War Office, anxious that conscripts should only be given a 'pocket money' level of income, as was the practice in continental systems of military conscription. The decision to pay the same rates meant that there was an increase in the cost of conscript forces and that the financial incentive for men considering regular and particularly short service engagements was undermined. A second concession, discussed in Chapter 5, was the decision in February 1947 that the National Service Act would not be permanent and would be reviewed after five years.

These concessions were not enough to arrest the growing revolt within the PLP which, guided by Callaghan and Crossman and drawing upon a reservoir of long-standing objections, was swelled by the slowing of the rate of release and the increased awareness of the industrial burden of conscription until it burst the banks of party discipline.

The government took just forty-eight hours to reverse its October decision and announce that it would move an amendment to reduce the proposed period of full-time service to twelve months. Professor John Mackintosh describes it as 'the one occasion on which back bench opinion influenced the Attlee government on an important matter'.[65] In fact that does less than justice to the backbenchers because, as noted, the government had taken pre-emptive decisions to minimize opposition. The mere existence of critical backbench opinion had been an influence on policy.

The vital role of the backbench revolt in the government's change of policy is undeniable. However, two other interpretations of the events of March–April 1947 have emerged. Robert Dowse has argued that it is possible to interpret the concession as 'a reaction to difficulties not only in the PLP but also within Government itself', and he cites the Cabinet battles over manpower and the defence estimates as the reason for this.[66] As there was 'something like an equilibrium of forces between the Defence Committee and the economic ministries', the absence at the critical moment of Bevin (he was in Moscow) and Morrison, who was a member of both the Defence and Economic Planning Committees (he was ill), meant that the 'opportunity to effect a compromise' was gone. What sort of compromise this could have been is not clear. Yet these considerations should not be discounted. A second interpretation is that Attlee now saw the eighteen-month period as inextricably bound up with the issue of the Middle Eastern strategy, and that the reversal of policy 'was the outgrowth of a conflict in which Bevin and the Chiefs of Staff confronted Attlee over the British military presence in the Mediterranean'.[67] The question of what exactly happened in those forty-eight hours is certainly intriguing.

There is no doubt that the decision was not taken on the basis of a considered reappraisal of either the economic or the military consequences of the eighteen-month period. It is therefore equally without doubt that but for the backbench revolt the government would not have changed its mind. When the issue was discussed by the Defence Committee on 2 April, the reduction had not been placed on the agenda and the services had not had time to prepare an appraisal of its implications.[68]

[65] John Mackintosh, *The British Cabinet* (Stevens, 1962), 494.
[66] R. E. Dowse, 'Attlee', in J. P. Mackintosh, ed., *British Prime Ministers in the Twentieth Century*, ii (Weidenfeld & Nicolson, 1978), 47–9.
[67] Frank Myers, 'Conscription and the Politics of Military Strategy in the Attlee Government', *Journal of Strategic Studies*, 7 (1984), 55–73.
[68] Slessor to Tedder, 10 Apr. 1947, AIR 8/800.

The army's position had not changed since October. The primary reason for conscription was to provide the trained reserves necessary on mobilization, but unless and until it obtained the necessary regulars to provide for existing commitments, eighteen months' service was essential. The position of the RAF, however, had changed somewhat. In October it had supported the longer period of service because it was useful and because it recognized that the army needed it. By April 1947 it was firmly behind the eighteen-month period. As Slessor told the Secretary of State for Air: 'The effect of cutting the embodied period of National Service from 18 to 12 months would be to reduce our effective strength in peacetime by some 25,000 men.'[69]

On 2 April 1947 the Chiefs of Staff restated the general case that they had made in October. Alexander chaired the meeting and with the support of Isaacs made it clear that political concessions were necessary to get the bill through the House of Commons.[70] The reduction in service was the necessary concession. The Defence Committee listened but did not record any agreement. Instead it 'took note that the Minister of Defence would report to the Cabinet the views expressed in the discussion about the suggestion that the period of whole-time service under National Service might be reduced from 18 to 12 months'. A week later Slessor wrote to Tedder: 'I understand from you that the Chiefs of Staff left the meeting under the impression that they would be given the opportunity of considering it further . . . I suppose no one imagined that the Cabinet would give a decision on such an important matter after such a cursory discussion.'[71] The idea that the Chiefs of Staff had been properly consulted and given their agreement was 'a most dangerous travesty of the truth'.

The Cabinet met the next day (3 April) to discuss the issue and decide on its volte-face.[72] Subsequently the press was to carry reports that the services had been consulted and had agreed, albeit reluctantly.

For the service chiefs this was adding insult to injury. On Montgomery's recommendation the Chiefs of Staff Committee refused to consider the military implications. As this had been a

[69] Slessor to Noel-Baker, 2 Apr. 1947, AIR 8/800.
[70] DO (47) 10th, 2 Apr. 1947, AIR 8/800.
[71] Slessor to Tedder, 10 Apr. 1947, AIR 8/800.
[72] CM (47) 35, 3 Apr. 1947, CAB 128/9.

political decision, so, he argued, it should be considered by the politicians and their memoranda forwarded instead to the Standing Committee of Service Ministers. Montgomery also insisted that the record of the Defence Committee meeting be adjusted to state exactly what had been said and agreed. When Alexander refused, the CIGS sent him a letter to be inserted in the official record stating the conditions on which the twelve-month period could be accepted.[73] Unless the commitments in Palestine and India were ended then the acceptance of the twelve-month period would require a complete redeployment of the army.

The government's action clearly angered the services. Hollis explained in a letter to Ismay that the Chiefs of Staff felt that Alexander had 'virtually double-crossed them' over the issue and it had taken a great deal of effort on his part to reconcile them with their new minister.[74] The reduction in the period of service exacerbated an increasingly serious manpower situation. As a result they pressed for an increase in the number of refresher training days and for a reversal of the decision to pay conscripts on the regulars' pay scale. The government was not prepared to yield on either issue.

The anger of the services was not attributable to the effect on manpower levels alone, nor indeed to the fact that the decision had been made solely for political reasons. It was also because they themselves were implicated. As Slessor told Tedder:

I have already heard the opinion expressed by responsible outsiders that if in fact the Chiefs of Staff had previously insisted on eighteen months service as the essential minimum and then agreed in 24 hours to reduce it by a third their original demand cannot have been an honest expression of our essential military requirements, and they will therefore suffer a loss of public confidence which will take a long time to recover.[75]

So concerned was he about the government letting this widely publicized and apparently authoritative misrepresentation go by default that he suggested that it was no longer practicable for the Chiefs of Staff to be treated as invisible and anonymous in

[73] Montgomery to Alexander, 9 Apr. 1947, CAB 128/9. For Montgomery's account see Bernard Montgomery, *The Memoirs of Field-Marshal The Viscount Montgomery of Alamein* (Cassell, 1958), 477–8.
[74] Hollis to Ismay, 16 Apr. 1947, Papers of Baron Ismay (Liddell Hart Centre for Military Archives, King's College, London), V/H23/3B.
[75] Slessor to Tedder, 10 Apr. 1947, AIR 8/800.

the same way as civil servants and their opinions. Nevertheless, he admitted that it would be 'most undesirable and dangerous' for the Chiefs of Staff to arrange for a leak of the true story to the press.[76]

Dissatisfaction with the Minister of Defence was evident. Ministerial responsibility for the handling of events was his. But the decision to reduce the length of service could have been made only by the Cabinet and indeed by the Prime Minister. That decision was a political one and involved a calculation of party feeling against existing defence and foreign policy. Given the position adopted by the Conservatives, there was no truth in Alexander's claim that the passage of the National Service Bill through Parliament was in jeopardy. Even allowing for those 'rebels' who supported the government on the second reading, the whips could have mustered sufficient support. Montgomery was essentially correct, if typically insensitive, in his reaction: 'I said I couldn't understand why the government was windy about a few rebels; they would still be left with a large majority and anyhow the Conservative MPs would see the Bill through for them. This last remark was not popular.'[77] This rather underestimated the strength of the opposition, although it is probably true that a three-line whip would have gained a loyal majority in the Labour ranks.

The decision, taken on party grounds in contrast to 'responsible' or 'statesmanlike' behaviour, was unique under Attlee's leadership. Although there were frequent conflicts with the Chiefs of Staff, particularly when arbitrary cuts in defence estimates and manpower ceilings were made, these were invariably carried out in the wake of economic crises, and, moreover, against a background of unparalleled peacetime military effort. The government, while it did not prevent a significant deterioration in the fighting capabilities of the forces (particularly, as will be seen, from 1947 to 1949), did not fundamentally object to the long-term design for defence policy. The pendulum between economic and defence needs was to oscillate. And although there were other decisions with which the services were unhappy (notably Indian independence), it was only on this one occasion that the momentum for the government was provided by party considerations

[76] Ibid. [77] Montgomery, *Memoirs*, 478.

(even if some of those considerations were themselves based on economic arguments). For this the government was pilloried by the opposition and attacked from within the PLP by those who had remained loyal and who were angry that such indiscipline was not just going unpunished but was actually being rewarded.

It is clear that the government would not have changed its mind if there had not been a revolt of such proportions. It is equally clear that the government did move to accommodate the rebels. Whether that meant there was a change of feeling is not quite so clear. The point about the 'equilibrium' between the Defence and Economic Policy Committees being upset by the absence of Bevin and Morrison is not wholly appropriate. Cripps and Isaacs were also members of both committees. Moreover, Morrison does not appear to have played a central role on conscription in October or on the *Economic Survey* in January. On both occasions he had supported the economic line; and, moreover, he was highly sensitive to backbench sentiment, as his attitude to National Service in 1949 was to illustrate.

Bevin's absence, on the other hand, may well have been critical. As has been shown, he had been the Chiefs of Staff's principal ally, particularly in early 1946 but also in October. It will be recalled that he warned the meeting of the 'three bodies' of the Labour Party in 1945 that if they failed to support conscription it would still go ahead and a future Labour government would support it. It is difficult to imagine him putting the PLP's sensitivities before his foreign policy. He had no experience of normal parliamentary affairs before 1945 and was hardly inclined to curtail his policies to suit the likes of Crossman. Without him on the spot the Chiefs of Staff were exposed.

Furthermore, Dalton's attitude may well have shifted. In October he had readily accepted the longer period. The absence of Treasury support had seriously undermined the opposition put forward by Cripps and Morrison to get Attlee and his colleagues to act on the manpower situation. Yet the industrial manpower deficit of 630,000 disclosed by the *Economic Survey* was within the anticipated range when Dalton accepted eighteen months' National Service in October 1946, at which point it was estimated that there would be a shortage of between 400,000 and 830,000. A mere 100,000 men in industry would not solve that problem. The argument itself had not changed, but the context had.

It is possible that when he had accepted the case for eighteen months, Dalton believed that the government would act in the sort of areas which he proposed in January. Dalton does not discuss these issues in his diary (other than by providing an account of the events in January). It does not appear that he contemplated the conscription of women, for example, until after October; and even if he did, it would have been imprudent to hint at it if he wished to see conscription adopted. Yet prudence aside, he made no attempt to bind the Cabinet to industrial manpower reforms or indeed to bring home the seriousness of the situation as he tried to do in January. It appears that his realization of the seriousness of the position developed only after October, and this may well have predisposed him towards a change; although even then neither he nor his colleagues would have abandoned the longer period without the party's intervention. Perhaps the most likely explanation is to be found in Dalton's absence. He was in Canada and the United States in September and October and returned to find that Attlee was determined to reach a decision. There was no prior indication that this would be needed and in 1945 Dalton had been quite clear that a decision on the long-term issue was not necessary for some years. It appears probable that he and the Treasury were taken by surprise and that he did not have sufficient time to comprehend fully the financial implications of the National Service policy.

The key person in the decision was Attlee, the more so given Bevin's absence. Attlee was the natural compromiser, who in defence issues was invariably faced with the need to balance different and indeed diverging needs. This was an inevitable task for any Prime Minister. As a Labour leader he also had a particular problem in leading the party as well as the nation. Pre-war experience and the memory of Ramsay MacDonald had a lasting effect on a generation of Labour politicians. It was inevitable that Attlee should be sensitive on an issue on which he himself had damned the Conservatives in 1939. Even if Bevin had been there, it is perhaps less than certain that he could have persuaded the 'little man' deliberately to wreck the internal unity of the party and undermine the government's foreign policy even though Attlee was opposed to a central aspect of British strategy in the commitment to the Middle East. Bevin retained a pragmatic outlook on these issues and it should be noted that in November

1948 when the Chiefs of Staff demanded an extension of conscription to eighteen months, Bevin was initially opposed to their recommendation.[78]

The view that Attlee's acceptance of twelve months' service was a discrete attack on the Middle East strategy is plausible, although there is no substantive evidence to support this interpretation. Moreover, Bevin does not appear to have shared the view that the government's reversal of policy was linked to his battles with the Prime Minister over the Middle East. When Attlee sent a handwritten letter to Bevin in Moscow explaining why he had bowed to backbench feeling in April 1947, the Foreign Secretary's response was sympathetic and somewhat phlegmatic:

> I quite agree with your analysis of the national service vote. I am sure you need not worry about it. I realised it was chiefly the Welsh and I always anticipated that they and a few COs would oppose it. It does me good to see you are in such fighting trim in the face of all your other difficulties. I am well.[79]

It should also be remembered that the financial drain of overseas commitments had recently reached crisis proportions. The government had proposed to withdraw from Greece and Turkey with the result that the Americans felt compelled to give financial support to the British to maintain their commitment, from which emerged the Truman doctrine. Against that background, decisions which placed domestic needs before overseas military ones were not surprising.

As events were to prove, the reduction in the period of service was short-lived and policy changed before the men in question were actually called up. Despite the decision of September 1947 to end the Palestinian commitment, the deterioration of relations with the Soviet Union and the efforts of the War Office were to sabotage the achievements of the PLP. Indeed, it is possible to argue that the paradoxical effect of the revolts may have been to prevent the government from subsequently abandoning or fundamentally changing the National Service scheme, a paradox that will be examined later.

Above all, it should not be forgotten that a Labour government which as a party in opposition had rejected conscription under the

---

[78] See ch. 8.   [79] FO telegram no. 589, 5 Apr. 1947, FO 800/493.

threat of war against Nazi Germany had introduced compulsory military conscription in peacetime for the first time in modern British history. As Montgomery later reflected: 'When all is said and done, one must pay tribute to the courage of the Labour government in introducing National Service in peacetime, in the face of great opposition within its own party. Attlee and Bevin pushed it through for us.'[80] Harold Laski felt that the conscription issue had demonstrated that 'Mr Attlee has many qualities, no doubt Mr Attlee has some defects, but he has a glorious obstinacy of purpose when he has made up his mind'.[81] On the other hand, the scheme that had been adopted was based on individual service expectations about a strategy that had yet to be agreed. These expectations were well beyond existing resources, even before the balance of payments crisis in 1947. In addition to those problems that would blossom in the economic crisis, the length of military service was now, in the eyes of the military, inadequate for one of the main purposes for which it was designed.

[80] Montgomery, *Memoirs*, 480.   [81] Harris, *Attlee*, 340.

7

The Convertibility Crisis and its Aftermath

ON 15 July 1947 the free convertibility of dollars and sterling came into effect, precipitating a haemorrhage of capital from Britain. By the middle of August the dollar drain was running at $183 million per week. As Kenneth Morgan says, 'Britain seemed to be going bankrupt, and fast.'[1] Moreover, 'in this crisis, the Attlee Cabinet reacted with little less than panic'. The economic crisis also provoked a political crisis within the government which threatened to undermine the Prime Minister's personal position. *Annus mirabilis* had become *annus horrendus*.[2]

The convertibility crisis arose as the international situation was becoming clearer and Cold War divisions sharper, even though the American commitment to Western Europe had yet to take shape. British foreign policy reacted to, and sought to bring about, changes in this demanding new environment. Alan Bullock's analysis of the development of Bevin's foreign policy describes its passage through three phases: a period of uncertainty and frustration from 1945–1947; a period of diplomatic achievement and indeed triumph from June 1947 to May 1949; and a period of consolidation with renewed challenges, in particular war in Korea, from then until his death in 1951.[3] Thus in the summer of 1947 the foreign policy of the Attlee government began to succeed as its economic policy began to fail.

For the service chiefs the changes in the international situation came as their own disagreements over policy and strategy were gaining momentum. The military had managed to agree a defence policy in 1947, but it was very quickly realized that this was

[1] Kenneth Morgan, *Labour in Power, 1945–51* (Oxford University Press, 1984), 345.
[2] Hugh Dalton, *Memoirs*, iii: *High Tide and After 1945–62* (Muller, 1962), part III. For other accounts of the crisis see Morgan, *Labour in Power*, ch. 8, and K. Harris, *Attlee* (Weidenfeld & Nicolson, 1982), ch. 20.
[3] Alan Bullock, *Ernest Bevin: Foreign Secretary* (Oxford University Press, 1985).

financially unrealistic, and harsh choices would be necessary. These changes had potentially serious implications for National Service.

The balance of payments crisis raised a number of important questions about the National Service scheme, including how many men would be conscripted in a given year and on what basis exemptions from service would be granted. It also affected and threw into sharp relief the fundamental issues of the long-term size and shape of the armed forces and the whole question of British strategy in war. It can be argued that decisions on all these issues should have been reached before the National Service Act was passed. On the other hand the balance of payments crisis compelled a radical revision of all manpower and budgetary calculations.

The guiding assumption, that the scheme should apply universally, remained in principle unchanged. Nevertheless, budgetary constraint was to lead to serious questioning of that assumption, though the political grounds on which it rested were not challenged. Indeed, they were reinforced. Having fought the bill through Parliament, the government and particularly Alexander (since January 1947 the Minister of Defence) was very much predisposed against fundamental changes that would be unpopular in the PLP. In examining this situation, and the growing reaction against conscription within the military, it is necessary first to look at the events of the autumn and winter of 1947–8.

These were to bring into stark and public relief the conflict between foreign policy and domestic economic objectives. Within government this conflict highlighted the divergence between economic goals and the long-term objectives of British strategy that the Chiefs of Staff were trying to devise. It also marked the beginning of a period of some years within defence policy in which there was divergence between the short-term provision of embodied forces and the long-term preparation of an ability to wage a major war. The immediate consequence of the crisis was to lead the services to press for fewer men as their manpower and budgetary ceilings contracted. Yet as the Cold War began in earnest the army in particular also pressed for a longer period of service. They were thus moving towards what the navy had always preferred—fewer men for a longer period. At the same time the effect of the constraints on the armed forces fuelled the growing military reaction against conscription, especially within the army.

No sooner was the wax dry on the Royal Assent to the National Service Act than a major economic crisis began, and the pendulum between defence/foreign policy needs on the one hand and economic/social goals on the other lurched dramatically in the direction of the economic imperative. The crisis was to entail a drastic curtailment of overseas commitments and came at a time when the long-term plans for the size and shape of the forces were entering a potentially crucial phase as they emerged into ministerial focus. The crisis led to a fundamental re-examination of the National Service scheme, although this did not extend to questioning the principle of conscription.

The balance of payments crisis was apparent by the end of July 1947 when the Cabinet began to consider the consequences of sterling convertibility and Dalton's proposals, which included drastic reductions in the numbers of troops overseas and in the armed forces as a whole. Before Cabinet, Dalton had met with his most senior colleagues and secured their support for the general proposal to make large and rapid cuts in many of the overseas theatres together with a quicker run-down of the services as a whole. To secure that agreement he had to threaten, and get Cripps to threaten, resignation. In the face of this prospect Attlee and Bevin accepted his plan to reduce the forces overseas by some 150,000 out of a current total of 500,000 by the end of the year.[4]

The Cabinet was told that the gross liability in foreign currency for the forces overseas was £140 million. Dalton believed it was essential to cut this by a half and reduce the number of troops abroad by 150,000 by the end of 1947. Alexander offered a cut of 120,000 by the end of the year, provided adequate shipping was available.[5] He argued that it would be very difficult to attain the 150,000 by the end of the year. He offered to reduce the size of the armed forces for 31 March 1948 from 1,087,000 to 1,007,000. This was dismissed as insufficient by Dalton. It was clearly the MOD's opening move, and in fact the 80,000 cut was the result of an examination initiated by Alexander in February and had been agreed by the Chiefs of Staff on 25 July.[6]

---

[4] Attlee to Alexander, 31 Jul. 1947, PREM 8/833.
[5] CM (47) 67, 1 Aug. 1947, CAB 128/10.
[6] Alexander to Attlee, 5 Sept. 1947, PREM 8/833.

The reductions were discussed on 4 August 1947 when the Defence Committee considered plans drawn up by Alexander in consultation with the Chiefs of Staff.[7] It was proposed to bring home 133,000 British servicemen and to make up Dalton's figure by repatriating 34,000 Indian troops from the Middle and Far East. On the somewhat arbitrary basis that five Indians corresponded to three Britons, this was deemed to represent a reduction of 21,000 men in overseas strength and met Dalton's target. The Chancellor, Defence Committee, and Cabinet duly concurred.[8]

The strategic and foreign policy implications of Dalton's cuts were considerable. In particular, Bevin had come under strong and immediate pressure from the Americans to postpone proposed withdrawals from Greece and Italy. Economic considerations prevailed, however, and the Cabinet accepted the first round of cuts. Though Alexander and the Chiefs of Staff had met Dalton's demands on overseas forces, they were still unwilling to go further on the overall strength. Dalton pointed out that this would mean 700,000 men in the armed forces located in the United Kingdom. This was politically difficult to justify and the Chancellor urged greater efforts. Alexander argued that he and the Chiefs of Staff were in the process of reviewing the ultimate size and shape of the armed forces and that to impose drastic cuts at this stage would be to jeopardize 'the fabric of the existing services'.[9]

At this point in the Defence Committee, Isaacs suggested that if speeding up the release scheme was impossible then the numbers in the forces could be reduced by slowing down the National Service intake. He referred to the exemption of miners and the option of deferment for students and apprentices, and suggested that these should be extended. In particular he advocated leaving a proportion of National Servicemen, at least temporarily, in other 'essential' industries, which could be done under existing wartime legislation. In response, Bevin reasserted the need to keep to the principle of universal military service; he foresaw 'great practical and psychological difficulties in any wide extension of the principle of exemption or deferment'. Instead he suggested that all young men should be given the option of deferring their call-up between ages eighteen and twenty-three.

[7] DO (47) 18th, 4 Aug. 1947, CAB 131/5.
[8] CM (47) 69, 5 Aug. 1947, CAB 128/10.
[9] DO (47) 18th, 4 Aug. 1947, CAB 131/5.

Dalton accepted that the size of the forces could not be reduced by retarding the releases, and supported the extension of exemption. Alexander was doubtful whether any further reduction was possible along these lines, but undertook to consider the ideas which were not unfavourably received by the military. The proposal to restrict the National Service intake was immediately examined by Alexander through the Principal Personnel Officers and Chiefs of Staff, and with the Minister of Labour. The preliminary conclusions were sent to Attlee in time for the Cabinet on Tuesday 5 August 1947.[10]

Alexander argued that there were particularly strong arguments against reducing the intake at once and then increasing it later. First, the provision of training would become increasingly difficult: training responsibilities would fall increasingly on regulars as experienced National Servicemen currently training new recruits departed. Second, to reduce the intake at this stage would mean depleting the forces in late 1948 and 1949, which would 'have a direct effect on the operational efficiency of forces at this critical time and on our ability to meet our operational commitments overseas'.

Bevin's proposal to extend the option of deferment to all young men was considered by the service departments and by the Minister of Labour to be quite impracticable. There would be no certainty about the size of the intake in any given year and therefore uncertainty about the strength of the forces as a whole. This, it was argued, would make it quite impossible to establish effective training arrangements. If men were allowed to defer their call-up until 1 January 1949 (when the provisions of the 1947 Act came into operation) then they would be required to undertake the part-time training and six-year reserve liability that was entailed. This would deter men from leaving their deferment until after 1 January 1949 and result in a bulge in the intake in late 1948 which the services would find impossible to deal with. Unless there was a corresponding expansion of the training establishment, deferment would lead to a serious overloading of that organization.

The other proposal was to extend the range of deferments to other 'essential industries'. This was strongly opposed by Alexander. Taking a list of such industries, ranging from iron and

[10] Alexander to Attlee, 5 Aug. 1947, PREM 8/833.

steel foundries to building, it was estimated that some 17,500 would be involved in the remainder of the year, including 7,500 men in the building industry. Total annual deferments in future years would number about 25,000. Alexander argued that while this was a practical proposition, it was 'open to the gravest objection of principle' in that it undermined the principle of universal liability. The Minister of Defence believed that the whole structure of National Service would be endangered in confronting the PLP with the abandonment of a principle on which the labour movement had accepted conscription. Yet the issue here was deferment, not exemption, and this indicates how sensitive Alexander and indeed his colleagues had become.

In addition there were administrative problems. Implementing a scheme of deferment by occupation would be a complex process, requiring an increase in the staff of the Ministry of Labour. There was also the same objection as to the deferment of all young men: namely, men could not be deferred beyond 1 January 1949 without bringing them under the auspices of the 1947 Act. They would therefore all be called up during 1948 and this would produce 'a completely unacceptable overloading of the service training machines'. To some extent the administrative problems could be overcome. It was possible to allow men who did defer their service beyond 1 January 1949 to avoid reserve liability, but this would have created anomalies between men in the same units. Adjusting the training establishment was the main alternative, but this was seen as problematic given the deteriorating manpower situation within the services.

When the Cabinet met on 5 August 1947 to examine and approve the Defence Committee's recommendations on overseas reductions and the size of the forces as a whole, it did not take a decision on the National Service intake.[11] It was becoming clear that the deferments that Alexander had in mind were much smaller than those which Dalton sought. In Cabinet on 7 August, the Chancellor argued that whereas any acceptable scheme of deferment would yield no more than 10,000 men by 31 March 1948, he was looking for a reduction of at least 100,000.[12] Dalton recorded the 'mulish resistance of Bevin and Alexander . . . half

[11] CM (47) 69, 5 Aug. 1947, CAB 128/10.
[12] CM (47) 70, 7 Aug. 1947, CAB 128/10.

backed up by the Prime Minister'.[13] He had got Attlee to instruct
Alexander to undertake feasibility studies of cuts of 100,000 and
200,000. To achieve anything of that order by industrial deferments would, as Isaacs pointed out, involve restoration of the
wartime schedule of reserved occupations. This would not only
mean discarding the principle of universal liability but would
require, Alexander maintained, a breach of the pledge that men in
the forces would be released on an age and service basis irrespective of whether they were serving at home or overseas. Alexander
wanted any decision deferred until he and the Chiefs of Staff had
completed their enquiry into the long-term size and shape of the
forces.

The feasibility studies on cuts in forces overseas progressed
through August and into September. Pressure remained on the
services, with ministers beginning to back Dalton where they had
not done so in January. Resignation threats aside, his position
within the 'inner' Cabinet was strengthened by Bevin. Although
the latter was inevitably concerned at the implications of the troop
withdrawals, the overall size of the armed forces was a cause of
alarm and surprise to him. Privately he told Dalton and Attlee that
the existing size of the forces was not in any way necessary to
support the conduct of his foreign policy.[14] A few days later, on
15 August 1947, he sent a detailed and personal letter to the Prime
Minister explaining his feelings at the time and recalling his views
and assumptions in 1945, when the Coalition government had
considered the issue of peacetime military conscription.[15]

For Bevin, even apart from the financial consequences of the
dollar crisis, the existence in the United Kingdom of 700,000
troops (the number after the agreed withdrawals) was something
he found great difficulty in understanding. While confessing that
he had no knowledge of the breakdown of this figure nor of what
the organization of the forces was, he pointed out that within five
years of reserve liability there could be an immediate call-up of
one million 'reasonably trained personnel'. Together with the
estimated 500,000 in the regular forces, this would provide the
largest striking force that Britain or the British Empire had ever
had. He told Attlee: 'The reason for maintaining a permanent

[13] Diaries of Hugh Dalton (London School of Economics), 8 Aug. 1947.
[14] Dalton to Attlee, 11 Aug. 1947, PREM 8/833.
[15] Bevin to Attlee, 15 Aug. 1947, PREM 8/833.

military formation of 700,000 in order to achieve this result even with the difficulties of transition, passes my comprehension.'

It is interesting that Bevin recalled that in 1945 he had assumed that no more than 500,000 men would be necessary to provide for comparatively small, well-organized standing forces capable of expansion in war. He also believed that instead of large garrisons stationed overseas the RAF and the navy would provide the predominant method of 'policing'. He argued that the idea of having a well-trained permanent force as a cadre, capable of being complemented by trained men on mobilization, was a far more efficient method than the one that Haldane had designed with the Territorials. He nevertheless felt that 'a complete overhaul of the reorganisation of the forces is absolutely essential' before the Chiefs of Staff 'ruin the entire prospect of obtaining an efficient force, and turn the whole country against them'—and, he might have added, against the government. While he had supported the figures for the transition period he described the tardiness with which the service chiefs were applying their minds to the problem as lamentable. In particular he attacked Montgomery, who, he commented, 'would be far better employed at home applying his mind to the organisation of the new army on a basis which the country can afford rather than on any of these other adventures'— a reference to the Field-Marshal's recent visits to Australia and New Zealand.

On the question of National Service intake Bevin remained keen on the option of universal deferment, given the current economic situation. He argued that preliminary training could be given during the period of deferment. This would not only reduce the size of the armed forces but ultimately mean troops spending a more effective year in their period of full-time training. Despite these doubts, Bevin continued to be the Chiefs of Staff's principal ally in Cabinet. This was unavoidable. However inefficient the military machine, he needed the troops for his foreign policy.

Meanwhile, Alexander continued to study Dalton's proposals and discuss with the service chiefs the long-term size and shape of the forces. With regard to the former, Alexander informed Attlee of his findings on 25 August 1947.[16] There were three outstanding difficulties in drastically reducing the number of men overseas:

---

[16] Alexander to Attlee, 25 Aug. 1947, PREM 8/833.

first, the repeated pledges given to the forces that releases of men abroad would proceed at the same rate as those of men at home; second, the shortage of passenger shipping (if 100,000 men were withdrawn it would mean suspending all reconversion for commercial shipping for six months); third, the various problems associated with deferring the call-up of National Servicemen.

Given these difficulties it would only be possible—and even then 'only with the greatest goodwill in the world'—to reduce the figure for 31 March 1950 by an extra 50,000. This would come from cutting forces overseas by another 31,500, providing the necessary shipping could be found, and by deferring the call-up of all the 17,500 intake who 'could be regarded as falling within the broadest possible definition of essential employment'. Alexander's reluctant acceptance of this reflected mounting Treasury pressure. To withdraw 31,500 would include removing the army completely from Japan. It would also mean making much greater use of the 'military necessity' clause, especially in the RAF and navy, to retain individual specialists and departure from the principle of consistency in releases. These findings were put as proposals to the Defence Committee on 18 September.

In tandem with these considerations, Alexander had been involved with the Chiefs of Staff since the spring in trying to determine the ultimate size and shape of the forces. He told Attlee that his discussions had shown beyond doubt that it would be necessary to take very drastic steps involving 'a radical change of policy', cutting the previously envisaged size of forces to ensure the necessarily large reduction in expenditure.[17] The general implications of this involved 'taking grave risks, particularly in defence of these islands, as our purely defensive forces will for the next few years be reduced to mere skeletons'. While the exact implications were being explored by the Chiefs of Staff, he felt that the likely cut in strength would be about 100,000. He warned, however, that if this were insufficient and if the demobilization pledge were adhered to, then the only effective way of imposing greater cuts would be to scrap National Service altogether and with it plans for trained reserves on the scale anticipated. This, so Alexander argued, would mean that Britain would have no hope of fighting a major war for fifteen to twenty years.

---

[17] Alexander to Attlee, 27 Aug. 1947, PREM 8/833.

Alexander's claim that the proposed reductions meant a complete departure from previous assumptions was something of an exaggeration. It had been accepted as a planning assumption since 1946 that there would be no major war for several years. Should hostilities break out, the forces would have to fight with what they had. The underlying assumption was that the risk of war would increase thereafter and by 1957 it would be necessary to be prepared for a major war. Alexander warned that the proposed reductions would mean that for the next five years 'all ideas of refashioning our forces in preparation for a major war should be dismissed and that we should not contemplate any measures towards a state of preparedness until our economic and industrial strength has recovered'. While this may have been true even under a reduced defence budget, research and development remained the government's stated priority. National Service would remain and continue to provide trained men. There was also the enormous number of men and women trained and experienced in the war, classified as 'Z' reservists, together with large stocks of equipment and supplies.

On 5 September Alexander reported in greater detail to Attlee on the discussions with the Chiefs of Staff.[18] He explained that these considerations involved the most fundamental principles of defence policy. They had been initiated in February, when Alexander had instructed the services to plan on a final defence budget of £600 million. This had been recognized as requiring examination of major controversial questions, such as the future of the battleship and the fleet aircraft carrier. The principles of future defence policy were prepared by 22 May 1947 and given general approval by Attlee at a Staff Conference on 11 June. The size and shape of the forces took some time to calculate because of various costing complications, and it was not until 15 August that the service departments circularized the results of their studies. For the government these were wholly unacceptable, but they revealed the long-standing basis on which the services had been planning. As Alexander wrote: 'It was obvious to me at once that fundamental recasting of those plans would be required inasmuch as they envisaged a total defence expenditure in 1948–9 of over £900 million and an average of £1,200 million in normal peacetime

---

[18] Alexander to Attlee, 5 Sept. 1947, PREM 8/833.

years.' Dalton's calculation that a million men in peacetime could be accommodated in a defence budget of £700–750 million was highly optimistic. Alexander told the Chiefs of Staff 'in no uncertain terms' that this was wholly unacceptable and required complete re-examination.

The Chiefs of Staff subsequently recast their plans to produce a projected defence estimate of £825 million for 1948–9 and of about £725 million in a normal peacetime year. These compared with the existing 1947–8 budget of £899 million. Pressure continued for the long-term budget to be brought nearer to the £600 million target. After further examination they explained that if the government were to insist on economies 'contrary to the considered advice of the Chiefs of Staff' the defence estimates could be reduced to £770 million for 1948–9, although this would entail serious risks. No indication was given of how the normal peacetime budget would be kept within £600 million.

On 2 September 1947 Alexander was presented with the £725 million figure again. Both he and Attlee considered this excessive given normal peacetime conditions when no significant preparation for major war was being undertaken. The manpower position, though not satisfactory, was less bleak than the financial situation. It was proposed to reduce the armed forces to 700,000–750,000 by 31 March 1949. Nevertheless, Alexander considered the 1948–9 defence estimate to be above what was acceptable, even allowing for terminal expenditure. Production charges had risen by 10 per cent and the revenue from War Office equipment sales had fallen substantially, from £110 million to £32 million. However, terminal charges (release benefits, contracts, and land requisition) amounted to only £110 million. Allowing for some latitude on the £600 million figure the 1948–9 figure should, it was calculated, be in the order of £675–690 million.

To reach the target would involve cutting up to £100 million off current proposals. Alexander himself believed that given continuing commitments, it would be essential to contemplate defence expenditure (and corresponding manpower levels) for 1948–9 'substantially in excess of the normal post-war target'. Nevertheless, with the Prime Minister's blessing he pressed the services to scrutinize their estimates further.

The results of these examinations went to the Defence Committee on 18 September 1947. They included a proposed cut in manpower at 31 March 1948 of some 70,000 troops.[19] This was Alexander's latest response to Dalton's demands for cuts of 100,000–200,000. It would leave the forces with 937,000 men as compared with the initial figure of 1,087,000.

Alexander argued that a cut of 200,000 men in the forces would be disastrous for both the navy and the RAF. The latter would be virtually immobilized. Moreover, it would mean complete and immediate withdrawal from the Middle East, including Palestine, and 'reduction beyond the edge of risk in Germany'. Even the 70,000 cut which he was obliged to recommend meant a substantial cut in the navy from 182,000 to 147,000. The RAF, 'already on the verge of immobilisation', would be spared significant cuts. The army would be reduced by an extra 37,000.

These decisions came when the withdrawal of operational units was reaching its climax as troops were pulled out of Austria, Italy, Trieste, Greece, and Japan and a substantial run-down occurred in Germany and in the Middle East. Alexander also planned an additional run-down in the army of some 46,000 between 31 March 1948 and 30 June 1948 to ensure that cuts in commitments were followed by cuts in administration. The Minister of Defence proposed that the Chiefs of Staff's slightly adjusted estimate of £827 million current expenditure be cut to £711 million.

The government's diverging objectives were apparent. Attlee argued that there had been insufficient understanding of the need to bring the forces within the financial and manpower limits that the country could afford. The Chiefs of Staff's failure to reach agreement came in for his, and indeed much other, criticism. The Prime Minister said he found it difficult to understand why even with the proposed reductions in expenditure the estimate for 1948–9 would be over £700 million when this meant virtually immobilizing the armed forces. In reply to his demand for an explanation of the assumptions on which the services were operating, Alexander spoke in general terms. He explained that the first priority was research and development; then came the RAF, which needed to be at a level sufficient to preserve its structure while maintaining 'the best possible show of deterrent strength'[20]; the navy should be at a minimum level required to safeguard

---

[19] DO (47) 68, 15 Sept. 1947, CAB 131/4 discussed at DO (47) 20th, 18 Sept. 1947, CAB 131/5.   [20] DO (47) 20, 18 Sept. 1947, CAB 131/5.

sea communications and other overseas commitments while preserving the nucleus from which it was to expand in war; and the army would be used primarily as a training organization for the National Service intake and to provide the minimum strength needed to meet overseas commitments.

Apart from the service ministers and the Chiefs of Staff, the main opponent of the Treasury was Bevin. He argued that he found it impossible to take an optimistic view of the international situation; moreover, if allowance were made for inflation and for terminal charges the figure of £711 million was not greatly at variance with the Coalition's rough estimate of £500–550 million. As for proposed expenditure, he thought it unwise to take an immediate decision on the main issue and voiced his doubts about some of the assumptions on which it was based. In particular, he saw little prospect of being able to withdraw the whole of the forces of occupation from Austria by 31 March 1948, or indeed until the Austrian treaty had been signed and ratified. As for the proposed reductions in Germany, given the pending negotiations with the United States over the Fusion Agreement it would be embarrassing to ask the Americans for relief on Britain's dollar expenditure in Germany while at the same time looking to US forces for assistance. The Foreign Secretary gave no indication of his doubts about the size of the armed forces.

The service ministers duly produced their departmental briefs. George Hall, the First Lord of the Admiralty, outlined the navy's tasks and announced that it might well have to limit its National Service intake to a purely token figure. Bellenger and Noel-Baker defended their respective manpower estimates, denying that they were excessive. More forcefully, Tedder, as Chairman of the Chiefs of Staff, emphasized that the sort of forces envisaged were neither qualitatively or quantitatively fit to wage a major war, and that the proposals rested on the assumption that there would be no major war for five years. He warned against any further speeding up of the release scheme, and in this was strongly supported by Alexander, who pointed out that given the limits on shipping, releasing even more troops would almost certainly involve abandoning the pledge on releases. This would have 'a fatal effect on the morale and efficiency of the services'.

On this he was supported by his colleagues. The view was taken that there could be no going back on the promise that within each service all men in a given group would be released at the same time (even though disparities between the services would continue to exist). The problems involved were later explained by Alexander in a letter to Attlee.[21] He argued that to reduce the forces to 937,000 while adhering to the pledge on parity between men at home and overseas would mean that the wartime scheme of age and service releases would have to be 'very much stretched'. In the army it would involve different rates of release for different groups. In some arms this would reach four or five release groups ahead of the general level. With the RAF the general level of release was likely to be much higher than in the army. In all three services there would have to be much greater use of the 'military necessity clause' in retaining specialists. All of this greatly increased the likelihood of discontent. However, though Alexander was clearly aware of these difficulties, he placed little emphasis on these problems in his memoranda to the Defence Committee or Cabinet.[22]

Dalton was not unsympathetic to the manpower target of 713,000 by 31 March 1949, but he 'viewed with some concern' the budget of £711 million, which he felt was more than the country could afford. He did accept Bevin's points on Austria and Germany but expressed 'grave concern' at the large number of troops stationed in Egypt. Clearly he was not finished with the defence budget. In his diary he commented that the Chiefs of Staff had not been co-operating together, despite directives from Alexander. 'I hear Montgomery won't work with the other two,' he noted.[23]

There was still the question of National Service and the proposal to extend the range of deferments to include a much wider selection of 'essential' industries and thus both save some 17,500 in the current year and help cut the 1948–9 intake to 150,000. Isaacs, who had suggested reducing the intake to control the size of the forces, did not support the idea of extending industrial deferment, although he recognized and indeed welcomed the benefits for industry. He explained about the problems of keeping men in a state of suspense over their call-up and the much greater difficulty of defining and defending the criteria on which industries or

[21] Alexander to Attlee, 25 Sept. 1947, PREM 8/833.
[22] CM (47) 78, 2 Oct. 1947, CAB 128/10.
[23] Dalton Diaries, 18 Sept. 1947.

jobs were to be categorized as essential. He suggested instead either raising medical standards (in which he was supported by Tedder) or a system of balloting as possible alternatives.

Bevin again raised the idea of allowing men to do part-time training before their full-time service, a view which Montgomery received reasonably well, arguing that the TA would be glad to receive men who had not yet had their full-time training. It was evident that these options needed further examination and a decision was deferred. Indeed, it was evident that in the face of Dalton's continuing pressure, further study of the size and cost of the forces would be necessary.

In the meantime the Defence Committee accepted the 937,000 manpower estimate for 31 March 1948, though it did not endorse the 1948–9 defence estimate. It should be noted that the figure of 937,000 was based on assumptions about withdrawals which had been questioned by the Foreign Secretary and in the belief that the National Service intake would be cut by 17,500, although no decision had formally been taken on how that was to be done. A working party was established to examine this.

Though Dalton had accepted the March 1949 manpower estimate he nevertheless pressed for a speedier run-down of the forces in the year up to then. This was discussed at Defence Committee on 29 September 1947[24] and at Cabinet on 2 October.[25] The Minister of Defence opposed a speedier run-down. He had examined in greater detail the commitments facing the forces during this period and this had reinforced his impression. The army in particular faced a series of problems and yet under the proposals would be reduced from 527,000 at 31 March 1948 (originally 590,000) to 401,000 by 1 October 1948 and to 339,000 by 31 March 1949.

However, it was not only in Austria (where some 12,000 men were deployed) that assumptions about withdrawal by March 1948 looked unduly optimistic. Similar doubts were now expressed about British forces in Greece (where the decision to withdraw had yet to be taken), Trieste, the Sudan, and India (where there were shipping difficulties in withdrawing troops who were supposed to have left by the end of 1947). As for Palestine, the

---

[24] DO (47) 22nd, 29 Sept. 1947, CAB 131/5.
[25] CM (47) 78, 2 Oct. 1947, CAB 128/10.

figure for March 1948 was deemed acceptable only if conditions did not get worse. It was estimated that reduction beyond the strength planned for March 1948 would be impossible.

The 527,000 estimate for March 1948 did not appear adequate. Moreover, the 339,000 target for March 1949 assumed that all special post-war overseas commitments (Germany aside) would have been liquidated. This, Alexander emphasized, was a bold assumption and furthermore meant that no additional commitments could be envisaged. These proposals entailed a reduction of 188,000 over the financial year and the release of about 300,000 men and women. They contained no margin for various transitional tasks, such as the administration of the Polish Resettlement Corps, or clearing ammunition dumps. Even then, 'a very great risk indeed is being undertaken in accepting the planned rundown of the army for 1948–9'.[26] To accelerate the rate of rundown, Alexander believed, would be 'premature and unjustified'.

As for the navy, the run-down to 147,000 (from 182,000) at 31 March 1949 would be achieved by 31 March 1948. Hence the navy was telescoping eighteen months of reorganization and redeployment into six months. To achieve that would require 'great sacrifice'. This gave rise to political conflict between government and opposition, as the latter attacked the dramatic reductions, particularly in the Home Fleet. As for further reductions, Alexander wrote: 'I do not see how the Navy can possibly do more.'[27]

Nor could the RAF be reduced at a faster rate. The original figure for the air force had been 315,000. The proposed reductions involved a run-down to 263,000 by March 1948 and to 227,000 by March 1949. To accelerate more quickly would mean a further limit on the National Service intake or a more rapid release. The latter would jeopardize the structure of the RAF, the service which Alexander had accorded priority in the defence effort.

The Defence Committee backed the Minister of Defence.[28] Dalton expressed disappointment at the prospect of the lack of further acceleration and reserved his position on the financial implications for the 1948–9 budget. In addition to the service manpower reductions Alexander proposed a cut in the industrial

[26] DO (47) 74, 25 Sept. 1947, CAB 131/4.   [27] Ibid.
[28] DO (47) 22nd, 29 Sept. 1947, CAB 131/5.

manpower engaged on service production, research, and development of about 100,000 down to some 350,000. Also at this stage it was agreed that the conscript intake for 1948–9 would be reduced to 150,000, split on the basis of 100,000 for the army, 48,000 for the RAF, and 2,000 for the navy. How this would be achieved rested on the findings of the manpower working party.

Alexander also re-examined the 1948–9 defence budget, provisionally set at £711 million on the manpower basis of 937,000 at 31 March 1948 falling to 713,000 at the end of the financial year. When the service departments and the Ministry of Supply completed their detailed examination, they found that the cost had been underestimated and that the actual total would be just over £723 million.

The gap between the Treasury and the services was considerable. The potential for conflict had been increased by the move of Cripps, first to the Ministry of Economic Affairs and then, with Dalton's resignation, to the Treasury. Cripps had conspired within the 'inner cabinet' in a bid to oust Attlee and replace him with Bevin, and had openly approached the Prime Minister to ask him to stand down.[29] Attlee survived and decided to move Cripps into more economically and politically crucial posts. As Chancellor, Cripps soon became synonymous with the period of domestic austerity after 1947, although he had inherited the mantle of Dalton, whose November budget was the most deflationary of the post-war years. In July 1947 Bevin had remarked to Dalton that Cripps was 'more than half way to Moscow'.[30] Yet his attitude to the defence budget was guided primarily by his departmental responsibilities and his recognition of the impact of the defence effort on Britain's economic and industrial recovery. On 15 December the new Chancellor wrote to Alexander urging that the defence estimate should be at the lowest possible figure and in any case 'should be appreciably less than £700 million'.[31] If that meant taking risks, so be it. Politically, Cripps was at his strongest at this time and his efforts bore fruit. The budget was reduced to £696.6 million after a revision of terminal charges.[32] This was accepted in the Treasury as having 'showed evidence of tight

---

[29] See Kenneth Morgan, *Labour People* (Oxford University Press, 1987), 162–75.
[30] Dalton Diaries, 26 Jul. 1947.
[31] Cripps to Alexander, 15 Dec. 1947, T. 225/73.
[32] DO (47) 97, 24 Dec. 1947, CAB 131/4.

squeezing'.[33] More importantly, the Chancellor was preparing for a longer and larger struggle over the long-term requirements. Alexander had to accept the reductions, but warned his colleagues that 'very considerable risks' were involved and that he might have to ask for a supplementary estimate if those risks 'matured against' the government or if additional commitments arose.

This left two questions: the National Service intake and the long-term size and shape of the forces. The manpower working party had completed its report and produced a simple solution that allowed the government to reduce the intake but escape the implications of tampering with the principle of universal liability. It was proposed that the surplus of men becoming available for call-up should be reduced by holding only three registrations in 1948, rather than four. This would cut the number of men available in 1948–9 by some 43,000 and raise the call-up age by three months. This would 'have the advantage of eliminating practically the whole of the year's surplus, without involving the selection of individuals or any interference with the principle of universal service'.[34] The task of reducing the intake to 150,000 in 1948–9 without creating anomalies in subsequent years looked within easy reach. Administratively, as well as politically, this was a far more acceptable solution than extending the range of industrial deferments or, as was later suggested, converting existing deferments into exemptions, or raising physical and/or educational standards of entry. It was accepted accordingly.

Nevertheless, it was emphasized that this could only be a short-term solution. After 1949 it would become progressively more difficult to keep raising the age of call-up. The number of men becoming available would rise steeply with those who had deferred their service becoming liable for entry. It was estimated on these assumptions that the numbers becoming available each year would rise progressively from 171,000 in 1948 to 240,000 in 1952. This clearly raised great problems for the services and for the scheme of National Service, which were bound up in the consideration of the long-term size and shape of the forces.

The nature of those forces remained undetermined. The Chiefs of Staff were unable to agree on dispositions within the £600

---

[33] Treasury brief for Cripps, 31 Dec. 1947, T. 225/73.

[34] DO (47) 87, 10 Nov. 1947, CAB 131/4, memorandum by Alexander on the control of the National Service intake in relation to service requirements.

million target that Alexander had given them, despite a good deal of work by the Joint Planning Staff. The root of the problem was quite simple: the growing imbalance between commitments and strategy on one hand and resources on each other. A total of £600 million was not enough to provide the forces which the service departments assumed to be necessary. In October 1946 conscription had been adopted to provide for peacetime forces of about a million, with an annual budget of £700–750 million. Of that million it had been planned that 300,000 would be conscripts of whom 120,000 would be under training and 180,000 would be embodied troops. The long-term aim of a £600 million budget, which predated the balance of payments crisis, was based on an initial figure of 200,000 conscripts (reduced to 150,000 in 1948–9) which would cost almost a third of the post-war defence budget. As the provision for defence decreased the proportion of the effort (in terms of both manpower and money) devoted to National Servicemen increased.

The inability of the Chiefs of Staff to reach agreement reflected their discord over priorities but was inextricably linked with disputes over strategy, as discussed in Chapter 4. The RAF and the navy were particularly aggrieved that the priority they were accorded in Alexander's rhetoric was not reflected in the respective and prospective budgetary allocations of the three services.

The Air Ministry and the Admiralty needed to plan on a longer-term basis, given the 'lead times' of their weapons systems (in particular the strategic jet bombers). Moreover, the strategic perspectives of these services did not require the kind of political decisions involved in commitments to Europe or the Middle East. The RAF and the navy did not accept the War Office's case.

Montgomery thus had to fall back on the argument that the army's essential wartime role was to resist invasion, provide anti-aircraft defences, aid the civil power, and protect overseas commitments. This assessment was attacked by the other services. The Chief of the Air Staff, supported by the First Sea Lord, argued that 'the risk of invasion by sea or by air was so negligible that in our present straitened circumstances we should be un-justified taking it into account in the provision of money, men and material'.[35] They also questioned the utility of anti-aircraft guns,

[35] DO (48) 2nd, 8 Jan. 1948, AIR 8/1587.

given the likely impact of high-altitude, high-speed bombers and the development of both surface-to-air missiles and surface-to-surface missiles which were impervious to gun defence. Nevertheless, the Chiefs of Staff were agreed on the need for Civil Defence as a role for the army and for the services as a whole.

On 1 June 1947 Montgomery had written to his friend Major-General de Guingand, 'I have gained my way in all vital issues and I reckon the post-war army is now well launched: Regular and TA.'[36] On 25 September he wrote to Bevin stating that in the changed circumstances 'a complete and fundamental re-design is essential'.[37] The result was described as a new National Army with the principal emphasis on training reserves so that there would be a large army to despatch on mobilization.[38] However, Montgomery's thinking drew increasing criticism in the Chiefs of Staff Committee. There was scepticism elsewhere. In the Foreign Office, Sir Orme Sargent warned Bevin that Montgomery's 'New Model Army' was no more than 'a glorified militia for home defence' which 'will be interpreted as the abdication of Great Britain as a world power'.[39]

The failure of the Chiefs of Staff to reach agreement was now apparent. Alexander, with Attlee's blessing, therefore attempted to get them to put before the Defence Committee sufficient material to 'enable the government to make firm decisions not in full detail but on the broad outlines of a long-term plan'.[40] Ministers were being asked to take decisions on key strategic issues because the services could not reach agreement. The information was put before the Defence Committee in a memorandum by Alexander and discussed on 8 and 14 January 1948.[41] With it was an additional paper by the Chiefs of Staff arguing the case for a minimum figure of £662 million for each year after 1948–9 together with the report of the official working party on the long-term issue of National Service intake.

The results of these meetings and of Staff Conferences held with the Prime Minister, Foreign Secretary, and Minister of Defence

[36] Nigel Hamilton, *Monty* iii: *The Field Marshal 1944–76* (Sceptre, 1987), 684.
[37] Montgomery to Bevin, 25 Sept. 1947, FO 800/451.
[38] Montgomery's thinking was set out in a series of papers he wrote at this time: British Army I, 8 Sept. 1947; CIGS/BM/28/1774; British Army II, 23 Sept. 1947, CIGS/BM/28/1801; and British Army III, 25 Sept. 1947, CIGS/BM/28/1807, FO 800/451.   [39] Sargent to Bevin, 13 Oct. 1947, FO 800/451.
[40] COS report to MOD, COS (47) 263, circulated as DO (48) 3, Jan. 1948, CAB 131/6.   [41] DO (48) 3rd, 14 Jan. 1948, AIR 8/1587.

were a budget victory for Cripps and a limited tactical success for Montgomery.[42] The £600 million budget was accepted; and the government eventually agreed that British forces already on the continent would stand and fight in the event of a war. The £600 million target was accepted in the face of the Chiefs of Staff's objections and despite the fact that even with £662 million, Tedder and Cunningham both emphasized that the navy and the RAF could accept the 'small allocation of money' (£180 million and £190 million respectively) for the immediate future only 'on the absolute and specific understanding' that it was the beginning of a twelve-year programme starting in 1949 that would have to continue as planned 'if these two services are to provide any form of deterrent or security as the danger of war increases'.

Even though the Chiefs of Staff emphasized the size of the 'rearmament programme' that would be necessary in the early 1950s, the Defence Committee decided that £600 million was the maximum provision for defence that could be afforded. Agreeing that target was one thing; implementing it was another. Nevertheless it appeared that the government had finally succeeded in achieving a financially realistic if risk-laden defence budget, not far from the original forecast for post-war expenditure. But even this (temporary) victory was not what it seemed. Not only did international relations significantly deteriorate in 1948, but given the sort of re-equipment programme that was envisaged by the services, it was evident that the government was only putting off hard, yet seemingly inevitable, choices. It was estimated that for 1954–5, for example, expenditure would be running at £830 million a year, even without provision for weapons of mass destruction and Civil Defence. When these were included the figures were in the region of £900–950 million per annum. It was evident that the battles over the budget were not yet finished.

The other outcome concerned Montgomery's attempt to gain agreement on the continental commitment. In this he was supported by Bevin and opposed by Attlee. Alexander sat on the fence, agreeing in principle but remaining doubtful of the budgetary consequences. Montgomery nevertheless noted his support with surprise.[43] The result was not what the CIGS wanted but

[42] COS (48) 16th, 4 Feb. 1948, DEFE 4/10. For Montgomery's account see Bernard Montgomery, *The Memoirs of Field-Marshal The Viscount Montgomery of Alamein* (Cassell, 1958), ch. 31.   [43] Montgomery, *Memoirs*, 501.

he did gain agreement that the army would stand and fight. However, ministers did not agree to send the TA divisions on mobilization. Nor did this represent the acceptance of the principle of a standing army in Germany. It was however a step in what for the War Office was the right direction.

On the question of National Service, the Defence Committee was presented with the MOD's endorsement[44] of the COS proposals and the report by the working party on National Service intake.[45] The first issue was the principle of National Service itself. On this some doubts were now being aired. With a £600 million budget, Tedder had told the COS Committee in August 1947 that 'if retention of conscription was to lead to completely unbalanced forces and to force so high an expenditure on the services the question of the continuation of the conscription scheme should be revised'.[46] Sir Henry Tizard, Chief Scientific Adviser to the government, actually recommended a reconsideration of the scheme.[47] Nevertheless, there was unanimous agreement among the Chiefs of Staff, the service ministers, and the MOD: peacetime military conscription should remain as a permanent feature of the armed forces. Although Alexander now asserted that the 'National Service scheme would have a considerable effect on the general outlook of the youth of the country, thereby increasing their usefulness as citizens in peace and war',[48] the reasons for the continuation of conscription remained to provide for commitments in peace and reserves in war.

In January 1948 the Chiefs of Staff estimated their long-term manpower requirement at some 685,000, which after pruning by Alexander came to 650,000. On the basis of existing trends of regular recruiting the Minister of Labour calculated that the regular strength of forces would be 487,000–507,000 by March 1950; by 1951, however, those trends were so bad that recruitment would be insufficient to replace wastage. In the longer term it was estimated that a regular strength of only 450,000 was likely. In this situation the position of the RAF was giving grave cause for concern.

Nevertheless, the services had to reject the idea of a 200,000 National Service intake within the manpower ceiling of 650,000.

[44] DO (48) 2, 5 Jan. 1948, CAB 131/6.
[45] DO (48) 1, 5 Jan. 1948, CAB 131/6.
[46] COS (47) 112th, 30 Aug. 1947, DEFE 4/6.   [47] Ibid.   [48] Ibid.

Conscription itself remained an arithmetical necessity given assumptions about commitments. But the rationale for conscription as the basis for wartime strategy appeared less certain. Alexander wrote that he did not see anything in the Chiefs of Staff's report 'to contradict the view that if war comes in the next ten to fifteen years it will be of great advantage to have at our disposal large numbers of men possessing this minimum of training and experience'. Given the increasing conflict over resources, to argue that long-term defence policy should be based on a scheme that was merely advantageous was a poor disguise of the failure of the government to co-ordinate policy with strategy. Yet conscription was still necessary as the RAF required National Service Airmen in both peace and war.

Given that conscription was to continue, the question then arose of how to limit the intake. It was estimated that the available pool would rise from 170,000 in 1948 to about 240,000 in 1952–3. It had already been decided to reduce the intake for 1948–9 by deferring one of the registrations. If the whole intake were subsequently absorbed, as envisaged in the 1947 Act, this would mean an average intake of about 200,000, with the army receiving 120,000, the navy 26,000, and the RAF 54,000. Alexander calculated that, after due regard to manpower and budgetary ceilings, the figures should be adjusted to 130,000, 25,000, and 45,000. These were firmly rejected by the service departments as still too high. Within the agreed financial and manpower ceilings they were not practical. In discussion the Permanent Secretaries at the War Office and Admiralty (Sir Eric Speed and Sir John Lang) were adamant that these targets were impossible.[49] They were only prepared to accept an allocation where the navy received a purely nominal intake of 2,000, the army got 110,000, and the RAF 30,000. With some leeway for increases in the latter two figures, Alexander estimated an eventual intake of 150,000. Given the estimate of a regular force of 450,000 this figure fell short of the Chiefs of Staff's requirement. They nevertheless accepted it as the inevitable consequence of the limits that they had opposed.

'The first obvious solution', wrote Alexander, 'would be to shorten the period of whole time service from twelve to nine or

[49] MISC (47) 3, 31 Dec. 1947, AIR 8/1587.

even six months.'[50] This would enable the services to absorb a much larger intake of National Servicemen within their budgetary and manpower limits while making conscription more palatable to industry and to the general public (and, of course, to the PLP). However, this length of service would allow only for basic training, discipline, and Civil Defence and thus would not help the forces and in particular the RAF provide the trained men to compensate for their lack of regulars. Alexander argued that it could not be considered for some years.

The problem therefore remained of how to limit the intake. The working party was unable to reach agreement on any long-term method as its work preceded the deliberations of the Chiefs of Staff. However, eight options were listed. These were examined in greater detail in Alexander's paper to the Defence Committee, where they were duly discussed.[51] Some of these schemes had been examined at various stages in the development of post-war conscription, and all had been dismissed as long-term options. Several—the introduction of the ballot, the widening of exemption to other industries, and the direction of surplus National Servicemen into existing essential industries—involved weakening the principle of universal military service. Indeed, Alexander argued that each involved abandoning that principle altogether. Administratively, he suggested that the ballot would be the easiest. Politically, they were all likely to be unacceptable in that each entailed abandoning universality.

Industrial conscription of any sort would have presented enormous political problems for the government as the unions had always based their acceptance of conscription on the condition that the compulsory direction of labour would be ruled out. A fourth proposal, to encourage those liable to volunteer instead for certain basic industries, presented less of an objection of principle. Nevertheless, as Alexander pointed out, it might well be seen as a veiled form of industrial conscription, and would mean considerable administrative difficulties as there could be no certainty about the response—there might be too many volunteers (in which case a ballot or other selective system would still be necessary) or too few (in which case the problem remained).

---

[50] DO (48) 2, 5 Jan. 1948, CAB 131/8.
[51] DO (48) 2nd, 8 Jan. 1948, AIR 8/1587.

The working party also suggested allowing men the option of auxiliary service as an alternative to full-time training. This raised important questions about the training organizations of the services, and how individuals would be chosen if the numbers exceeded the places available. Neither the working party officials nor Alexander gave it very serious consideration, but the idea did re-emerge later in the year, when it was taken up by Cripps.

The sixth possibility was to exempt those who had already been deferred (i.e. apprentices and students). Alexander did not favour this as these deferments had been granted on 'individual not national' grounds. To exempt all future students and apprentices would of course undermine the principle of universality. It would also have been particularly unfair on those who, though eligible for deferment, had chosen to complete their military service before beginning their studies or apprenticeships.

In addition to these proposals, there were those which in Alexander's opinion did not raise the same question of principle. The Minister of Defence argued that it would be entirely justifiable to raise medical standards and take only men from medical Grade I and eliminate, or at least reduce, the number of illiterates recruited into the forces under National Service. It was inevitable that any standard of entry was arbitrary. However, if the standard were sufficiently high then some men eligible for regular service would be ineligible for National Service; and the arbitrary nature of the standards did lend itself to bureaucratic adjustment that did not require potentially embarrassing political announcements. By this means Alexander calculated that it would be possible to reduce the annual intake by as much as 20,000–25,000. Whatever its merits, this measure was still insufficient and so additional measures were required. Foreseeing this, it was suggested that further use should be made of the postponement of registrations. Though warning that this tool should be used with discretion and that there would be problems with deferments beyond 1953 if National Service were abandoned after the expiration of the 1947 Act, Alexander argued that this option should be adopted in conjunction with the raising of medical standards.

The Minister of Labour also submitted a report on the practicability of deferring registrations. Isaacs' conclusions supported those of Alexander, and the Defence Committee duly decided to follow the line of political least resistance. On raising the medical standard of entry, it was left to the Minister of Defence to consider whether it would be expedient to introduce higher medical and educational standards before 1950. In the event, some adjustment was agreed, but this did not extend to exempting all men in the Grade II category.

The balance of payments crisis had made it clear that the planning assumptions of the Chiefs of Staff and the financial needs of the country were diverging. It can be argued that the military's plans were beyond the resources of the nation. Counterarguments might be that defence was an overriding priority and, for example, the housing programme or the extension of public ownership should have been sacrificed to provide the services with what they needed. Given the political objectives of the Labour government that was, however, unthinkable.

The conflict between military requirements and social and political objectives was to be the basis on which the Labour Party was to split in 1951. In late 1947 this choice was not nearly so stark, yet it is interesting to note that the services initially wanted a normal peacetime budget of £1,200 million which compared to the £3,600 million spread over the three years of the initial phase of the Korean rearmament programme (which was based on some American aid). Although the services were to reduce their figure, the result was that key decisions were only deferred. However, the figure that was imposed on the Chiefs of Staff was so low that they were unable to reconcile their different strategic perspectives within it and, as has been seen, the Defence Committee had to address the critical decisions of strategy and policy. Yet this did not resolve the problem, as will be seen in Chapter 8. The change in the assumptions about the provision for long-term defence policy with the adoption of the £600 million budget and 150,000 intake had been strongly reinforced by the balance of payments crisis. However, ministers did not reconsider the principle of conscription, only the workings of the National Service scheme.

While the government remained wedded to National Service the principle of conscription was increasingly questioned within the services. Opposition was growing within the army and to a lesser extent the RAF. In the former this reflected disappointment with the experience of trying to establish a mass army in peacetime. It was exacerbated by the budgetary pressures and particularly by the decision to train National Servicemen in regular units.

These 'bastard organisations'[52] were ascribed to the government's volte-face over the length of service, although they were in fact attributable to budgetary constraint.

Whatever the specific reason, National Service was increasingly seen within the army to be bad for regular morale. Shinwell admitted to Liddell Hart in April 1948 that 'most senior officers had changed their opinions about its value'.[53] In December 1948 Ismay wrote to Martel saying: 'I have felt for some time that conscription does not really work in this country and that the proper answer is to have a small long service Regular Army under conditions which will attract good men,'[54] though earlier in the year he stated that after the war for 'psychological reasons alone we were right to have conscription'.[55]

Many serving officers were reluctant to express their opposition, even in private correspondence, and others were not particularly disenchanted. However, General 'Bubbles' Barker (the General Officer Commanding (GOC) Eastern Command) clearly agreed with Martel and indeed in 1949 proposed a scheme to the Army Council designed to phase out conscription over a five-year period.[56] Major-General J. C. O. Marriott, the GOC London District, replied to Martel's appreciation of the state of the army and the burden of conscription with the comment: 'Personally I couldn't agree with you more.'[57] Yet even in army circles there was no unanimity. In rejecting an article from Martel for the *Army Quarterly*, its new editor, Brigadier Barclay, claimed that he had spoken to 'lots of people' but had 'yet to discover anyone who agrees conscription should be abolished'.[58]

According to Lt.-Gen. Martin, the military correspondent of the *Daily Telegraph*, Montgomery himself had begun to develop serious doubts. Liddell Hart was told by Martel on 29 March 1948 that the CIGS had admitted to Martin that the decision on conscription had been a mistake and that he wished that he had

[52] Lt.-Gen. Sir Evelyn Barker to Martel, 28 Apr. 1948, Papers of Sir Giffard Martel (Imperial War Museum, London).

[53] Liddell Hart, Notes for History: Talk with Shinwell, 22 Apr. 1948, Papers of Sir Basil Liddell Hart (Liddell Hart Centre for Military Archives, King's College, London), 11/1948/9.   [54] Ismay to Martel, 7 Dec. 1948, Martel papers.

[55] Ismay to Martel, 16 Apr. 1948, Martel papers.

[56] Barker to Martel, 28 Dec. 1949, Martel papers.

[57] Marriott to Martel, 18 Aug. 1948, Martel papers.

[58] Barclay to Martel, 25 Feb. 1950, Martel papers.

not started on that line.[59] This may well be true. Montgomery's attempts in the winter of 1947–8 to design the post-war army must have brought home to him the intractable problem of turning the regular army into a training organization for his 'New Model Army' while at the same time trying to provide embodied forces to meet foreign policy commitments within a shrinking budget and when the Cold War was just beginning.

Yet whether or not this was the case, these were essentially private doubts. The mathematics of the argument for conscription were overwhelming and grew more so through the year until in October 1948, Montgomery states that he got the military members of the Army Council to threaten their collective resignation unless the government agreed to eighteen months' service.[60] The attitude of the War Office remained that whatever the intrinsic merits of a regular army there was no quick and easy way back from conscription. That was certainly the view of the new CIGS, Sir Bill Slim.[61] In December 1949 Field Marshal Wavell (now in retirement) agreed that there was a powerful case for a strong regular army but did not consider it 'practical politics' to abandon it at that time.[62] The view that whatever the intrinsic disadvantages of National Service it could not simply be abandoned was certainly shared by Lt.-Gen. Martin, who himself had believed conscription to be right but by 1947–8 had come to recognize the deleterious influence it was having on the army.[63]

Potentially of greatest importance was the fact that Shinwell now believed that conscription was a burden and should be abolished. He told Liddell Hart that his views had changed since he had been at the War Office (though it will be remembered that he had been opposed in 1945) and that if he were Minister of Defence Britain would not have conscription.[64] Although this overestimated the powers of the department, his views did lead him to oppose Montgomery in October 1948, and indeed when he became Minister of Defence to attempt to move the services to an

---

[59] Liddell Hart, Notes for History, 29 Mar. 1948, Liddell Hart papers, 11/1948/7.
[60] Montgomery, *Memoirs*, 479. Montgomery diary entry 1–30 Oct. 1948, Papers of Viscount Montgomery of Alamein (Imperial War Museum, London), BLM 187/1.   [61] Slim to Martel, 19 May 1950, Martel papers.
[62] Wavell to Martel, 28 Dec. 1949, Martel papers.
[63] Martin to Martel, Jun. 1949, Martel papers.
[64] Liddell Hart, talk with Shinwell and his PPS, Wigg, 25 May 1948, Liddell Hart papers, 11/1948/13.

all-regular system. By January 1948 he had already expressed his support for a ballot to control the size of the intake.[65]

The idea that conscription was a burden and that the services should be run on a professional full-time basis also appears to have gained some ground in the RAF. Air Vice-Marshal Sir George Pirie, Air Member for Supply, told Liddell Hart in March 1949 that whereas two years before he had been in favour of conscription, he had completely changed his views on seeing results which were 'ruinous to the service'.[66] Although the ceilings imposed by the government were not foreseen, the preference for an all-regular Air Force had been long-standing. Opposition to conscription grew as the manning problems of the RAF mounted and as National Service was seen to be at the expense of properly paid and equipped regulars.

However, Slessor in particular argued that the RAF needed National Service to provide for its forces both in peacetime and at the outbreak of war. As regular recruiting continued to fall to what were seen as alarming levels, the case for conscription in the RAF remained a numerical imperative. On the other hand, the reduction in the defence budget did raise doubts about conscription which were rooted in the RAF's disquiet at the size and cost of the army. As noted, Tedder warned Alexander in August 1947 that if the retention of National Service led to completely unbalanced forces and too high defence expenditure the continuation of the conscription scheme should be reviewed. This view was shared by Cunningham.[67] Nevertheless, in November and December Tedder reaffirmed his support for the principle of conscription, largely because the RAF was increasingly dependent on its National Service intake. Tedder wanted both a reduction in that intake and a review of the army's role in wartime. Both the air force and the navy saw the link between the continental commitment and a large and costly conscript army as a threat to their own designs.

One view, expressed by Shinwell and others, was that it might be possible to end conscription, but for Alexander.[68] He had been

[65] Shinwell to Alexander, 9 Jan. 1948, DEFE 7/64.
[66] Liddell Hart, Notes for History, talk with Air-Marshal Sir George Pirie, Air Member for Supply and Organisation, 15 March 1949, Liddell Hart papers, 11/1949/10.   [67] COS (47) 112th, 30 Aug. 1947, DEFE 4/6.
[68] Liddell Hart, Notes for History, 25 May 1948, Liddell Hart papers, 1/634.

pilloried for the government's behaviour in April 1947 and his stay
at the MOD was not getting any happier. He was faced with
fundamental problems that were based on assumptions beyond his
control. As noted, he was extremely sensitive to any proposal that
interfered with the perception of universal National Service. He
was not liked by the Chiefs of Staff and Montgomery recounts
how he planned to get rid of him.[69] It was said that the Chiefs of
Staff 'disagreed on every subject except one—that Alexander was
n[o] b[loody] g[ood]'.[70] In parliamentary terms Dalton noted in
May 1947 that Alexander's 'stock is fallen very low'—he is
'pompous, unconvincing and incompetent in the handling of
detail in his National Service Bill'.[71] In December 1948, after the
announcement of the extension of the length of service, Paget
reported to Liddell Hart that 'all the talk was that Alexander
would resign. Personally I have heard this sort of talk before and I
don't think he will.'[72] In December 1948 Morrison told Attlee it
would be popular to 'change the lot' in the defence ministries.[73]
Attlee himself had believed for some time that Alexander might
have to be moved to the Lords.[74] Yet 'King Albert' or 'Albert
Victorious' (to use Dalton's irreverent but affectionate nicknames
for his colleague) survived and even entertained hopes of suc-
ceeding Bevin at the Foreign Office. There is little doubt that
after the events of April 1947 Alexander's continued existence as
Minister of Defence was entangled with the issue of National
Service. For the government to have radically changed or indeed
abandoned National Service could well have meant his political
demise.

It can be argued that the £600 million budget called for a radical
revision of thinking and a fundamental re-allocation of resources
that would have ended universal National Service. Indeed, that is
precisely what Alexander's private secretary Richard Wood maintained. As early as June 1947 he warned the Minister of Defence
that 'in the long term National Service is not merely of no advantage to our country it may be a positive danger'. The failure

---

[69] Montgomery, *Memoirs*, 483.
[70] Liddell Hart, Notes for History, 25 May 1948, Liddell Hart papers, 1/634.
[71] Dalton Diaries, 23 May 1947.
[72] Paget to Liddell Hart, 7 Dec. 1948, Liddell Hart papers, 1/563.
[73] Morrison to Attlee, 29 Dec. 1948, Papers of Herbert Morrison (Nuffield College, Oxford).   [74] Attlee to Morrison, 15 Sept. 1947, Morrison papers.

properly to apportion priorities 'would cripple our power for effective offensive action' and give us 'a false sense of security'.[75] In September 1948 he made another (equally unsuccessful) attempt to persuade the minister and promised not to say another word if the Chiefs of Staff turned the idea down.[76] However, Alexander was in no mood to 'set the cat among the pigeons', especially when, as Wood warned, there was the danger that it might appear (and might leak out) that he was 'wavering over the National Service issue'. If Alexander was indeed reluctant to conduct a necessary reappraisal of conscription policy, then, paradoxically, the real significance of the backbench revolts may have been to weld the government more firmly to National Service. In terms of policy, the PLP revolts could therefore be seen as wholly counter-productive.

The charge that but for Alexander National Service could have been brought to an end is nevertheless weak. Both the RAF and the army needed conscripts to meet their peacetime commitments and to provide trained reserves on the outbreak of war. Although the army's long-term wartime needs could be questioned, those of the RAF were less amenable to objection once strategic bombing and home defence were accepted as central defence objectives. After 1949, when the commitment to Europe began to take shape, the army's role became better defined and a strategic rationale for the trained reserves in war emerged more clearly. Moreover, by that stage the onset of the Cold War, mathematical logic, and the army's determination had strengthened the government's dependence on conscription.

Alexander was in a new department that was weak in bureaucratic resources. He was not a politically strong member of the government or a member of the 'inner cabinet'. Although his role was important it was beyond his powers—institutional as well as personal—to affect a fundamental reversal of policy. Abandoning conscription would have required a change in the configurations of power within the government, which was indeed made more likely with Dalton's replacement by Cripps. However, it would have also required the political eclipse or radical change in the outlook of the Foreign Secretary. Furthermore, in early 1948

---

[75] Wood to Alexander, 5 Jun. 1947, Papers of Viscount Alexander (Churchill College, Cambridge), 5/12.
[76] Wood to Alexander, 6 Sept. 1948, Alexander papers, 5/13.

Attlee needed to consolidate his own position after a quite serious threat to him from Cripps the previous autumn. A decision to abandon National Service could well have precipitated a crisis of confidence in his leadership within the PLP.

Yet the events of 1947–8 had shown the National Service Act to have been overhasty. Some of the problems could be dealt with by reasonably straightforward administrative action, but the long-term budget on which conscription had been based had now been significantly reduced. This raised serious doubts about the policy in the long-term, especially as some of the strategic objectives for which National Service had been established had yet to be agreed by the Chiefs of Staff or the government. On the other hand, although the different needs of embodied forces in peacetime and trained reserves in war could (and indeed should) have been analytically separate, no such distinction could yet be made in policy terms. As will now be seen, that was to become even more evident as the Cold War developed.

8

The Onset of the Cold War

EVEN as Alexander was embarking on the attempt to develop the long-term size and shape of the armed forces within an economically acceptable budget, events were conspiring to jeopardize the basis on which defence policy was being planned. The Cold War was beginning in earnest. On 22 January 1948 Bevin made his public plea for a Western Union, the first open step towards the Brussels Treaty signed on 17 March 1948. By then the communists had staged their coup in Czechoslovakia and East–West relations were disintegrating. In June Yugoslavia was expelled from the Cominform and on 17 July a state of emergency was declared in Malaya. On 24 June the Soviet forces began their blockade of Berlin.

The short- and long-term assumptions of the government's defence policy were being undermined. Commitment to the land defence of Western Europe had been accepted but only nominally. It was not translated even into the promise of any reinforcement divisions until 1949. Until then the Middle East remained the strategic priority. A permanent commitment of the standing army in Europe was not envisaged, although Montgomery had gained agreement for the army in Germany to stand and fight so long as it remained (and there were no indications of when a political settlement would allow withdrawal).

As for the cuts imposed on the 1948–9 budget, the assumptions about withdrawals looked increasingly shaky, and the risks that had been accepted in the size and organization of the forces threatened to 'mature against' the government. It had been recognized that these assumptions might prove overoptimistic particularly with regard to commitments in Greece, Trieste, and Austria. This indeed turned out to be the case.

On 27 February 1948 Shinwell wrote to Alexander pointing out that the garrisons in Trieste (5,000 strong) and Austria (7,500) would definitely be needed in July 1948.[1] The troops in Greece would also have to remain but by redeploying forces in the Middle East (i.e. from Palestine) this could be accommodated within existing manpower and budgetary limits. The withdrawal from Palestine was to be completed by 1 August 1948 but did not entail any compensatory cuts in overseas manpower as the forces were redeployed within the Middle East. Thus, Shinwell argued, it would be necessary for the army to overshoot its manpower target for July 1948. The release of troops during this period involved the last of the wartime groups. In less than three years five and a half million men and women had been demobilized with 'the minimum of avoidable friction and disturbance'.[2] Certainly when compared with the experiences of the Great War it was a notable triumph.

The manpower problems of the forces (especially the army and the RAF) were mounting at a time when the threat of war loomed into sharper focus. By July, when the state of emergency was declared in Malaya, the government had agreed to an emergency programme designed to put the forces into a better state of readiness if the Berlin situation deteriorated into war. Montgomery asked Alexander bluntly if the government were prepared to go to war over Berlin.[3] The answer and moreover the reaction of the government were equivocal. Previous assumptions about the likelihood of 'unpremeditated war' were called into question and the services pressed strongly to have the release of men and women suspended to strengthen the forces with trained and experienced personnel at a critical time.

The question of stopping releases was discussed on several occasions, culminating in a working party report[4] to the Defence Committee on 21 July.[5] It was proposed to suspend releases (of men and women) between then and September. This would mean the retention of 92,000 trained men and women, both regulars and National Servicemen (including those who had voluntarily extended their service). It would put the forces in much stronger

[1] Shinwell to Alexander, 27 Feb. 1948, PREM 8/833.
[2] Alexander to Attlee, 31 May 1948, PREM 8/833.
[3] Bernard Montgomery, *The Memoirs of Field-Marshal The Viscount Montgomery of Alamein* (Cassell, 1958), 482.   [4] DO (48) 43, 17 Jul. 1948, CAB 131/6.
[5] DO (48) 12th, 21 Jul. 1948, CAB 131/5.

shape and in particular help the RAF to sustain the airlift. It did not entail any significant change in policy towards the reinforcement of the army in Germany in the event of war.

However, neither Attlee nor Bevin was at this stage willing to suspend releases. To take such a public step would in effect be announcing a state of emergency. As Alexander pointed out, 'a decision to stop releases would in fact be the first step in a policy which involved switching the economy from a peace to a war footing'. The government was at this stage unwilling to take such action and Attlee had the report withdrawn. However, the Defence Committee did agree to the RAF's request to retain some 2,500 technicians to sustain the airlift. The Chiefs of Staff urged the government to take a variety of measures. These ranged from calling up the Regular Reserves to even remobilizing the four million or so Z reserves. Not surprisingly the Defence Committee saw this to be even more dramatic than the suspension of releases.

The crisis continued and on 29 July the Chiefs of Staff formally warned the government that 'if the Russians continue the blockade and action to freeze us out of Berlin after the present approach to them the sequence of events following this attitude may well lead us into war in the near future'.[6] However, the state of the armed forces was such that they were not in a position to 'fight with what they had' and that if war came there would be 'complete disorganisation leading to disaster unless certain steps are taken at once'. They felt it their duty to inform the government that the state of the services gave cause for alarm and necessitated (among other things) stopping releases, calling up selected reservists, and expanding the Army Supplementary Reserve from 4,000 to 11,000.

The government did agree to a limited re-equipment programme designed to place the forces on a better footing for action. The suspension of releases was discussed on three occasions in Defence Committee during July, but no decision was reached. When the stoppage of releases was agreed, on 23 August, the reason was to strengthen the hand of the Foreign Secretary over the ensuing six to nine months rather than to prepare for war.[7] Even then it was decided not to call up the reserves.

---

[6] DO (48) 49, 29 Jul. 1948, CAB 131/5.
[7] DO (48) 17th, 23 Aug. 1948, CAB 131/5.

The Defence Committee recommended that there should be a general suspension of releases for a period up to 31 March 1949. This went to Cabinet on 26 August 1948. By then, however, Montgomery had emerged with an entirely separate proposal to slow down the rate of releases and prevent 'administrative chaos' in the army during 1949, which Shinwell formally proposed to Cabinet.[8] The Secretary of State suggested that the rate of releases should be retarded rather than suspended. This should 'be directed towards bringing the maximum length of service down to two years by 1 January 1949' and would leave the army with some 400,000 men. His aim was to stabilize the length of National Service at two years from 1 January 1949. Politically this was a great deal more controversial than suspending releases. The provision of 400,000 men during 1949 compared with the previous figure of 339,000 and the working party's subsequent recommendation of 410,000 at 1 April 1949 falling to 376,000 by 1 July. From the War Office's point of view the CIGS's scheme offered a much easier administrative proposition. Yet it was clear that this was, as Hollis warned Alexander, 'a try-on to secure what CIGS had shown himself so eager to obtain, namely National Service for two years'.[9]

The Cabinet endorsed the Defence Committee's recommendation to suspend releases and referred the matter to a working party to examine how this should be done.[10] Given the Moscow talks planned for later in the month, it was decided not to announce the decision until later. Men in the Class B release category would not be affected. The Cabinet also decided to undertake a 'comprehensive review' of National Service and established another working party to examine this. At Bevin's insistence, the terms of reference were widened, though not to include the principle of conscription. Nor did they involve a fundamental reappraisal of the strategic aspects and the military need for trained reserves in war.

The working party on the suspension of releases reported to the Cabinet the following week.[11] It recommended that the personnel in the forces should have their period of service extended by a

[8] CP (48) 216, 2 Sept. 1948, CAB 129/29.
[9] Hollis's brief for Alexander, 25 Aug. 1948, CAB 21/2071.
[10] CM (48) 57, 26 Aug. 1948, CAB 128/13.
[11] CM (48) 58, 3 Sept. 1948, CAB 128/14.

period of three months. Unlike previous proposals this would not apply to regulars (including women) and National Servicemen on voluntary re-engagements. The scheme would immediately and progressively strengthen the forces with experienced and skilled men during the ensuing six critical months, while attempting to minimize the administrative dislocation and impact on service morale. The report was a majority one: the War Office representative argued for the Montgomery plan in the mistaken belief that the Cabinet had rejected the idea of the total suspension of releases.

The War Office argued that 'it would in any case be improbable that the army could get down to an overall one-year colour service of its National Service component by 31 December 1949 without major administrative and organisational difficulties'.[12] However, neither the RAF nor the navy supported this. Nor did they agree with the War Office interpretation of the Cabinet decision. They argued that Montgomery's proposals would have no effect at all on the strength of the other two services during the ensuing six to nine months. Both needed a complete suspension for a given period. Although the RAF's main needs were in 'shortage trades' the majority scheme would enable the air force to preserve its existing structure over the next few months. The two services agreed that after the Cabinet announced its decision on the suspension of releases, this should come into operation as soon as possible after that announcement.

The Cabinet rejected the War Office proposals and endorsed the majority report. Montgomery defended his own scheme but Shinwell was prepared to accept the other view. The only opposition came from Bevan, who argued against either suspension or retardation, saying that the former would have serious political and economic consequences. As it was impossible to rely on any certain improvement in the international situation in the next six months, he considered that it would not be possible for the government to end suspension. On balance, the benefits from the proposal would be more than outweighed by the subsequent embarrassment which the government would have to face.

This particular argument proved to be without foundation. Nevertheless Bevan was not wholly wrong about the duration

---

[12] CP (48) 216, 2 Sept. 1948, CAB 129/29.

of the military manpower crisis which led to the more politically difficult decision to extend National Service to eighteen months. His concern undoubtedly reflected feelings in the PLP, although the nature of the crisis facilitated an easier reception for the proposals than would otherwise have been the case. The Cabinet acted for reasons of foreign policy and the need to back Bevin's negotiating position. This was sufficiently pressing to come before party politics or economic concerns and there was no prior attempt to consider the cost of the extension or the industrial consequences caused by the loss of manpower.

The manpower situation of the services was continuing to deteriorate and Montgomery, after his failure in September 1948, spent his remaining weeks as CIGS trying to gain acceptance of an extension of the length of military service. Montgomery informed the COS Committee that it would not be possible for the army to carry out its tasks in 1949 within its existing manpower ceilings.[13] To fulfil existing commitments alone would require 409,000 troops (subsequently revised to 433,000). If the 1947 Act were introduced with the planned twelve-month period, the army would move from a strength of some 420,000 at 1 January 1949 to only 297,000 at 1 January 1950.[14] Assuming commitments remained as envisaged, and the rate of regular recruiting did not further deteriorate, the army would be some 124,000 men short of its requirements. Even with an extension to eighteen months the total strength at 1 January 1950 would be only 345,000, some 76,000 men short. Indeed, even two years' National Service would still mean a shortage of 9,000 men. The Army Council was told that the twelve-month period was absurd; even an eighteen-month period was not acceptable.[15]

Montgomery's concern was not just with existing policy. He also looked to the possibility of new commitments arising in the face of further Soviet or communist-inspired activity. There had already been great difficulty in providing a single brigade for Malaya and this was with an army of over 400,000. With the Guards Brigade now despatched, it would not be immediately possible to form another brigade as a strategic reserve without disruption of the training organization. The current plan was to

---

[13] COS (48) 199, 6 Sept. 1948, DEFE 4/16.
[14] Note for Secretary of State, 27/GEN/3211, 4 Oct. 1948, annex to AC/M (48) 5, 5 Oct. 1948, WO 163/63. [15] Ibid.

provide a reserve of two brigades, one built up over the next two or three months, the other in early 1949. As for the decision to send the Guards to Malaya, Liddell Hart privately told Montgomery: 'No critical article could have a tithe of the effect of the announcement in showing how bare is our cupboard.'[16]

One solution to the problems would have been a dramatic increase in regular recruiting, and indeed the services continued to press for improvements in pay and conditions. This, however, would be effective only in the long term. So even assuming commitments did not increase, the government was faced with the choice of increasing the period of service or significantly changing its approach to the use of military force in support of foreign policy. The atmosphere of Cold War crisis, the global perspective of the perceived communist threat, and the possibility of war itself did not make for radical changes.

The army's position was sympathetically discussed by the Chiefs of Staff on 8 September 1948[17] and the plight of the three services brought to the attention of the Prime Minister. At a Staff Conference on 24 September Attlee and Alexander met the service chiefs to discuss their warning of three days earlier that 'the present state of forces gives the gravest cause for alarm'.[18] Tedder told Attlee that the risk of war had increased to the point where it was 'almost dangerous', challenging existing assumptions about the risk of war in the period 1947–52. With the forces in their present state, the ability to fight with what was available in any 'unpremeditated war' was also weakened. All three services emphasized their inability to react effectively to the Soviet Union.

The navy argued that its fighting capability was very superficial. It was insufficiently trained and had inadequate fuel and equipment. In particular, the new First Sea Lord, Admiral Lord Fraser, emphasized the offensive capability of the Soviet submarine fleet. As for the RAF, it was argued that unless immediate steps were taken to arrest existing manpower trends it would find itself unable to meet current commitments, let alone assume further ones. In the event of war it would be unable 'to take the first

[16] Liddell Hart, Notes for meeting with Montgomery, 31 Aug. 1948, Papers of Sir Basil Liddell Hart (Liddell Hart Centre for Military Archives, King's College, London), 1/519/38a.   [17] COS (48) 124th, 8 Sept. 1948, DEFE 4/16.
[18] COS (48) 212, 21 Sept. 1948, PREM 8/834, discussed at COS (48) 136th, 24 Sept. 1948, DEFE 4/16.

shock' while its bomber force would be 'utterly inadequate to carry out even one of the major tasks which would immediately fall upon it'.[19] As noted, the army would be unable to meet existing commitments with its allocations of manpower.

What the services demanded of Attlee was action on pay and conditions to remedy the regular recruiting position, together with an extension of National Service aimed at preparing the armed forces to react in an emergency. Some of the arguments were familiar. The Chiefs of Staff, particularly concerned over the condition of married officers and NCOs, argued strongly for much better housing and housing allowances. Attlee, supported by Alexander, said that existing service pay had given the forces the best deal that they had ever had in comparison with civilian pay. He had been much impressed by the reports of the waste of service, and in particular army, manpower. Montgomery's reply that the men were misusing rather than wasting their time would hardly have reassured the Prime Minister.

On the issue of National Service, Attlee was even more disobliging. Having argued that defence policy had hitherto been based on the maintenance of a sound national economy, he pointed out that the recent decision to delay the call-up had been made because there were too many National Servicemen for the army and air force training organizations to cope with; yet now the services were asking for an increase in that burden. This was only partially true, as the problems of the intake were a consequence of manpower and budgetary ceilings imposed by the government which at the same time insisted on universal service.

However, Attlee was correct in saying that the existing state of the armed forces could hardly be blamed on the adoption of the twelve-month period, as the new act did not come into operation until 1 January 1949 and its immediate implications would not take effect for another year. Attlee's reaction to Montgomery's claim that an army of 400,000 would mean at least two years' conscription was most unsympathetic. Alexander calculated that the cost of these manpower levels would amount to some £840 million even before the re-equipment envisaged by the Chiefs of Staff for the period up to 1957. This was a considerable increase over the Treasury goal of £600 million or the latest compromise of

---

[19] COS (48) 136th, 24 Sept. 1948, DEFE 4/16.

nearly £700 million. At a time when the balance of payments was becoming manageable, the measures proposed by the Chiefs of Staff were received with little sympathy. The Staff Conference decided nothing.

Nevertheless, Montgomery was not idle. On 19 October 1948 he succeeded in getting the military members of the Army Council to threaten resignation unless the length of service was increased.[20] By then he was well aware of ministerial opinion, having met a hostile Shinwell a fortnight earlier.[21] The Secretary of State was not only opposed to the extension, but later used the crisis to try to end conscription, as he had told Liddell Hart he would earlier in the year. According to Montgomery's diarist the CIGS informed the Secretary of State of the threat of resignation on 21 October, and he 'must have told the Minister of Defence and probably the Prime Minister'.[22] A somewhat different account is provided in the official biography of Slim.[23] Ronald Lewin describes Slim's first morning at the War Office, when he was greeted by General Sir Gerald Templer, the Vice-Chief of the Imperial General Staff, with the words: 'Sir, I am very sorry to tell you that I offered your resignation on your behalf last night.' Lewin argues that Montgomery was prepared to accept twelve months, and that it was only the action of Slim, Templer, and Steele, the Adjutant-General, which 'extricated the army'. This will be considered later.

When initially presented with the implications of existing manpower trends, Shinwell said that it was simply out of the question even to attempt to obtain approval for any extension of National Service, especially when it would prejudice the possible closing of the balance of payments gap 'in two or three years' time'.[24] Politically, he believed it would be even more difficult to have a longer period of service than when the National Service Act had been introduced—an argument advanced with the Labour Party very much in mind. At the same meeting Speed argued that while two years was out of the question, eighteen months was

[20] Montgomery, *Memoirs*, 479–80.
[21] AC/M (48) 5, 5 Oct. 1948, WO 163/63.
[22] Montgomery diary, Papers of Viscount Montgomery of Alamein (Imperial War Museum, London), BLM 187/1, ch. 78.
[23] Ronald Lewin, *Slim: The Standard Bearer* (Leo Cooper, 1976), 266–70.
[24] AC/M (48) 5, 5 Oct. 1948, WO 163/63.

not impossible. Shinwell, however, expressed dissatisfaction at the large number of men (some 40,000) employed on administration, at the lack of amalgamation of common services, and at the number of troops in the United Kingdom in general.

Shinwell had been an early critic of conscription and since arriving at the War Office had become convinced that all-regular forces were needed. He was therefore much more sympathetic to the army's plea for an increased regular component, and to its scheme to guarantee civilian employment for men on the completion of their colour service. General Templer suggested that in time that measure in itself might ensure the recruitment of sufficient regulars to reduce National Service to twelve months. Yet, as he and the CIGS emphasized, it was the short-term inability of the army to meet its commitments after 1949 that required the extension of conscription.

Despite his objections, Shinwell was none the less prepared to accept that with the suspension of releases it would only be logical to expect those conscripted after January 1949 to be treated the same. Politically this could be defended on grounds of equality of treatment rather than appearing as a reversal of the April 1947 decision. He was thus prepared to accept an extension to fifteen months, but this was not acceptable to the military. The gap between Shinwell and the army's position had narrowed, but the Army Council reached no agreement. Subsequently the Secretary of State argued that in order to facilitate an extension of the period of service, the 1947 act should not come into operation. This would solve the short-term problem, though Shinwell's aim remained to phase out conscription altogether.

The next day the Chiefs of Staff examined the manpower requirements of the forces.[25] They concluded that the army needed 433,000 (including 12,000 ATS), the navy 160,000 (of whom 135,000 were to be regulars) and the RAF between 213,000 and 225,000 (depending on the exact length of service). The army figure of 433,000 could be met in 1949–50 only by increasing the National Service component. However, neither the navy nor the RAF could hope to reach its estimated minimum peacetime requirement; both were highly technical services that had to rely on regular

---

[25] PPO (P48) 27, 28 Sept. 1948, CAB 21/2071, discussed at COS (48) 143rd, 6 Oct. 1948, DEFE 4/17.

personnel in particularly crucial areas. The National Service intake was therefore constrained by the number of experienced instructors available to train the conscripts.

While the manpower situation of the navy had always been the least difficult among the three services, it could expect a strength of only 148,000 during 1949–50. Even on the assumption of two years' National Service this was some 12,000 short of peacetime requirements. With eighteen months the navy's strength would be 147,000; with the envisaged twelve months only 142,000—some 18,000 short. An intake of more than 10,000 conscripts was considered impossible. This was a change in the Admiralty's position, as before 30 August 1948 it had been prepared to accept only 2,000. From October 1948, with regular recruiting falling below projected targets and with higher wastage trends than before the war, the navy was taking 6,000 conscripts a year.

The position of the RAF looked a good deal grimmer. The immediate prospect for the Air Staff, occupied with the Berlin airlift that took up almost the whole of Transport Command, was alarming. Even to man the existing 'nominal' front line of 1,160 aircraft would require some 216,000–222,000 airmen. To reach the target of 1,858–1,891 aircraft (the figure imposed in the wake of the £600 million target) the RAF would need 250,000. However, if the trend of regular recruiting remained unchanged, the air force would be down to 166,000 by January 1950 and 153,000 by January 1952. This was quite inadequate for the Air Staff, already engaged in the Cold War with the Berlin airlift and the commitment in Malaya, and with operational forces also deployed in the Ogaden and Aden. Furthermore, they were concerned with future contingencies in Italian Somaliland, Transjordan, Tripolitania, West Africa, the Persian Gulf, and the Middle East. There was also the need for capability in home defence, strategic bombing, and a tactical air force for possible deployment in Western Europe.

Adoption of an eighteen-month period of service would enable the RAF to retain a substantial number of trained men in the forces. Two years would 'provide a further valuable alleviation of the recruiting problem and lead to a greater overall efficiency by virtue of the greater stability and increased experience provided'.[26]

[26] PPO (P38) 27, 28 Sept. 1948, CAB 21/2071.

Nevertheless, the real problem for the RAF, even more than for the army, lay in its dangerously low levels of regular recruiting and regular re-engagement. Indeed, the requirements of the air force—225,000 with twelve months' service and 61,000 conscripts, 218,000 with eighteen months and 68,000, and 213,000 with two years and 71,000—all assumed a very marked improvement in regular recruitment, which was believed to be unrealistic. If the level of trained men in the RAF remained static, it would result in a 'wholly unacceptable dilution of trained strength'. Unless regular recruiting improved and there was an increase in re-engagements then the number of National Servicemen would have to be reduced, with serious implications for the manpower situation.

The Chiefs of Staff had been asked by Alexander to consider various options to meet these problems. They replied in some detail, explaining the problems that National Service presented to each of the services in terms of training liability and overseas commitments.[27] It was argued that after 'all possible economies' had been made and 'all acceptable risks' taken, in order to meet the existing and foreseeable commitments for the next three years, a minimum of some 815,000–830,000 service personnel would be needed. The three-month extension would mean a total strength of some 820,000 on 1 January 1949, including about 375,000 conscripts, all of whom would be released by 1 January 1950 if the period of service remained at twelve months. With the intake of 150,000 National Servicemen and regular recruiting at its current level, the total strength on 1 January 1950 would be 615,000. Aside from the unprecedented turnover of personnel during the year, it would leave the forces some 200,000 men short of their estimated requirements. This, it was argued, would be 'militarily catastrophic'.

At a Staff Conference Alexander held with the Chiefs of Staff on 16 October 1948,[28] the Minister of Defence asked for an examination of three possible courses of action: an increase in National Service to fifteen months; an increase to eighteen months; and the postponement of the introduction of the 1947 act for one or two years or indefinitely. They replied that the fifteen-month option

---

[27] COS (48) 125, 19 Oct. 1948, PREM 8/1021.
[28] COS (48) 145th, 16 Oct. 1948, DEFE 4/17.

did not offer a solution. It would leave the army 70,000 short on
1 January 1950 and 100,000 short on 1 April 1950. Even if overseas commitments were considerably reduced, it would still be
impossible for the army to take a higher National Service intake
than 110,000, and reducing commitments was not what the Chiefs
of Staff had in mind.

They also rejected the idea of postponing the implementation of
the 1947 act and maintaining conscription under wartime legislation. It would do nothing to remove the existing instability of
the services or the 'serious psychological effect' of that instability.
There would also be an impact on the TA unless the men were
also expected to serve a period of part-time liability. Any extension of full-time service for the post-January 1949 entrants (under
the 1947 act) would adversely affect the TA. The service chiefs
nevertheless declared the idea of postponing the National Service
Act to be 'most undesirable'. They wanted an unequivocal commitment to the principle of National Service as the basis of long-
term planning.

The Chiefs of Staff's suspicion was not without foundation.
Shinwell saw the 'postponement' of the 1947 act and the maintenance of conscription until the 'present emergency' was ended
(about two years) as publicly and politically acceptable if it were
accompanied by an announcement that conscription for the army
would be ended altogether at a stipulated time in the future.
Indeed, he suggested that with increased regular recruiting, it
might be possible to do without any National Servicemen by the
middle of 1953. Apart from some part-time service in the TA, this
meant ending conscription in 1951. How the RAF was to cope
was not explained.

Alexander, however, sided with the service chiefs. He rejected
any idea of ending conscription, arguing that it would undermine
the Western Union and threaten the American willingness to assist
the Europeans—one of the first explicit justifications of military
service in terms of the American commitment to Europe.[29]
Shinwell was a lone and isolated opponent and the Chiefs of Staff
carried the case for the introduction of the 1947 act.

So far as the navy and air force were concerned the eighteen-
month period was the 'absolute minimum', and even this meant a

[29] SM/M (48) 13, 21 Oct. 1948, CAB 21/2071.

further deterioration in their state of preparedness for war and a general slowing-down of administrative services. There would also be a decrease in the efficiency of the training machine. Eighteen months would enable National Servicemen to be sent to all the overseas theatres (with the possible exception of the Far East); it would nevertheless leave the army some 50,000 men short of its requirements. Only the two-year period would really be sufficient.

The eighteen-month period entailed cuts in the army's overseas commitments and in particular reducing the garrisons in Germany, the Middle East, and the Far East. On a proportionate basis this would involve cuts of 8,000 men from Germany, 3,000 from the Middle East, and 2,000 from the Far East—reductions in both administrative units and in 'teeth arms'. This, it was argued, would involve serious risks. It was nevertheless the best that the military could hope for.

The cost involved was a central concern for the government. Cripps provided estimates for the different options. Two years' National Service would cost £40–50 million; eighteen months would mean £30 million in 1949, somewhat less thereafter. These figures did not include the consequences of the loss of production and other aspects of industrial dislocation. Assuming £500 was the annual value of a man's production, two years' service would mean a further loss of about £60 million; eighteen months, £40 million running down to £30 million.

These costs were in addition to the proposed increases in pay and marriage allowances which the services claimed would facilitate greater recruiting and re-engagement and which amounted to some £15 million. The increases were paid only to regulars, which meant that the services had now succeeded in obtaining differential rates of pay between regulars and conscripts. Taken as a whole this meant a considerable increase in the burden of defence expenditure and a further obstacle to achievement of the government's economic objectives. Opposition was inevitable and was strengthened by the fact that Cripps was now Chancellor, though this reduced the significance of his former department. The new President of the Board, Harold Wilson, was a junior member of the Cabinet and does not appear to have concerned himself with defence in the way that Cripps had done, at least until the Korean rearmament programme provoked his resignation.

The decision on the extension of conscription was taken by an *ad hoc* Cabinet committee which first met on 25 October.[30] Alexander opened the discussion with a resumé of the services' position, arguing that it was no good demanding a long-term plan from the Chiefs of Staff and expecting that they fulfil existing commitments while denying them the resources to do so. He explained how since early 1947 he had pressed them to formulate proposals on the respective roles of the services within a strategy to be agreed by ministers. The failure to reach agreement within the proposed 650,000 manpower ceiling and £600 million budget had been further complicated by the short-term cuts arising from the balance of payments crisis. The deterioration in the international situation had rendered it impossible to end certain commitments and already imposed new ones, notably in Malaya.

His colleagues were anything but sympathetic. Led by the Prime Minister, they presented a formidable case against the extension of military service. Attlee began by referring back to the initial rationale of the 1947 act, recalling that National Service had been primarily intended to provide trained reserves of manpower at the outbreak of war. Though recognizing that the change in the international environment might necessitate stronger armed forces in the next three years, he argued that it would be impossible to prepare for both short- and long-term contingencies. Further, Attlee correctly pointed out that, while some of the overseas commitments had not originally been anticipated, commitments in Italy, India, Burma, and Palestine had all ended. Less correctly, he argued that existing commitments (and in this he optimistically cited the example of Malaya) might not last three years. More effective use could be made of 'native manpower', particularly in Africa, and, as the recent report on the army's use of manpower seemed to confirm, the period of service following the twelve weeks of basic training could be used far more efficiently.

If Attlee was unsympathetic, Cripps was deeply hostile. He argued that to increase conscription to eighteen months or two years would mean 'a very radical recasting of UK economic plans including cuts in the capital investment programme' and, even more politically explosive, 'possibly in food consumption levels'.

[30] Gen 254/1st, 25 Oct. 1948, PREM 8/1021. The committee consisted of Attlee, Cripps, Isaacs, Alexander, Shinwell, Hall, and Henderson. Morrison and Bevin were also members but did not attend the first meeting.

The additional expenditure would make substantial increases in taxation necessary if an inflationary budget was to be avoided.

Cripps was not satisfied that the Chiefs of Staff had tried to work out joint manpower plans for meeting overseas commitments. In his view, Britain should wait until the American and Commonwealth governments had reached their decisions and he pointed out that the French were limiting defence expenditure to well below anticipated levels. Behind these arguments was the general Treasury belief that military alliances and pacts should entail burden-sharing with the aim of a reduction in the British effort. In practice the opposite was the case.

Finally, the familiar Treasury line on the defence budget was emphasized: the Cabinet needed to determine the amount that the country could afford in manpower and financial resources in the next three years. The Chiefs of Staff should then submit proposals setting out the respective roles of the services within that limit. This view was supported by the ministerial committee and, in the wake of the services' inability to reach agreement, led to the creation of the Harwood Committee, which was given the task of making a comprehensive study of the strategic and military implications of a £700 million budget.[31]

The loss of industrial manpower was described as 'very serious' by Isaacs, although he did not provide any figures until later in the week. It was left to the service ministers (now Shinwell, Hall, and Henderson) to provide any counter to the economic arguments. Shinwell was most reticent. He argued that it was imperative to reach an early decision, but gave little support to the services. Instead he said that too much manpower was spent on administrative duties and that overseas commitments could be met with smaller forces. He further criticized the Chiefs of Staff for having failed to reach agreement on the respective roles of the services. In his view the most important thing for the army was to stimulate regular recruiting. George Hall was likewise unhelpful, arguing that the extension of National Service was not essential for the navy to discharge its responsibilities. Only the Secretary of State for Air, Arthur Henderson, provided any real ministerial backing for the military. He warned that the RAF would be hopelessly unbalanced by the end of 1949 owing to its regular recruiting and

[31] See ch. 9.

re-engagement difficulties. The meeting concluded in agreement with Cripps, but did not reach any formal decisions.

The committee met again a week later with Bevin and Morrison in attendance.[32] Alexander opened with his endorsement of the service chiefs' view that long-term reorganization would have to be subordinated to the needs of the next two or three years. By now, he informed his colleagues, the Chiefs of Staff were prepared to accept that on economic and political grounds two years' National Service was unacceptable. He suggested that the problem should be approached with two main questions in mind: whether commitments could be reduced, and whether the demands of the forces were 'compatible with the economic position'.

In response to the first point Bevin argued that, while it was difficult to forecast how the international situation would develop in the next two years, he himself believed that the danger had receded in the last few weeks, even though the Berlin crisis was still unresolved and 'there was no knowing where the next crisis might occur'. Indeed, with the strengthening of communism in China, the attention of the United States might be diverted away from Europe. In his opinion the really critical period was up until 1951.

Nevertheless, he felt there was a tendency to exaggerate the defence commitments that resulted from his foreign policy. While the Austrian and Trieste commitments had persisted beyond anticipated dates, this had been offset by the withdrawal from Palestine. Indeed, he argued, the estimate of total overseas commitments was less than had been made in 1946. While claiming that overseas obligations involved no more than 100,000 men out of the total of 650,000, he argued that apart from forces actually maintained overseas it was the appearance of military strength that was necessary for diplomacy. He was particularly concerned over the loss to Malaya of the Guards Brigade, which had been earmarked for Germany if serious trouble arose.

However, he did not support the Chiefs of Staff. Though appreciating the great need for skilled men, especially in the RAF, it seemed to him very wasteful of manpower to extend the period of service in order to provide the comparatively small proportion

[32] Gen 254/2nd, 1 Nov. 1948, PREM 8/1021.

of trained men. The need for skilled servicemen and NCOs could be met by an effective recruiting campaign and by better inducements to join the services as a career.

On the general questions of defence and foreign policy, it was agreed that the proper formula was to decide what proportion of national resources was required to fight the Cold War and then use the remaining resources to prepare for the 'shooting war'. Cripps argued that on past experience it was unprofitable to ask the Chiefs of Staff for their demands, as, invariably, these could not be met. The better course was to inform them how much was available and get them to produce a 'concerted plan founded on the best possible allocation of available resources between the three services' rather than by simply adding together the separate requirements of each of the services as defined by the respective departments. As past experience had shown, and as the Harwood report would bring home, this was easier said than done. Cripps again found support among his colleagues. The departure of Montgomery (at the end of October) may well have raised hopes in this and in other areas of planning and co-ordination.

The discussion then turned to the specific question of whether the period of service should be increased. Isaacs estimated that eighteen months' service would mean a maximum extra number of men in the forces of some 131,000 in January 1950, falling to 103,000 in July; two years would mean 100,000 in January 1950 and 177,000 in January 1951. These men would enter the forces at the expense of industry.

Alexander recounted the service chiefs' view and put the cost of the defence budget for 1949–50 at £760–770 million, based on eighteen months' service. Twelve months' service would leave the army 'in a serious state of disorganisation'. Fifteen months would only delay problems and still leave the services well short of requirements. The attitude of the service ministers had not changed, though Shinwell did elaborate on his own ideas. The threat in the near future, he argued, could be met by recourse to the large numbers of trained and experienced men in the Z reserves. The main objective should be to stimulate regular recruiting.

There was no indication of any change in ministerial sentiment. There was a general belief, clearly shared by the Secretary of State of War, that great improvements could and should be made in the field of manpower economy. There was also agreement with the idea of using some 65,000 Colonial troops (the non-white soldiers from the West Indies, East Africa, West Africa, and Malaya) outside their indigenous areas, albeit only in administrative and noncombatant roles, as had been happening in Egypt.

No formal decision was taken, but the mood of ministers was evident. The following day, 2 November 1948, the Chancellor met with the Minister of Defence to discuss the defence ceiling within which the services would have to work in the next few years.[33] Cripps told him that £700 million would be available for the forthcoming year; Alexander informed the Chiefs of Staff of this later that day. They promised to study the proposal 'on its merits' but were aware that on their existing plans it would be inadequate. Their immediate concern was with the extension of conscription. On this they were adamant. They declared that 'with a shorter period of service both the army and the RAF would disintegrate'. The decision on conscription, they argued, was so fundamental that it should be taken irrespective of manpower or financial ceilings.

It was this view that the service chiefs presented to the ministerial committee later that week.[34] Tedder put their case. While declaring, inevitably, that his colleagues were fully conscious of the need for a sound economic base for national defence, nevertheless, if there were a substantial reduction in the proportion of experienced men resulting from the twelve-month period, then the services would become completely ineffective over the following two or three years. Eighteen months' service would itself present a 'serious handicap'. To go below that would be disastrous. The twelve-month period would mean the loss of 50 per cent of the experienced men in the forces during 1949. Overseas service, it was claimed, could be undertaken only by regulars; this would further damage morale and affect recruiting and re-engagement. Indeed, Tedder argued that it was difficult to see how enough experienced men would be available to train the new recruits and conscripts. Under these conditions National Service would involve a 'gross waste of manpower'.

Nevertheless, the services were prepared to accept that keeping men in the forces might prove to be an intolerable burden

[33] Memorandum for Gen 254/3 by Alexander, 2 Nov. 1948, PREM 8/1021.
[34] Gen 254/3rd, 5 Nov. 1948, PREM 8/1021.

on the economy. It followed that to keep within budgetary and manpower restraints it would be necessary to reduce the intake. Given the financial circumstances, they would prefer to have a smaller number of National Servicemen and 'get more out of them'. Aware of the political difficulties involved in encroaching on the principle of universal liability, and that extending the range of deferments would produce considerable administrative difficulties in the long term, the Chiefs of Staff argued that they could reduce the intake by significantly raising the standards of entry. This pre-empted the comprehensive review of National Service that officials were undertaking. Moreover, the eighteen-month period still entailed reductions in overseas commitments. Tedder spoke of cutting the British Army on the Rhine (BAOR) from 60,000 to 40,000 or scaling down the forces in the Middle East.

There was now a significant change in the reaction of the ministerial committee. The timing of this accords with Lewin's account of Slim's action when the new CIGS went to see Attlee with his resignation in his pocket.[35] This change in ministerial attitude indicates that it was Slim's threat, not Montgomery's, that was decisive. The accusation that Montgomery accepted twelve months is more difficult to sustain for, as has been seen, he had since July been engaged in a constant battle over the length of service and the size of the army.

As Montgomery's diarist recorded, the Cabinet had not taken a decision when Montgomery left the War Office and indeed he won a bet (of two shillings and sixpence) with a member of his staff who predicted there would be a decision by 1 November.[36] Lewin's account notwithstanding, it is worth noting the remarks of Monty's diarist, written on 19 November: 'There can be little doubt that if eighteen months' service is decided upon by the Cabinet, most of the thanks will be due to CIGS for his unremitting struggle.'[37]

Ministers now agreed that on current assumptions it would be impossible for the forces to attain a reasonable standard of efficiency in 1949 or 1950 and that owing to changes in the international situation, and the resulting need to place the forces in

[35] Lewin, *Slim*, 269.
[36] Montgomery diaries, 1–30 Oct. 1948, Montgomery papers.   [37] Ibid.

a better state of preparedness in the next two or three years, it was therefore necessary to review the policy on National Service. In order to preserve the efficiency of the forces, a smaller number of National Servicemen would be retained for a longer period. There was no recorded dissent from this.

The discussion turned to the various ways of adjusting the National Service intake. The first suggestion was to extend the principle of total reservation as applied in coalmining and agriculture. Other vital industries could benefit at a time of economic difficulty. Compared with occasions when this option had been studied before, the international crisis made public understanding more likely. The problem remained of knowing where to draw the line without undermining acceptability of the scheme.

Shinwell again argued that the existing method should be retained 'for the duration of the emergency' which he believed would be no more than two years. As before, he received no support. There were two other specific suggestions. First, the idea of raising medical standards was pressed by Slim; second, Cripps suggested that National Service should comprise two different categories: some men would have a short training period (of six months or so) with the colours followed by a long period with the reserves, and others would serve two or three years with the colours and have no reserve liability. Deciding which individuals were placed in which category would be done by ballot. The idea of different periods of military service so far had not received serious consideration. It gained initial support from Tedder who correctly saw it as fulfilling in principle the two basic needs of the services. This raised fundamental political questions (about balloting and universal service) and equally basic questions about the size and shape of the forces. Cripps clearly had an economic motive in mind and wanted a very different ratio between the two categories than did the services. He strongly pressed the need to keep within strict financial limits for the forthcoming year. The issue of controlling the intake clearly needed further study and so was referred to the working party already at work on the problem. The meeting did however conclude by agreeing in principle, and deciding to recommend to Cabinet, the increase in the period of National Service from twelve to eighteen months.

Before this proposal reached Cabinet an equally vital battle over the size of the defence budget had developed. Cripps had told

Alexander that £700 million was the maximum that the country could afford for 1949–50. When the service departments had subsequently submitted their provisional manpower estimates for 1949–50, the MOD had calculated that this would cost £833 million, including research and development, and £12 million for increased pay and allowances, but excluding atomic energy.[38] This was predicated on a service manpower strength of 715,000 at 1 April 1950 and an average strength of 750,000 during 1949–50. While this was well below the 820,000 for which the Chiefs of Staff argued, it was based on the assumption of eighteen months' conscription.

After making allowances for various cuts in administration and production Alexander arrived at a figure of £788 million, some £45 million below his estimate of their projected requirements. To bridge the gap between £788 and £700 million he argued that it would be necessary to reverse or drastically slow down some of the special production and stockpiling measures approved during the summer, together with a reduction in normal maintenance, and perhaps even more dramatically by a further substantial early reduction in the forces, possibly in the order of 100,000. He warned that this would 'practically knock the bottom out of the army and the air force as regards the skilled and experienced National Servicemen now serving and render both incapable of meeting their overseas commitments'.

Cripps was unmoved and stuck to his £700 million. Alexander's response came after further consultation with the Chiefs of Staff and the Service Ministers Committee.[39] He referred to the initial service estimate of 820,000 which was now generally agreed to be impracticable. Taking the more realistic target of 750,000, he emphasized that to reduce the forces below that would render them incapable of carrying out their tasks and unbalance them 'almost to the extent of ceasing to exist as coherent forces'. He and the service ministers were in unanimous agreement that £700 million would mean not only the cancellation of the July emergency programme but, in the case of the army and the RAF, manpower targets for 31 March 1950 (250,000 and 150,000 respectively) that would be little above their regular contents. 'In

[38] DO (48) 83, 6 Dec. 1948, CAB 131/6.
[39] Alexander to Cripps, 15 Nov. 1948, PREM 8/1021.

this event National Service would virtually be at an end because we could neither train or pay for anything but such a small intake as to make it ridiculous.'[40]

Nevertheless, neither Alexander nor the departmental ministers were unaware of the economic circumstances and after lengthy deliberation they improved on Alexander's initial cut of £45 million. Allowing for the proposed pay increases and based on the current levels of requirement and commitments, 'as a result of a very great effort' they got the estimate down to £750 million. Though this still required further negotiation with the services the Minister of Defence anticipated that the army would get slightly over £300 million and the Ministries of Supply and Defence £60 million, leaving just over half the remainder of £390 million for the RAF and the rest for the navy.

The £750 million figure would none the less mean 'drastic cuts and sacrifices'. For example, the emergency equipment pro-gramme for the army would have to be reduced to one-third of its projected target. This would invite severe criticism in Parlia-ment and elsewhere. Moreover, the service ministers were by no means satisfied that their allocations would allow them to meet their minimum reasonable demands. Yet cuts in their equipment programmes were unavoidable. To cut manpower would not only produce proportionally small savings (cutting 30,000 from the average annual manpower budget would save only £10 million) but would involve a very drastic run-down of the forces which would leave them quite inadequate in the face of their commit-ments. The equipment problem was exacerbated by the fact that as wartime stocks were now becoming exhausted it would be necessary to meet existing needs from current production.

Alexander's conclusions were presented as the defence estimates to the Defence Committee on 8 December 1948.[41] Before then the question of National Service had to be resolved. It was again discussed by the ministerial committee[42] before going to Cabinet on 18 November. By then the 'decision' had already been leaked to the press.[43] The committee met to discuss the detailed report on National Service prepared by the working party under the chair-manship of the Permanent Secretary at the MOD, Sir Harold

[40] Ibid.   [41] DO (48) 23rd, 8 Dec. 1948, CAB 131/5.
[42] Gen 254/4th, 17 Nov. 1948, PREM 8/1021.
[43] *News Chronicle*, 16 Nov. 1948.

Parker.[44] The main problem was how to reconcile the numbers of men available for call-up with the numbers that the services could accept within the manpower ceilings imposed by financial limits. To that end the various proposals for limiting the intake were examined in detail.

Ministers agreed with the working party's conclusions that extending the total reservation was not a practical solution, for reasons that were familiar. Consideration was again given to the idea of exempting apprentices. This was favoured in industry and in the Ministry of Supply and was treated sympathetically in the report and in the ministerial discussion. While there was scope for extending deferment by administrative means to men engaged on scientific research the loss of apprentices and potential tradesmen was regarded as too disadvantageous for the services. Moreover, it would be unfair on other young men in industry and particularly unfair on those who had already opted to do military service before taking up their apprenticeships.

Although the working party supplied a detailed account of the American system of selective service, it gave little consideration to a ballot, which was dismissed as politically unacceptable. This view was shared by ministers. However, it was noted that if the position arose in which numbers available far exceeded numbers required then 'the ballot might well be the only practicable solution'. The proposal was rejected by the committee but with the qualifying phrase 'except as a last resort'—the nearest the government had yet come to seriously considering selective service.

The committee held that public opinion would not accept a situation in which the choice between complete exemption and a lengthy period of service would be decided simply by luck. Cripp's suggestion about the two categories of service did minimize this problem, but still had serious disadvantages. The men who had only received six months' full-time training would be unable to provide the useful service that the forces needed at the time. Moreover, unless the number of men doing six months was substantial, the average number of conscripts would be greater than under existing proposals. This would be more expensive. If the whole intake were absorbed between the two categories, it

[44] Gen 254/1, 13 Nov. 1948, PREM 8/1021.

would make the services less efficient and less able to carry out their tasks, 'possibly at an increase in cost'.

The smaller the intake the fewer the difficulties. Nevertheless, it would mean a larger training establishment producing a proportion of men with no operational value. This was a particular problem in the RAF. It would be impossible, it was claimed, to avoid excessive training liabilities by abandoning the period of basic training altogether and sending the men straight into the reserves. This would leave the TA with an even lower level of operational efficiency. Moreover, it would exacerbate what the working party regarded as the fundamental political objection to the idea, namely, that the 'general public' would not regard the alternatives as fair equivalents. The greater the inequality, the greater the objection to the use of a ballot. Ministers found no reason to question this assumption.

Shinwell's proposal that the 1947 act should be repealed or substantially amended and the men called up under existing wartime legislation was rejected. This would have meant announcing a maximum two-year period of conscription, which would have ensured flexibility and provided the numbers that the services required. Shinwell also proposed a reserve liability on those finishing their full-time service from 1 January 1950. There were political problems with this as it meant an entirely new obligation on men called up under the transitional scheme. The Secretary of State defended his proposal, arguing that after the initial two-year period of call-up, the length of service could be gradually tapered off 'to the point when perhaps National Service might be dispensed with altogether'. Though this presented the services with the advantage of a two-year period in the immediate future, the threat to National Service itself was apparent. There was little support for Shinwell's proposal among ministers. They took the view that it would be unfair to the individual, who would be kept in doubt over his future; it would, moreover, impose an insufficiently firm basis for planning the forces. Politically, repeal of the National Service legislation would be highly embarrassing and make its reintroduction a matter of extreme difficulty. Extending conscription to two years even as a *quid pro quo* for its subsequent abolition would have been very difficult indeed.

Instead, the working party turned to the formula that had been adopted in 1947—raising standards and deferring registrations.

In suggesting that general medical standards should be raised, the working party rejected the War Office proposal to restrict the intake by raising the mental capacity of conscripts. Under the existing scheme of medical classification, men whose 'mental capacity or intelligence' was 'in any doubt' were rejected after a psychiatrist had confirmed their condition. However, there was a significant number of men who, though not considered backward, were 'below average'. For years the navy had weeded these men out and the RAF was in the process of introducing a similar scheme. Only the army would be left with the 'dullards' who were consigned to the Pioneer Corps. The problem was that this selection process was carried out once the men had already been accepted into the army. If the test could be carried out before entry, and those who failed declared unfit, the intake could not only be reduced in size but improved in quality.

However, it was felt that to do so would undermine the principle of universal conscription and would 'put a premium on ignorance' for those wishing to avoid National Service. It would impose a disproportionately heavy share of the national burden on 'the intelligent classes of the community'. Ministers endorsed this argument.

Under the recently introduced Pulheems system of medical assessment the men were measured separately under various headings—eyesight, hearing, locomotion, etc. They were then placed in grades. Of the men posted to the services 87.5 per cent were placed in Grade I; the rest, who usually had some minor defect of vision or locomotion, were put in Grade II. Unlike the 1947 report, the working party rejected as out of the question the idea of exempting men in Grade II. Instead they proposed a 'modest' raising of standards. No details were given except that the envisaged adjustment 'would be welcomed by the services' and would reduce the numbers available for call-up by about 7 per cent. This was not seen to impair the principle of universal service because it involved administrative adjustment rather than fixing a particular standard (as the War Office proposed). This was a curious distinction, but one apparently accepted by ministers. Adjusting the standard provided a formula that was both bureaucratically convenient and politically straightforward.

On the assumption that this was accepted, the number of men available in the next three years was calculated. The service departments concluded that the maximum annual intake that they could accept during that period would be 175,000. With eighteen months' service, it was estimated that by 1 July 1950 the strength of the forces would be 790,000, with an average of 769,000 during 1949–50 and 737,000 during 1950–1. These figures were dependent on a level of regular recruiting that was expected to improve with the increases in pay and allowances.

On the basis of four registrations a year the intake of 175,000 could be accommodated in 1949–50 but not in the following two years. It had been realized for some time that there would be more National Servicemen than could be absorbed. When the problem had been considered in 1947 it had been decided to omit one of the quarterly registrations, and this had already come into effect, reducing the intake by some 35,000 and raising the call-up age to eighteen years and three months. Given an intake of 175,000 it would not be necessary to drop one registration; in the two years after that two more registrations would have to be postponed. The 150,000 intake that the Defence Committee had meanwhile decided upon meant that the number of registrations per year would eventually have to be adjusted.

Under the 1939 Military Training Act the call-up age had been fixed at twenty years and it was argued that this had advantages for the services, for industry, and for the individual. On the other hand, it was strongly argued in Parliament that call-up at eighteen would cause least interruption to civilian life. The working party saw no problem in deferring registrations until the call-up age approached twenty. With an intake of 175,000 there was no immediate difficulty as any gap would be closed by the measures already announced. Even with an intake reduced to 135,000 the age of call-up would (by the beginning of 1952) still be only nineteen years and six months. Given that the position was so uncertain, the working party considered it unprofitable to examine what might be necessary thereafter.

A number of other issues arising out of the eighteen-month period was discussed by ministers. Extending the period of service raised the question of reserve liability—the length of the liability and the annual and aggregate periods of training during that time. The services had slightly different needs in these respects, although no one suggested different aggregate (as opposed to annual) liabilities. The RAF's main concern was not to overload its training capabilities and Tedder's inclination was to reduce the length of time for which men were liable (from six years) but to keep the period of training at sixty days. Shinwell suggested sixty days' training within a three-year liability. This was questioned by Slim, who advocated a five-year period 'to avoid problems with industry', and by the Admiralty, who felt that it would be difficult to take the navy's reserves to sea for three periods of twenty days in three successive years. A compromise was agreed of four years' liability with sixty days' service distributed on an annual basis at the discretion of the services.

The report also examined another idea of Shinwell's, to merge National Service reserves with voluntary elements of the TA. While it recognized that this had certain attractions, it noted that the success of the scheme would depend on an increased training liability for the conscripts. Apart from the administrative and political problems, the cost would have been substantial. Experience in the army already suggested that training conscripts and regulars in the same units was less than satisfactory. The working party was also unfavourably disposed to the idea that apprentices and students who chose to defer their National Service should be required to undertake part-time training during their years of deferment. This was a more universal scheme at age eighteen but another burden on the TA.

The other important question raised by the MOD report was the period of time over which National Service would be retained at eighteen months. The officials endorsed the Chiefs of Staff's view that it was essential to be able to plan on the assumption of an eighteen-month period for the next three years unless there was a striking improvement in the international situation. Nevertheless, with the Treasury stressing the need to bear a reduction in mind if circumstances permitted, the committee was 'not prepared to enter into a binding commitment'. The eighteen-month figure would thus be imposed as a maximum to be varied downwards on the basis of an Order in Council. The planning requirements of the services were to be met by the issue of a directive to service departments making it clear that eighteen months would be retained for three years unless there was a striking change in the international situation. Although this decision did nothing to ease service doubts about the long-term issue, it nevertheless featured in the government's defence of its decision in Parliament and to the Labour Party.

Returning to the question of the defence budget, the ministerial committee meeting of 15 November 1948 provided the first opportunity for confrontation over the Treasury's £700 million target and Alexander's response. Cripps was insistent that £700 million was the maximum that the country could afford (excluding the increase in service pay and allowances). Alexander was equally insistent that on the basis of existing commitments, and including the increases in pay and allowances, the minimum possible figure was £750 million, and by December that had been adjusted to £770 million. The service departments backed Alexander. Shinwell spoke of the War Office's acceptance of £300 million as entailing 'very serious risks'. Hall and Henderson had similar views on their allocations. The Foreign Office was anxious that 'everything possible should be done to maintain overseas defence commitments and stiffen the resolution of allies'—a reference to the current negotiations over NATO and in particular over the American commitment. It is interesting to note that by this time the Americans had re-introduced the draft with service for twenty-one months.

The gap between Cripps and Alexander was by now only some £35–38 million, but neither was prepared to compromise further. There was no indication of how that gap was to be crossed except that, as Alexander reported, the Chiefs of Staff were preparing to appoint a small working party 'to bring fresh minds to the problem of balance between the three services and try and clarify the issues involved'. This was the genesis of the Harwood Committee, which however held out little hope of producing any conclusions that would be of help in 1949–50. The second round on the defence estimates took place in the Defence Committee on 8 December.

In the meantime the Cabinet had yet to take a formal decision on the extension of the length of National Service. It met on 18 November to hear that the ministers involved believed that it was necessary to extend conscription to eighteen months and reduce the National Service intake by raising medical standards and deferring registrations as and when necessary.[45] The Cabinet was not provided with any details and ministers were clearly expected to endorse a decision taken in a Cabinet committee. However, such

[45] CM (48) 74, 18 Nov. 1948, CAB 128/13.

was the strength of opinion on the subject, perhaps exacerbated by the leaks to the press, that ministers succeeded in deferring the Cabinet's endorsement of the decision. They also got the decision communicated to the PLP on 24 November before it was presented to Parliament on the following day. There is no indication in the official record of who was responsible for this.

The Cabinet met again four days later equipped with a memorandum from Alexander outlining the situation.[46] Cripps once more emphasized that acceptance of the new period of service did not imply his agreement to a higher defence budget. On conscription Alexander put the case forcefully and there is no record of opposition to the proposal. Nor did ministers attempt to question any of the more fundamental premisses about foreign policy commitments. Disquiet at the decision was channelled into criticism of the forces' training programmes. In endorsing the ministerial committee's decision the Cabinet invited the Secretary of State for War to submit to the Defence Committee a detailed statement on steps to ensure that more effective use would be made of the training period.

The defence estimates were put to the Defence Committee on 8 December. Alexander had examined the implications of the £750 million target more closely and under pressure from the Chiefs of Staff concluded that to stick to that figure would mean curtailment of the emergency programme launched in the summer. He now argued that the minimum acceptable figure was £770 million. Even then, so Tedder argued, it would 'just, but only just, enable the three services to perform their essential tasks'. To convince ministers he elaborated on these tasks.

The first was to play their part in the Cold War. Included under this heading were the occupational commitments in Germany, Austria, and Trieste, together with emerging problems, notably Malaya, and, in an unselfconsciously global view, those places where 'unexpected commitments might arise at any moment, say Hong Kong, West Africa, the Italian Colonies or the Antarctic'. In other words, the Cold War meant staying put in most places and being able to intervene in a good many others. It has been argued that one of the characteristics of the Chiefs of Staff during the immediate post-war years was that they frequently deliberated on

[46] CP (48) 276, discussed at CM (48) 75, 22 Nov. 1948, CAB 128/13.

matters outside their appropriate area of concern and in particular impinged on foreign policy.[47] This could be seen as one such example. To some extent this was inevitable, given the often symbiotic relationship between foreign and defence policies. Moreover, it frequently went unchallenged by ministers who shared crucial perspectives and assumptions. Global horizons and the habits of an imperial past couched in the language of the Cold War present had become fused together into a civil–military consensus.

Second, the forces were required to 'inspire confidence in our ability to meet Treaty obligations' and to provide both strength and equipment for European allies. Other essential tasks were to be able to fight with what they had in an 'unpremeditated' war (which the July programme had been designed to improve); and to be ready to fight a 'premeditated' war in eight to ten years' time, by when it was estimated that the Soviet Union would possess atomic bombs. To be able to perform these various roles, each of which implied a different set of priorities not only among but within the services, the Chiefs of Staff and the service departments estimated a minimum budget of £770 million.

Cripps was unmoved. While not able to discuss the budget with the committee, he was 'satisfied that unless the Cabinet were prepared to make drastic cuts in other sections of the budget' it would not be possible to go beyond £712 million. The only proper approach was to decide how much could be given to defence and then for the services to plan accordingly. The MOD's figure instead represented the simple aggregate of the services' requirements. This process, Cripps argued, reached the 'palpably absurd conclusion that expenditure of the enormous sum of £712 million would nevertheless mean that not one of the three services would be an effective force'.[48]

However, by now the Chancellor was isolated. Attlee confessed that he was unable to see why £60 million should make all the difference. Nevertheless, he said that it would be impossible to abandon the July emergency programme. Even Isaacs did not support the Chancellor, as a budget of £712 million would jeopardize the call-up scheme by reducing registrations to one a

[47] For discussion of this see P. Darby, *British Defence Policy East of Suez 1947–68* (Oxford University Press, 1973), ch. 1.
[48] DO (48) 23rd, 8 Dec. 1948, CAB 131/5.

year. Noel-Baker, 'far from wishing to see a reduction wanted to see an increase', as he felt that 'every penny spent on defence helped to ensure our economic recovery'. This was an astonishing view for any minister to take (let alone a man who was to win a Nobel Peace Prize and become the doyen of the peace movement in the 1980s). It was, he believed, 'perhaps not insignificant' that Soviet pressure had begun to increase so soon after Britain had cut its defensive strength in 1947—a one-dimensional and ethnocentric perception of Soviet behaviour.

Bevin's position was more subtle. While accepting that the defence burden was so heavy that 'under modern conditions' no one country could be expected to bear alone the cost of maintaining adequate forces, he believed that the next two years would be crucially important for the build-up of Western defence. Given that the 'mood of the country' was willing to provide for that defence—a view shared by the Prime Minister—it was essential to carry out the emergency programme and not jeopardize the rebuilding of Europe. Shinwell, previously and subsequently critical of the scale of the forces, donned the mantle of departmental minister and argued the serious risks of further cuts.

Cripps was outmanœuvred. He did manage one concession before Alexander brought the estimates to Cabinet in January 1949 by negotiating a further cut of £10 million. The figure of £760 million was duly accepted. Although this had required compromise on the part of the services they had nevertheless completed their victory on the issue of National Service.

The National Service Amendment Act was by this stage moving relatively easily through the legislative process. The second reading was on 1 December 1948 and the debate in committee on the sixth, when the third reading also took place. The extension of conscription was discussed by the PLP on the eve of the first reading and although there was considerable disquiet from some MPs the government did not find difficulty in securing the necessary support. On the floor of the House it was helped by the Speaker's decision to call a pacifist rather than a 'liberal technical' amendment. Forty-one MPs voted for the amendment but eight who had been rebels in April 1947 voted according to the whip. It was indicative of the government's nervousness that this was only a two-line whip. On the third reading only nineteen MPs voted against the government, fewer than on the third reading of the 1947 act. There was no repeat of the spring of 1947, no coalition of opposition factions that could be mobilized. Sentiment on the subject was, however, still considerable. In March 1948 Labour MPs had signed an EDM calling for an end to conscription.[49] But in December the PLP supported its leaders with less of the rancour and bitterness that had been generated before.

It was clear that the general mood of the party had changed since early 1947 when doubts about both foreign and domestic policy had reached a watershed. Nevertheless, there was clearly a great deal of unhappiness at the government's decision and feeling was still running against conscription. Yet the deterioration in relations with the Soviet Union, and in particular the Berlin crisis, provided a very different context for MPs and within Whitehall.

The extension of the length of service represented a victory for the services, though it was not achieved without an element of compromise on their part. The problems of the defence effort were becoming manifest as the government struggled to accommodate diverging objectives while the Cold War gathered pace. Dependence on National Service increased but the problems associated with that dependence were deepening.

[49] Robert Jackson, *Rebels and Whips* (Macmillan, 1968), 60.

9

Defence Policy, National Service, and the Cold War 1949–1951

THE Berlin blockade was a turning-point in East–West relations and Western security policy. By standing firm against the Soviet Union the British and Americans laid the foundations for the political and military structures which provided the framework for Western European security and the US commitment to Europe.

By 1949 British defence policy was concerned with two principal objectives. The first was the preparation of armed forces that would be required in the long term to fight a major war. The second lay in the global perspective of Britain as a world power and was based on the view that any withdrawal from areas of strategic interest would create a vacuum inviting communist expansion. In this Cold War British armed forces were necessary to prevent communist exertion of political and military leverage. To withdraw from the Middle East would open up both the Muslim world and the continent of Africa; to withdraw from the Far East would be to surrender vital economic interests; to withdraw from Europe would be to sacrifice everything for which the war had been fought and leave the military security of the United Kingdom in peril.

Military forces were needed in peacetime to deter aggression and preserve British interests. Imperial interests were transformed into the 'negative sum' of the Cold War where the lessons of the 1930s were taken to mean that the prevention of aggression required the ability to act quickly and seemingly to intervene on a global basis. The interests involved were a complex of strategic, economic, and psychological factors. The Middle East, for example, was to be held in peace and war for several very different reasons. With the range of bombers then available, it provided bases for operations against the Soviet Union which would include targets beyond the range of bombers in the United Kingdom. When long-range bombers became available Egyptian bases would enable the RAF to strike beyond the Urals. Second, if the Middle East were lost, it was argued, the Soviets would be able to expand into Africa. Third, the supply of oil was increasingly crucial to the British economy. In addition there was an element of self-interest on the part of the services. For the War Office, until a full-scale continental commitment emerged, the Middle East remained the *raison d'être* for the commitment of an army overseas in wartime. This was reinforced by the feeling among military leaders, who had so recently fought for the Middle East, that it was a natural and traditional area of British interest.

How far the global Cold War perspective was shared by the key military and political leaders is a matter of great interest. Although in 1946 Attlee and Dalton had favoured withdrawal from the Middle East, the deterioration of relations with the Soviet Union in 1947 and the events of 1948 had brought home to them, and to most of their colleagues, the pervasive nature of the communist threat. The only circumstances that would allow British withdrawal in these conditions would be when Commonwealth or reliable indigenous (or conceivably American) forces were able to replace them.

By 1949 these perspectives were widely shared in Cabinet. Philip Noel-Baker, previously and subsequently identified with the cause of disarmament, told his colleagues in November 1949 that he thought that 'every penny that has been spent on defence since the war had contributed to economic reconstruction some-where in the world, to the revival of world trade, and to the consolidation of the West under the Brussels Treaty and the Atlantic Pact, on which the peace of the world now depended'.[1]

Yet that is not to suggest that there was no criticism. This was particularly evident when the economic consequences were considered. Nor is it to suggest that foreign policy itself did not have its dissenters. Bevan, for example, disdainful of Britain's support for the various 'unstable and reactionary governments of the Arab states', urged that Britain's Middle Eastern strategy should be founded on Israel.[2] While this reflected a strong pro-Zionist senti-ment within the Labour Party, it clearly took no account of the

---

[1] DO (49) 20th, 15 Nov. 1949, AIR 19/583.
[2] CM (49) 3, 17 Jan. 1949, CAB 128/15.

need for Arab oil or of the real difficulties in transferring military allegiance from the Arabs to the Israelis. The Chiefs of Staff were themselves keen on a stronger relationship with Israel, though not at the expense of links with the Arabs. What is significant about Bevan's suggestion is that, radical though it was, it nevertheless was within the parameters fixed by a Middle Eastern strategy designed to thwart Soviet designs in that region.

Dissent did surface from time to time, reflecting various threads of backbench disquiet. Yet as there was no Cabinet committee on foreign affairs, and as the Defence Committee proved an inadequate forum for the discussion of strategic priorities, the major questions of foreign policy were discussed only infrequently. This reinforced the hand of the Foreign Office, which had in Bevin the most formidable member of Attlee's Cabinet. As for the Ministry of Defence, it was still a new department with a limited role and limited resources. In Alexander it had a minister who was by temperament, ability, and frame of mind unlikely to attempt radical and far-reaching reforms of the armed forces.

Fundamental problems remained about the size and nature of the British defence effort. These were exacerbated as old commitments persisted and new ones arose. In 1948 additional British troops were sent to Malaya. By 1949 commitments had arisen in Aqaba and Abadan. The strategic reserve was despatched to reinforce Hong Kong. Although the withdrawal from Palestine had taken place, those troops were all redeployed in the Middle East. There were still British forces in Greece and occupational commitments persisted in Germany, Austria, and Trieste. Since the signing of the Brussels Pact there was increasing European pressure to make an effective contribution to the ground defence of Western Europe. With the NATO treaty of April 1949, decisions on that contribution would soon have to be taken.

Moreover, as peacetime commitments persisted the problems of preparing the forces for their role in war within the financial limits envisaged by the Treasury were steadily mounting. The defence estimates for 1949–50 had been agreed at £760 million, though this was a compromise that satisfied no one. The Treasury was only reluctantly coming to accept the idea of an eventual defence budget of some £700 million. The Chiefs of Staff regarded even £800 million as inadequate to discharge the tasks of prosecuting the Cold War, preparing for a 'shooting war' after 1957, and retaining at least some capability to fight in the event of 'unpremeditated' war in the meantime.

Fundamental questions, especially about the role of the atomic bomb in British strategy, remained. In September 1949 the Joint Planning Staff reported to the Chiefs of Staff on the significance of the atomic bomb on the respective services.[3] The guiding assumption remained that nuclear weapons would not revolutionize modern warfare so far as to remove the need for large conventional armies and navies. 'The bomb' would enable the RAF (and the United States Air Force) to pursue with even more devastating effect the role of strategic bombing. Even if this was to be decisive in deterring or in waging a major war, conventional forces would still be needed to prevent the Red Army overrunning the whole of Western Europe and the Middle East.

Defence planning was based on the assumption that the Soviet Union would be in a position to wage war by 1957. This was taken as the date by when Britain's armed forces would need to be ready for war. That preparation was one task required of the services. The second was to provide the military forces in being to maintain occupational commitments and prosecute the Cold War. In addition, prudence required that they be able to fight with what they had as effectively as possible. The problem lay in deciding on the priorities among these objectives. This was greatly complicated by the absence of an agreement in the West on strategic priorities and on the necessary force levels in each of the regions of Western interest. It seems obvious that decisions on British strategy could not be taken until the broader issues had been resolved. But the practical needs of military planning and British foreign policy meant that it was necessary to reach conclusions that inevitably begged wider questions about Britain's role in Western strategy.

One of the central issues was the nature and extent of Britain's contribution to the defence of Western Europe. The history of Britain's post-war continental commitment was a complex one. The original fears of those like Slessor who believed that permanent peacetime conscription was for the specific purpose of a 'continental strategy' were shown to be exaggerated. The decision

---

[3] JP (49) 45, 23 Sept. 1949, DEFE 6/8. For the development of British nuclear strategy see Ian Clark and Nicholas Wheeler *The British Origins of Nuclear Strategy 1945–55* (Oxford University Press, 1989).

on National Service predated any agreed strategic doctrine, which emerged only in the summer of 1947 and even then in a form which was economically unrealistic.

Although a commitment of sorts to fight on the continent was made in early 1948, it was the Middle East that remained the strategic priority, with the four TA divisions available three months after mobilization earmarked for that theatre, in preference to Europe. It had been recognized that particularly with the development of rocket weapons and atomic bombs, the defence of Western Europe was important for the security of the United Kingdom. Nevertheless, until the winter of 1949, the Chiefs of Staff were prepared to recommend only a token increase in the strength of the BAOR, though even this was not acceptable to the government.[4]

Yet without an effective British–American contribution to the ground defence of Western Europe, the French remained reluctant to provide sufficient divisions. For the Joint Planning Staff, it was the French provision that was to be the very cornerstone of Western European defence.[5] Bevin was less concerned with military preparation for a major war. For the Foreign Secretary the main objective was to secure American involvement, as well as to encourage the West Europeans to participate in structures that would help provide collective security.

Within the government pressure to reinforce the BAOR came from the Chiefs of Staff. In January 1949, they and the Foreign Secretary had opposed the despatch of a brigade to strengthen the Dutch.[6] Moreover, they had been reluctant to make any guarantees about the despatch of the TA on mobilization. In 1949 that position began to change. The Joint Intelligence and Joint Planning Staffs were asked to re-examine the nature of the threat posed by the Soviet Union to the Middle East in war.

This re-evaluation concluded that the speed at which the Soviet threat would materialize in the Middle East had been exaggerated.[7] It was now believed that the Soviet forces would have much greater problems in establishing a rail line of communication through Turkey. The scale of the threat remained, and so did

[4] DO (50) 20, 20 Mar. 1950, CAB 131/9.
[5] JP (50) 22, 10 Mar. 1950, DEFE 4/29.
[6] DO (49) 2nd, 10 Jan. 1949, CAB 131/8.
[7] COS (49) 168th, 14 Nov. 1949, DEFE 4/26.

British concern in the theatre. But the pace at which it would develop was judged to have altered. This meant that two of the four TA divisions available after mobilization could be assigned to Europe. It was claimed that the defence of Western Europe had become more important for the security of the United Kingdom, although this was not based on any fresh evaluation of that particular threat. What was new was that the Soviet Union had exploded an atomic bomb.

This had taken military and political leaders by surprise. It came at a time when negotiations within NATO over deployments were gathering pace. Having prevaricated since the very beginning of the Western Union discussions on the issue of a British commitment, the Chiefs of Staff now believed that a decision and some form of commitment were unavoidable. It was necessary to make firm guarantees to send additional British divisions to defend Europe as far east as was possible but no further west than the Rhine.

Despite the agreement of the services on the need for these guarantees and the endorsement of the new Minister of Defence, Shinwell, that commitment remained limited. There were no plans to send the 40,000 men required to bring the BAOR up to its wartime establishment. The regular army division which would be available from the autumn of 1951, at the same time as the territorials, was not included in their proposals and indeed the French were not initially told of its availability.[8]

Moreover, the two TA divisions would not be ready until some three months after mobilization, although it was hoped to reduce that period. This meant that they would be unlikely to reach the defensive position on the Rhine until after the Western defence had collapsed. Indeed, as the Chiefs of Staff pointed out, in such circumstances they would not need to be sent. Although the decision to switch these divisions from the Middle East to Europe was important, it was clear that there was a long way to go before Britain was committed to a permanent standing army in Germany. In military terms the implications for National Service were not significant. There was no change in the plans for mobilizing the TA or in the need for conscripts for that purpose. But in so far as it was a step towards a firm and binding commitment, it

[8] COS (50) 43rd, 16 Mar. 1950, DEFE 4/29.

reinforced the requirement for trained reserves on mobilization and for a system of military training to provide them.

The conflict between defence requirements and economic constraints was looming larger, particularly as the government faced yet another economic crisis, this time over devaluation. Yet it had been more than apparent in the autumn of 1948 that financial and defence objectives were diverging. As a result it was decided to establish an inter-service working party on the size and shape of the forces in the next three years, 1950–3.[9] This was chaired by Sir Edmund Harwood, the Permanent Secretary at the Ministry of Food,[10] and had the task of constructing a detailed defence budget on an annual allocation of £700 million in the next three years.

One of the reasons for establishing the working party was to defuse Treasury pressure. The Chiefs of Staff were well aware that £700 million was insufficient for the defence effort on which they had agreed. However, by demonstrating the consequences for foreign policy that such a budget entailed, they would be able to strengthen their case. On the other hand, there was the danger that the adoption of such an arbitrary figure would acquire a psychological momentum in Whitehall and in the minds of the Treasury, as had happened with the Coalition government's loosely worked-out estimates for post-war defence.

The Harwood Report was finished in February 1949 and discussed by ministers in July. The study had taken several months to complete and represented the most fundamental and detailed set of reforms that the Attlee government was to consider. It has been characterized as the first post-war defence review.[11] It was certainly the first attempt to apply the long-standing Treasury demand that defence policy should be based on what the country could afford and then the military strategy hammered out. The starting-point was the figure of £700 million for which Cripps had been pressing.

Although Harwood was not directed to examine foreign policy commitments, the scale of the reductions envisaged meant drastic cuts in all theatres of operation (in peace and in war) and entailed

[9] DO (49) 47, 21 Jun. 1949, CAB 131/7, first discussed by ministers on 5 Jul. 1949, Gen 296/1st, CAB 130/53.

[10] The other members were: Air Vice-Marshal R. Ivelaw-Chapman, Rear-Admiral C. E. Lambe, and Brigadier J. H. N. Poett.

[11] Peter Hennessy, *Whitehall* (Fontana, 1990), 415.

virtual withdrawal from the Far East. These recommendations were highly controversial. Furthermore, all three services were to be substantially reduced, and the priority and resources further shifted to prosecuting the Cold War and preparing for 'unpremeditated war' in the immediate future at the expense of preparation for major war after 1957. The exception to this was the strategic bombing capability.

Wartime and many peacetime capabilities would be smaller than hitherto deemed necessary. However, it was argued that this would be more than compensated for by the roles envisaged for the United States and to a lesser extent the Commonwealth and the Colonies. It was assumed that the United States 'would be at war with Russia wholeheartedly and practically simultaneously with ourselves'.[12] This was most important where air and naval forces were concerned. Assumptions about the American role were based on an act of faith. There was as yet no formal agreement between the British and Americans with regard to their respective military roles in peace or war. On the navy Harwood nevertheless argued: 'Our naval contribution in war must be complementary rather than competitive and be confined to those tasks which are essentially a domestic responsibility.' The navy would be reduced from its existing target of 146,000 at 31 March 1950 to 90,000 by 1952–3. These would be all regulars and all male. The implications of these cuts were considerable, involving a severe curtailment of wartime and peacetime tasks. The idea that the navy's role would be reduced to 'domestic responsibilities' presented very great challenges to the traditions and expectations of the admirals, even though Harwood's interpretation of 'domestic' was a broad one.

One controversial proposal was the disbanding of the Royal Marine Commandos, 'despite its high standard of discipline, ceremonial and its age-long tradition', although some 1,500 marines were to be retained on ships. Accepting that this would be a 'terrible step to take', the only alternative was to retain their identity by incorporating them in the army, which would have met with as much horror in the admiralty as the threat of abolition.

The Harwood proposals were not just the consequences of cuts that they envisaged. As the report concluded:

---

[12] DO (49) 47, para. 24, 21 Jun. 1949, CAB 131/7.

It is quite clear that since 1945 the navy has supported a peacetime force which could not possibly have been sustained if a proper programme of capital re-equipment and refitting had been put in hand. Moreover there are still a large number of dispersed shore establishments which are legacies of the last war and which will never be abandoned unless and until a real contraction takes place. Our recommendations therefore include many measures which would in any case have been necessary if the navy is to be properly re-equipped, efficient and battleworthy for another war.

Some of the most radical and far-sighted ideas lay in the retraction of peacetime commitments east of Suez. At the start of the war the role of the navy would be confined to 'home waters'. This meant British ports, the Channel, and North Atlantic shipping lanes, including the Canada, Gibraltar, and Norway routes, together with the Mediterranean (Gibraltar, Malta, and the Levant ports). There would be no British role in the Persian Gulf, the Indian Ocean, Australia, or the Far East. Responsibilities for these would fall on the United States or the Commonwealth or combinations of the two.

The wartime fleet would contain no battleships (as opposed to the currently planned five), twelve rather than fourteen aircraft carriers, and half as many modernized cruisers, although there would be a larger number of smaller ships. In peacetime the fleet would be concentrated in a 'peripatetic task force' based around three aircraft carriers, a cruiser, and sixteen destroyers. It was envisaged that this group would cover the North and South Atlantic and the Mediterranean. The reserve fleet would be some ten ships larger in size although smaller in terms of manpower. There would be no battleships except, possibly, as potential platforms for new weapons systems or (rather more bizarrely) for the purpose of Royal tours. Harwood recommended careful review of the future of the battleship and by the following year the Admiralty had accepted that they would no longer be necessary.

These main recommendations were accompanied by a variety of proposed cuts in administration, personnel, and training, and indeed it was here that Harwood had most impact. Harwood also proposed the abolition of the Women's Royal Naval Service (WRNS), though women were to continue to serve in the army and the RAF. In Britain the Sheerness, Portland, and (possibly) Chatham dockyards would be closed. Training would be concentrated in Portsmouth and Devonport. Overseas, Singapore and

Trincomalee dockyards would be abandoned, and the Bermuda and Simonstown yards placed on a 'care and maintenance' basis. The naval air stations on Malta would be closed. The Combined Operations role would be much reduced and naval flying and ground training commands integrated with their RAF counterparts. There would be no National Servicemen in the navy.

With the RAF Harwood was likewise not concerned just with the imposition of cuts, but also with changing the air force's roles in the light of political and other developments. The more radical suggestions involved the peacetime deterrent role and the general personnel structure of the RAF. Harwood shared the Chiefs of Staff's view that the importance of a genuine deterrent was undeniable. A strategic bomber force with sufficient strength and range to reach the vitals of the Soviet Union was 'one of the strongest deterrents against war'. It was accepted that the eventual front-line bomber strength should remain as envisaged (528 long-range jet bombers).

However, there was disagreement with existing plans for the interim build-up of the strategic bombing capability: 'Bluntly, this country has neither a strategic bomber near enough to production, nor indeed the financial resources to maintain a force of bombers likely to deter Russia from embarking on war during the period 1950–2 nor probably until very much later.' So long as the RAF's ultimate aim was a strength of '528 large and very costly bombers', there would be a heavy and increasing drain on finances, manpower, and training capacity. The cost of an effective interim capability would be too great.

Furthermore, it was argued that the proposed interim force did not constitute an effective capability. It was to consist of Lancasters and Lincolns. The latter could not reach a sufficient number of Soviet targets and lacked speed, armament, and accuracy. The Lancaster did not have the range of even the Lincoln. Both would be equipped only with non-nuclear payloads. This situation had been overtaken by events to some extent, as in March 1949 the Defence Committee approved the Air Ministry's proposal to accept an American offer of surplus long-range B-29s.[13] It was agreed to accept 194 aircraft to maintain a strength of

[13] DO (49) 13, 2 Mar. 1949, CAB 131/7, discussed at DO (49) 7th, 9 Mar. 1949, CAB 131/8.

eight squadrons (replacing six Lancaster and two Lincoln) from
1949 to 1955. Negotiations over the purchase began accordingly.
The B-29s (known by the RAF as Washingtons) had an operational range of 1,300 km and were able to hit a much wider range
of strategic targets from Middle Eastern and British bases. In the
event, in the face of Treasury pressure, only seventy of the aircraft
were purchased.

This development rather outflanked the Harwood report as the
working party had recommended that as long as the Lancaster and
Lincoln were the only types available, no expansion of Bomber
Command should take place. The existing 144 aircraft would be
able to perform non-strategic bombing tasks. However, when the
new strategic bombers began to arrive, Harwood proposed that
the front-line strength should be no higher than 208 aircraft. It
was also proposed to reduce maritime forces to a 'barely adequate
level'. Transport Command was to be left untouched and Fighter
Command's front-line strength likewise endorsed. As for the
defence of Western Europe, it was suggested that a Tactical Air
Force of some sixty-four aircraft be provided by 1952–3 to
demonstrate Britain's resolve in support of the Western Union.

The other main proposed reform of the RAF concerned its
personnel structure. Harwood examined the implications of reducing existing manpower levels from 250,000 down to 190,000, a
process which had been designed 'in order to maintain a proper
balance between running costs and re-equipment expenditure'.
The air force was to retain the teeth but trim the tail, and the
report insisted that

there must be imaginative and quite ruthless elimination of some complete units, telescoping of others, reduction of redundant intermediate
formations, even though this process may involve breaking with tradition, reversal of recent decisions, overthrow of little 'Empires', departure
from conventional ideas and the acceptance of certain risks.

Structural reform was not sufficient. An attempt had to be made
to reduce the RAF's dependence on National Servicemen as part of
the overall concern with getting rid of conscription in general.

The position of the army was recognized to lie at the heart of
the question of priorities imposed by the need to fight the Cold
War, prepare for the 'shooting war', and remain able to respond to
a Soviet attack in the near future. Harwood accepted that the army

deployed overseas was fully stretched with its occupational and Cold War tasks and that for the next three years there was little likelihood of that pressure diminishing. Harwood's solution to the problem of priorities followed the trend in War Office and Chiefs of Staff thinking. The main priority should be given to fighting the Cold War and preparing for an 'unpremeditated' Soviet attack. While for all the services the divergence between Cold War and 'shooting war' capabilities was reflected in the balance between 'teeth' and 'tail', it was most apparent in the army where the former required supplies of infantry and the latter laid greater stress on mechanized units and on administrative provision to enable the expansion of cadres in war. Even then, Harwood's claim that the proposal would be sufficient to meet Cold War commitments rested on the assumption that no further obligations would arise or existing commitments, such as Malaya, expand.

With a 'fire brigade' consisting of one armoured regiment and two brigades in the United Kingdom, it was recognized that a satisfactory state of preparedness before 1957 would not be possible, even after the change in priorities: 'It was clear from the start that we could only continue to undertake all of our present Cold War tasks with the reduced manpower and money available if there was a very complete overhaul of army organisation and expenditure at home and abroad.'

The army, at present 390,000 strong, would be reduced to 360,000 on 1 April 1950. In addition to administrative cuts, this meant reducing commitments in all theatres of operation. In Germany, BAOR would be cut by 12,000 men to 43,500. This would mean some transfer of responsibility for internal and border security and might mean a change in the military organization and system of control. The total peacetime garrison for the Middle East would be 42,500. This could be achieved only at the expense of existing plans for building an adequate basis in war, and would therefore necessitate American and/or Commonwealth contributions.

The Colonial garrisons were likewise scrutinized with the aim of replacing British forces with indigenous Colonial troops. Gibraltar would lose its infantry garrison. The infantry battalion in the West Indies was to be replaced by local troops, despite the Colonial Office's objection that 'the very rapid growth of political and Trade Union consciousness in the area has resulted in considerable political instability'.

As already envisaged, the regular army reserve would be used to bring the active army from peace to war establishment. The Territorial Army would provide five Home Defence divisions for anti-aircraft, internal security, and civil defence. Five more TA divisions (including one armoured) would be available for overseas service. Two of these would be sent to the Middle East but further reinforcements for that theatre would initially have to come from Britain's allies. As for Europe, it was felt that it would be in the interest of both the United Kingdom and the Western Union if Britain's contribution were provided exclusively by air and sea contingents. However, in order to demonstrate good faith in the Western Union, it was thought necessary to guarantee two additional divisions to reinforce the occupational forces. These would be supplemented by the nucleus of a Tactical Air Force.

Taking the services as a whole, Harwood proposed a reduction from the planned strength of 750,000 at 31 March 1950 to annual average strengths of 652,500 in 1950–1 and 565,000 by 1952–3. An essential part of this contraction, in keeping with the need to maintain front-line and peacetime strength, was the proposed reduction in National Servicemen from a content of 267,000 at 31 March 1950 to 122,000 by 1952–3. This was based on an eighteen-month period of full-time service and would require an annual intake of 121,000 in 1950–1, 91,700 in 1951–2, and 81,350 in 1952–3. As there would be 192,000 men liable for service in 1950–1, 201,000 available in 1951–2, and 205,000 available in 1952–3, it was evident that in a short time less than half of those liable would be needed. Raising medical standards and reducing the number of registrations was seen as a partial and interim solution. Harwood recommended an amendment of the National Service scheme to produce a 'smaller and more flexible intake' by means of selective service. There was no detailed discussion of this, although it was recognized that a ballot would be likely.

More importantly, Harwood did not see even this form of National Service as a permanent feature of the defence system.[14] National Servicemen had been required in the first place to provide the trained reserves of manpower necessary on the outbreak of war, but had been used to augment regular forces. With

[14] On 30 Oct. the *Sunday Times* carried a report claiming that Harwood had reached agreement on the role of the services and concluded that conscription was essential.

a disproportionate number of regulars involved in training men whose active service life was of relatively short duration, the effect on an army whose level of regular recruiting was increasingly inadequate was to lower the efficiency of the forces.

On these grounds it was therefore necessary to move towards all-regular forces sufficient to meet peacetime needs. It was also necessary to find an alternative method of providing the trained reserves of manpower that were necessary on mobilization. Harwood believed that 'unless a fundamental change is made in the conditions of service of the regular soldier there is no possibility of the army being able to do without National Service'. In order to produce the required number of regulars Harwood advocated a combination of increased pay and 'a different approach to the career aspect of the recruiting problem'.

The report did not suggest a specific pay increase but argued that making service pay adequate would involve introducing rates not only comparable to those paid in civilian life, but sufficient to compensate for the disadvantages of service life. If pay were the only consideration increases of 35–40 per cent would be necessary. These costs could be offset against savings in training and other commitments. But a smaller pay increase would be sufficient if a satisfactory solution could be found to the career aspect of regular recruiting.

Harwood argued that these proposals offered a solution both to the problem of pay and to that of providing the reserves of trained manpower in war: 'The broad conception would be that service in the armed forces is not a thing apart but merely one of a number of forms of public service and that men joining the regular forces, subject to certain conditions, should be assured at the outset of a continuity of public service throughout their active lives.' There was no indication of which 'specified categories of public service employment' would be involved, though this might include the new public corporations.

It was claimed that this scheme would provide 'more mature, balanced and experienced men' for civilian public service. Moreover, taken together with an increase in pay, it would mean that 'the services should find no difficulty in recruiting sufficient men over a period of five or six years to do away with National Service while at the same time providing the trained manpower reserves required for essential tasks'. This would be possible as those tasks would themselves be reduced. The TA would be scaled down and its Home Defence divisions, with reduced quotas of artillery and other arms, would require fewer reserves.

As noted, the fundamental and wide-ranging recommendations of the Harwood Report were the result of the attempt to adopt a Treasury figure of resources available and then decide on defence policy. The approach itself was not opposed by the Chiefs of Staff. But the allocation they were given certainly was. They knew that £700 million was insufficient. Indeed, as the working party had acted independently and not had its proposals costed by the service departments, it was discovered that it had under-estimated the cost of its defence budget by an annual average of some £55 million. This meant that the Harwood proposals were based on a very similar annual budget to the compromise £760 million agreed for 1949–50. Yet it seemed that even that sum meant radical changes in British defence policy.

Harwood accepted that the suggested forces would not be able to meet all the contingencies of the Cold War, unpremeditated war before 1957, and 'shooting war' thereafter. However, in the judgement of the Chiefs of Staff the proposed forces failed to provide against any of these dangers.[15] As far as the Cold War was concerned, the forces would be inadequate to support British policy in any number of areas. On the need for American support in peace and war, the Chiefs of Staff had previously and in more forthright terms been urged by Tizard to accept that global responsibility for world security would have to fall on the United States.[16] Yet the service chiefs themselves regarded American and Commonwealth forces as vital. However, acceptance of the American predominance did not, for the Chiefs of Staff, entail the immediate and substantial reductions that it did for Harwood or Tizard. While American assistance in the Middle East, for example, was indispensable, until that assistance appeared it was 'essential to ensure by the example we ourselves set that the Americans do not weaken their resolve'.[17] The problem lay not just in the difficulties for military planning, but in the very real difficulties involved in getting American military commitments on a global scale, particularly in areas of British Imperial and post-Imperial interest.

[15] DO (49) 50, 22 Jun. 1949, CAB 131/7.
[16] COS (47) 251, 2 Dec. 1947, PREM 8/659.
[17] DO (49) 50, 22 Jun. 1949, CAB 131/7.

The arguments of the Chiefs of Staff were unavoidably based on political judgements. As far as the BAOR was concerned, they argued that any reduction in the occupation forces would weaken the Western Union, contrary to the wishes of the Harwood Report. To abolish the East Indies squadron would create a void in Southeast Asia and the Indian Ocean. Naval forces in the Far East would be 'inadequate to support our policy in normal times, quite apart from the growing Chinese communist threat'. Withdrawal from Simonstown 'would have political effects in the Union of South Africa, where the presence of these forces is the only tangible sign of the benefits which South Africa receives in the defence field, from remaining a member of the Commonwealth'.

With regard to wartime forces, it was argued that the number of fighters would be barely sufficient to cover the existing radar belt (in south-east England), and when that was extended would be inadequate. Reducing the number of regular and TA anti-aircraft regiments (from 222 to 150) would cause a deterioration in a situation in which a large number of vital areas was already undefended. The wartime fleet that Harwood envisaged could not be achieved as the building and modernization programme after 1952 would be too great for the shipbuilding capacity to undertake before 1957. Even then the Chiefs of Staff argued that there would be shortages of carriers, cruisers, and minesweepers and no provision for offensive anti-submarine warfare and amphibious task forces.

As for the principal theatres (Europe and the Middle East), even if it were possible to count on 'some months'' warning of an emergency, no reinforcements of either area would be possible. Given the proposed reductions in the active army, all the reinforcements would have to be provided by the TA, which would mean a lapse of four months before the divisions were fit for active service—slightly longer than planned. The tactical air force envisaged by Harwood was described as well below the reasonable expectations of Britain's allies. Such criticisms were equally applicable to existing planning; indeed, when the Chiefs of Staff subsequently did recommend a guarantee of two divisions to Western Europe, they did not include any provision for additional tactical air support.[18]

---

[18] DO (50) 20, 20 Mar. 1950, CAB 131/9.

The Harwood Report stood little chance of being accepted. The government would have required bold and dynamic leadership to discard so dramatically the advice of its professional military advisers. Yet the working party's efforts were not without results and resulted in administrative savings estimated at £40 million. They must have brought home to ministers that if the British government wished to possess military forces on the scale envisaged by its professional advisers and implied by its foreign policy then a considerably larger defence budget would be necessary.

It is certainly the case that many of the radical proposals were far-sighted. It can be argued that contraction on the scale suggested would have solved some of the main problems that British defence and foreign policy faced in the following decades. An early recognition of Britain's reduced role in the world and the concomitant need for American troops and commitments was an opportunity that was, arguably, lost in the rejection of the report.

Yet there were clearly enormous questions to be answered about the nature, extent, and indeed desirability of an American global role. The United States was to show little enthusiasm at the prospect of sending forces to the Middle East. Even after the NATO treaty had been signed and the Americans began to prepare for a long-term campaign in Europe, their short-term plans rejected on military grounds what was for the continental countries the vital political objective of defending the Rhine.[19] It was hardly surprising that the British Chiefs of Staff opposed radical and dramatic ideas when there were such unresolved differences of interest and perspective involved.

Of course, having been a wartime partner of the United States, and by no means a junior partner, it was difficult for Britain to readjust to a subordinate role. It was not surprising that there was a degree of ambiguity about the likely relationship with the Americans. This was well illustrated when it came to the central issue of strategic bombing. As the Chiefs of Staff commented: 'The bombing force even when it is equipped with modern aircraft and armed with atomic weapons, will be small even for its primary task of supporting the USAF in the offensive against the main targets inside Russia.'[20] This implied that the RAF would not provide an independent nuclear deterrent and accepted the

[19] Ibid.   [20] DO (49) 50, 22 Jun. 1949, CAB 131/7.

pre-eminent American role. But the questions of why it was necessary to provide a supporting role and on what criteria it was to be judged sufficient indicated an ambiguity that lay at the heart of British thinking about the 'independent deterrent'.

One of the fundamental problems for Harwood, as for other would-be reformers, was that such proposals were invariably divorced from the context of foreign policy. This was not necessarily an insurmountable problem, but at that time, for Britain to have reduced its armed forces significantly and to have reduced actual commitments would have been greatly to weaken if not to undermine the attempts to persuade allies to provide military forces of their own, in Europe, the Middle East, and elsewhere. As Winston Churchill privately informed Giffard Martel in June 1949: 'I am entirely opposed to the abolition of National Service at the present time. I should consider it a great blow to what is left of British prestige throughout the world.'[21]

While there were many, particularly in the Treasury, who looked to alliances and pacts as means of ultimately reducing the scale of British commitments and expenditure, it remained evident that building those relationships required Britain at least to do its share and more often take a lead. Britain was, for all its economic problems, the least damaged of the European belligerents. These practical political considerations reinforced the British Imperial (and post-Imperial) self-image of leadership by example.

This was apparent in Europe and the Middle East. It was by now also apparent that conscription itself symbolized Britain's commitment to those theatres and to its foreign policy in general. In Europe the British had played an instrumental role in building the political framework for a military alliance. Even though their own commitments remained limited, the British persistently urged their European allies to provide the military forces to defend Western Europe. In Britain a prerequisite for the provision of those forces was an adequate period of compulsory service.

The British repeatedly pressed their European allies, especially the French, to extend the period of their full-time military service so that the conscripts could be used to provide divisions necessary to defend Western Europe. In August 1950, when the Attlee

---

[21] Churchill to Martel, 21 Jun. 1949, Papers of Sir Giffard Martel (Imperial War Museum, London).

government was extending National Service to two years during the Korean war, the French retained only a twelve-month full-time period and did not have annual part-time training of their conscript reserves. According to Montgomery, who was now Chairman of the Western European Commanders-in-Chief Committee, the Dutch had 'no army of any sort that could even begin to fight in the field, even against naked savages'.[22] The call-up had been suspended in the Netherlands the previous year and it was only now in the process of being re-introduced, though with two years' service. Also according to Montgomery, the situation of the French army was so 'thoroughly bad' in 1950 that the idea that they would be able to create fifteen new divisions by the end of 1953, as planned, was 'sheer nonsense'.

As for the Middle East, the British had for some time been trying to persuade their Commonwealth allies to share the defence burdens. They had little hope of success—at least where the Antipodeans were involved—until the American position (particularly in the Pacific) had been made clear and Australia and New Zealand had received adequate guarantees about their own security, which were contingent on the peace settlement with Japan. The only real achievement here had been New Zealand's decision to introduce conscription for the explicit and public purpose of providing troops for the defence of the Middle East in war. New Zealand was the only Commonwealth country to introduce peace-time conscription before the Korean war, and this was largely due to the personal decision of the Labour Prime Minister, Fraser. Neither Australia nor South Africa was prepared to follow Britain's example; and in 1946 MacKenzie King had reacted angrily to the suggestion of compulsion in Canada, which was hardly surprising given the problems that had arisen there during the war. Even the New Zealand system was designed to provide only some 8,000 men for the army reserve.[23] These were to be selected by ballot (as had been the practice in wartime) to serve a basic training period of fourteen weeks with three years' part-time training and a seven-year reserve liability. The decision was taken after secret consultations with the British Chiefs of Staff, but only after it had been accepted in a national referendum in August

[22] Montgomery to Attlee, 14 Aug. 1950, PREM 8/1154.
[23] COS (48) 152, 8 Nov. 1948, PREM 8/1158.

1949. Yet even this was not translated into a firm commitment to the Middle East as New Zealand was still waiting on the American position.

Conscription was now viewed by the British government as the means by which societies could provide troops for the enlarged commitments of the Cold War. In the European context Montgomery told the assembled Chiefs of Staff and Ministers of Defence of the Western Union on 4 August 1950 'that as things are today, no nation can hope to fulfil its defence obligations unless it will at once have two years' National Service with the colours'.[24] It was interesting that the British with their traditions of voluntary service were now haranguing their European allies on the need for compulsory service. Yet without an adequate period of military service, it was apparent that Europe's defences could not be built up on the scale required.

To have attempted to persuade European and American allies of the need for conscript armies in Western Europe while at the same time abolishing National Service in Britain would have greatly weakened Britain's credibility. It is worth recalling that when conscription was being considered by the Defence Committee in 1946 Bevin had told his colleagues that

a plan should be prepared for the Zonal Defence of the Empire and its communications in which the Dominions should assume their full share of responsibility. He felt confident that if this country gave a lead it could rally the Dominions to our support and our determination to defend the Empire would be our greatest contribution to the peace of the world. Furthermore it would have a salutary effect on the United States which was at present seeking a clear objective for its foreign policy and the Western European Nations would be heartened by our example and encouraged to support us in our stand against the communist threat.[25]

In 1950 it was again hoped that Britain's example of two years' National Service would be followed by its European allies. Indeed, it had been hoped that the Western Union states would act together to raise their respective periods of service. If these hopes were founded on expectations of immediate and positive action, they were to be disappointed.

---

[24] Montgomery to Attlee, 14 Aug. 1950, PREM 8/1154.
[25] DO (46) 27th, 16 Oct. 1946, CAB 131/1.

But that did not mean that conscription was not important. Once the decision to maintain National Service had been made, a decision to bring it to an end would have signalled a reversal of foreign policy, as it would have meant reductions in Britain's military strength in peacetime. To have persuaded allies that Britain would be able to maintain existing force levels without National Service would have been extremely difficult. For the French, especially, it would have rekindled long-standing suspicions.

While the establishment of an effective West European defence and an effective Commonwealth defence in the Middle East remained crucial British objectives, the abolition of National Service presented great difficulties. Nevertheless, it should be noted that Shinwell, the new Minister of Defence, who had harangued his European colleagues on the need for effective West European defence and two years' National Service, was himself keen on the idea of an all-regular British army. Indeed, at the same time he was lecturing the French, he was pushing the Chiefs of Staff into further consideration of abandoning National Service.

It was only when a solution began to emerge to the problem of the political chicken and military egg of Western European defence that Britain could seriously consider ending conscription. Even then it took the trauma of Suez to strike the decisive blow, signalling as it did, among other things, an end to a British Commonwealth strategy in the Middle East. Although Harwood proposed a phased abolition of conscription and although the objective remained more efficient armed forces, the problem of ending National Service while urging allies to make greater defence contributions remained a fundamental difficulty.

The dilemma facing the government persisted. The divergence between economic and defence objectives was intractable. For the Chiefs of Staff the defence budget was only barely adequate to fulfil existing foreign policy obligations. It was inadequate as a long-term basis for a 'shooting war' without the guarantee of additional resources to provide for re-equipment. For the Treasury even that figure was too much and when the devaluation crisis erupted in September 1949 the Cabinet was presented with the choice between cuts in social security and cuts in defence.

The state of existing defence capabilities was politically embarrassing to the government. This was an additional factor in

precluding open and informed discussion, since the government
had little incentive to advertise the nation's weakness. Although
there remained a crucially bipartisan approach to the fundamental issues of foreign and defence policy, this did not prevent the
opposition, alarmed at the paucity of existing capabilities, from
exploiting the situation. Other sections of opinion within the
Labour Party and among reputable military critics were equally
unsympathetic. By now, for example, the *Manchester Guardian*,
which had initially supported the introduction of peacetime military conscription, had turned against National Service which, it
argued, was responsible for inefficient armed forces and in particular an inefficient army.[26] The *Daily Mail*, which had been
publishing Martel's criticisms for some time, urged the abolition
of conscription on 18 October 1949. The inefficiency of National
Service had long been recognized by the military. The Chiefs of
Staff themselves argued that

regular forces backed by the necessary auxiliary formations and reserves
provide undoubtedly the most economical and efficient method of meeting our commitments in peace and the requirements of our strategy in the
early stages of a war. To use the National Servicemen as we must at present to supplement the regular forces in their peacetime tasks is both
expensive and inefficient because it results in an undue proportion of
manpower being absorbed by training establishments at the expense of
the front line.[27]

By the autumn of 1949 the government's defence policy was
open to the charge not only of inefficiency but also of inadequacy.
Given increasing political criticism and a defence budget that cost
too much yet provided too little, disaffection with the scheme of
compulsory military service was hardly surprising. On the other
hand, previous discussions within government had clearly demonstrated the intractable nature of the problem and the strength
of the Chiefs of Staff's arguments. Nevertheless, an attempt was
made by Morrison to get the government to end full-time
compulsory training. There was also a further review of the
National Service scheme designed to reduce the intake of conscripts and cut expenditure.

[26] *Manchester Guardian*, 23 Dec. 1948.
[27] DO (49) 50, 22 Jun. 1949, CAB 131/7.

The autumn was becoming the traditional season when the government re-examined the size and nature of the National Service intake. This arose from consideration of the defence budget. In 1949 the examination again took place against the background of economic crisis, on this occasion precipitated by devaluation. After the pound had been devalued in September, a fresh round of cuts had been imposed on the armed forces which had made it necessary to lower financial and conscript manpower ceilings. When the problem had been considered earlier in the year, it was agreed to reduce the intake. This could be done by omitting two quarterly registrations in the period 1950–2, which would raise the call-up age by six months to eighteen years nine months.

By November 1949 financial pressure to reduce the manpower ceiling had grown. It was at this time that Morrison attempted to persuade his colleagues to bring full-time National Service to an end. With unhappiness in the party and an election not far away, the idea of radical reform to secure financial and political benefits was not without attraction. In October the Defence Committee established an inter-departmental committee under Godfrey Ince, the Permanent Secretary at the Ministry of Labour and National Service, to investigate methods of controlling the National Service intake.[28]

The options were no different from what they had been in 1947 or 1948. Neither were the arguments. In particular the principle of universal liability was still a fundamental political prerequisite for a scheme of peacetime military conscription. The use of a ballot was again rejected, although it was noted that in certain circumstances it might prove unavoidable if no other method could be found, and when the numbers liable far exceeded the numbers required. It was recognized as the simplest scheme to operate; it was also noted that selective service appeared to work on the continent and in the United States, where the draft had been reintroduced in 1948. On the question of raising both educational and medical standards, the report echoed previous conclusions. While it was accepted that there were obvious advantages, particularly where illiterates and 'dullards' in the army were concerned, the principle of universal liability held sway.

[28] DO (49) 74, 21 Nov. 1949, CAB 131/7.

Once again the government's options looked clear. Omitting one or more registrations presented neither administrative nor political problems. The government was faced with a surplus of about 65,000 men over the period 1950–3 (slightly less after development of the apprenticeship schemes). If the low-calibre men could be eliminated then the surplus would be reduced to 50,000. As each registration yielded an average of 35,000, it would be necessary to omit at most two registrations, increasing the age of call-up by at most six months to eighteen years nine months. It would not be necessary to raise the call-up age in 1950 and the same would probably apply in 1951. Omission of the registration would then take place early in 1952, with a possible second omission early in 1953. The complexity of the situation meant that speculation beyond that date was not considered worthwhile.

This in fact was largely what had been anticipated earlier in the year. Again attention was given to the eventual call-up age, and it was strongly urged that call-up at age twenty was the 'most advantageous from all points of view'. It would be necessary to move gradually towards that age so as to avoid missing out any particular age group. It was argued (contrary to the conventional political wisdom) that a higher call-up age would be beneficial for industry. While employers were reluctant to take on school-leavers at fifteen for permanent jobs only to lose them three years later, with a five-year period of potential employment that reluctance would be reduced. There was no reason to suppose that the considered decision of the 1939 Military Training Act was not sound, although it would have been impossible to arrange the 1947 Act to call up men at twenty as using wartime legislation would have meant forgoing any intake for two years and allowing eighteen- and nineteen-year-olds to get away without any service. There was some ministerial disagreement on this, as Bevin had always believed industry would benefit from as low a call-up age as possible. Nevertheless, the recommendations of the Ince report were accepted by the government. However, these decisions were overtaken by the Korean rearmament drive, and far from the age for call-up rising, it was lowered by one month in February 1951.

Given his responsibility for economic affairs Morrison had long been worried about the economic consequences of the defence budget and of conscription in particular. In October 1946 he had given support to Cripps over the length of service.[29] His concerns were shared by his Permanent Secretary, Max Nicholson, who described existing defence policy as combining 'some of the most burdensome features of pre-war continental armies with the old British conception of seapower and a new conception of a highly technical and mechanised force'.[30]

Moreover, as Leader of the House of Commons Morrison was well aware of feeling in the Labour Party and the desire to 'render our defences defensible against public criticism' appeared to weigh as heavily with him as the desire 'to support the development of the most effective practicable measures of military security'.[31] A general election was not far off. Whatever the political problems of reversing decisions on National Service (and being seen to do so for purely electoral gain), abandoning conscription would have provided significant electoral benefits and afforded the opportunity of outflanking the Conservatives.

In November Morrison attempted to persuade his colleagues to end full-time National Service. Ammunition was provided by the Harwood Report and even more by the initial budgetary targets for 1950/1 and the following years, which were already posing choices between social security and defence that would later throw the Labour Party into such bitter internal conflict. Morrison's arguments were submitted in a memorandum to the Defence Committee and discussed, with Alexander's reply,[32] on 25 November.[33] Morrison was clearly aware of the political and military sensitivity of his proposals and went to some lengths to assure his colleagues of his support in general for foreign and defence policy. Before the Defence Committee he wrote in friendly style to Alexander (on Nicholson's suggestion[34]) to emphasize that he was 'very anxious to help in any way possible'.[35] Yet his recommendations inevitably involved scaling down commitments.

[29] DO (46) 28th, 17 Oct. 1946, CAB 131/1.
[30] Nicholson's brief for Morrison, 18 Oct. 1949, CAB 124/131. On Morrison's relationship with Nicholson, Attlee told Dalton that Morrison 'reads out briefs in Cabinet without really understanding them'. Dalton's view was that he 'eats out of the hand of his twittering little bird watcher': Diaries of Hugh Dalton (London School of Economics), 8 Sept. 1947.
[31] DO (49) 69, 3 Nov. 1949, CAB 131/7.
[32] DO (49) 70, 7 Nov. 1949, CAB 131/7.
[33] DO (49) 22nd, 25 Nov. 1949, CAB 131/8.
[34] Nicholson to Morrison, 10 Nov. 1949, CAB 124/131.
[35] Morrison to Alexander, 15 Nov. 1949, CAB 124/131.

His line of attack was a subtle one. He did not question the principle of conscription *per se* and indeed in his letter to Alexander declared that he was 'strongly in favour of retaining National Service'.[36] Instead he suggested that there should be some form of compulsory part-time training, in the TA, for example. While recognizing that this would involve very great difficulties in the transition period, he nevertheless argued that 'it seems worth careful investigation as the most promising means of ultimately securing better balanced and more efficient forces with less strain on our economy'.[37]

The responses of Alexander and the Chiefs of Staff were predictable, familiar, and, as far as the Defence Committee was concerned, irrefutable. National Service was still the only means of providing the two manpower needs of the services. First, it was the only effective means of building up the reserve of trained men required in a future emergency. If the conscripts had not had a period of basic full-time training, they would be of little value as trained manpower. Second, conscripts were needed to supplement regular forces to provide for peacetime and Cold War commitments. At this stage the armed forces comprised some 750,000 persons, of whom 300,000 were National Servicemen. At a previous Defence Committee Alexander had submitted proposals to reduce that total to 682,000 (with 230,000 National Servicemen) by April 1951.[38] He estimated that an all-regular force would need to comprise only some 600,000. But this would mean finding another 150,000 regular servicemen, an increase of about a third.

The fundamental question to which Morrison and indeed many of the military and political critics of conscription outside government failed to provide an adequate answer was how to provide these forces. Furthermore, while one of the motives for the opposition to National Service was to reduce its cost, any attempt to phase out conscription would have required additional financial incentives for regular recruiting. Alexander claimed that any chance of increasing regular recruiting on the scale envisaged would add £30 million to the pay bill. This increase would have to take place immediately, whereas the reductions in the National Service intake would need to wait until there were sufficient

---

[36] Ibid.   [37] DO (49) 69, 3 Nov. 1949, CAB 131/7.
[38] DO (49) 19th, 19 Nov. 1949, CAB 131/8.

regulars. While this could be defended as a short-term cost designed to ensure a long-term saving, the fact of fierce and continuing conflict over the defence budget meant that Alexander and
the service chiefs were bound to be reticent. From a political point
of view, substantial increases in service pay might also affect
civilian wage negotiations and the government's incomes policy in
the period up to the election.

Most importantly, there was no guarantee that even dramatic
increases in service pay combined with improvements in service
conditions would procure the necessary immediate and substantial
increase in regular recruiting. Certainly Alexander shared the
Chiefs of Staff's view that, with full employment, expectations of
regular recruiting were based on little more than wishful thinking.
Subsequent rates of regular recruiting in the 'professional army'
of the 1960s and 1970s do little to question the soundness of
that judgement. Harwood's view that the 'career aspect of the
recruiting problem was a potential solution' was based on nothing
more than speculation.

Morrison was clearly aware of these objections. His paper called
for an investigation by the Chiefs of Staff into the practicability
of his proposal, but carefully avoided the issue of regular recruiting. However, in his letter to Alexander, he addressed himself to
these questions. He argued that it was possible to exaggerate the
importance of pay increases as a method of attracting the right
type of recruit: 'Interest and opportunity of service career and
prospects of a favourable entry into civilian life at the end of it
may be even more important.' In particular, he indicated that he
would be happy to explore the possibility of persuading the
socialized industries to 'give facilities for an intake of suitable ex-
servicemen at a convenient age', something which the Post Office
had been doing and which had been canvassed previously, notably
in the Harwood Report and by the Secretary of State for War.
Such a proposal was clearly not contingent on an end to conscription. Moreover, whatever its intrinsic merits, it could hardly
amount to a transformation of military service that would facilitate the necessary increase in regular recruiting.

To some extent this typified the debate between those who
argued for all-regular forces and those who accepted conscription
on the grounds of mathematical imperative. There was a tendency
for the former to revert to generalities about improvements in

conditions of service. There had been great reluctance at the idea of following pre-war continental examples where conscripts were paid significantly less than regular servicemen. Initially, in order to defuse political opposition, it had been decided that the conscripts would receive the same rate of pay. This changed in November 1948 when, in the face of mounting manpower problems among the regulars, the government had given them a pay increase but not done likewise with the conscripts. Subsequently, with National Service extended to two years and with every prospect of conscripts seeing active service (initially Malaya did not count as active service), it was decided that for the additional six months' full-time service the conscripts would receive the regular rate of pay.[39]

The case for an all-regular force invariably involved the suggestion of an improvement in conditions. Yet this in itself posed unavoidable political problems. Aside from the impact of service pay increases on wage negotiations, any improvement in service conditions could only come at the expense of civilian programmes (unless it came from the defence budget). This was especially evident in housing. While it was widely recognized that the living quarters of troops and their families at home and abroad were appalling, and indeed deterrents to recruiting and re-engagement, it was equally evident that improvements in service housing could only be made at the expense of a civilian housing programme that remained a crucial political priority both for the government and for the electorate. Even had such improvements in service conditions been made, there is still little evidence to suggest that military service would have been significantly more attractive to sufficient numbers of people. Even if a change in popular perceptions of service life could be affected, it could only be a long-term transformation.

Yet the argument did not end there. Morrison, for example, had already raised the question of developing police formations along the models of the Palestinian Police and the Royal Ulster Constabulary to replace army units in occupational and certain kinds of Cold War commitments.[40] Furthermore, he suggested greater use of Colonial, allied, and Dominion manpower to

---

[39] CM (50) 53, 11 Aug. 1950, CAB 128/18.
[40] Morrison to Alexander, 15 Nov. 1949, CAB 124/131.

relieve the burden on the United Kingdom. These ideas had of course arisen before (most recently in the Harwood Report) and had self-evident benefits.

The equally obvious problem was that the government had no control over allied or Dominion governments, many of which were unwilling to enter into commitments. As noted above, although New Zealand had introduced conscription for the purpose of providing forces for the Middle East and although South Africa and Australia looked likely to send divisions to that theatre, no Dominion commitments had yet been made. While conscription remained anathema for Canada, as a NATO signatory it was expected to provide some contribution to West European defence, though the negotiations over NATO force levels were still at an early stage. Until the end of 1949 the British themselves remained unwilling to commit any further divisions to Europe. And with the Americans loath in their short-term planning to commit themselves to a defence of the Rhine, the suspicions of Britain's European allies were hardly surprising.

Colonial manpower offered a more attractive proposition, in so far as the British government could exercise more direct political control over the decisions involved. Indeed, several of the government's critics within the Labour Party were keen on this idea, not least because they viewed it in terms of racial and political equality. Attlee himself was clearly in favour of a greater Colonial contribution.

However, there were inherent problems in using Colonial forces. In the first place there was the question of the cost. Expenditure on Colonial forces would have to come at least partially, more probably largely, from the British Exchequer. Although Colonial troops could be paid less than British conscripts, there would still be costs to be borne. Nevertheless on military grounds the Indian Army and the Gurkhas provided the best examples of the value of Colonial troops. Yet there was considerable reluctance, especially in the Colonial Office, to place reliance on such troops in politically sensitive areas where their political reliability might be in question. These doubts were one element behind the government's reluctance to press any form of conscription on the Colonies.

While it might be imagined that Colonial conscription could be viewed as an instrument of social and political control, the opposite view was widely (and almost certainly correctly) held. The Colonial Office was in fact reluctant to see Bermuda adopt a system of compulsory service.[41] Where there were demands for local militias (e.g. in Gibraltar and the Falkland Islands) these were judged solely on grounds of military necessity and were confined (notably in Kenya) to Europeans. The military requirements were concerned with internal duties (i.e. combating subversion); these forces were not, as more radical critics proposed, considered for external roles.

To be able to deal with internal threats, it was necessary to have politically reliable forces. It was believed that compulsion did not provide reliable troops. In addition, it was recognized that there would be enormous political problems in imposing compulsory military service on the Colonies. The policy on conscription was laid down by the Overseas Defence Committee in 1948. As Creech Jones informed the Governor-General of Gibraltar, Sir Kenneth Anderson, on 15 September 1948:

Compulsory military service has political aspects not only locally but also in the United Kingdom and I do not intend at present to apply it as a general policy for all Colonial territories. That intention however, does not rule out the possibility of compulsory military service being imposed in any territory where special circumstances might apply.[42]

Where conscription was considered this arose out of local initiatives, in Kenya, Gibraltar, Bermuda, and the Falkland Islands.

There was some feeling that as conscription existed in Britain, so British subjects abroad should be expected to 'do their duty'. At the same time, as the commander of the Falkland Islands militia explained to the Governor-General, Miles Clifford, 'on the outbreak of war when the force was embodied and conscription introduced every possible excuse was put forward by all and sundry as to why they should not be called up and the percentage of those seeking active service was extremely small'.[43]

There was also the more important military objective of providing forces for internal security in wartime. As in Whitehall, there was little inclination towards using Colonial forces overseas.

[41] Departmental Colonial Office Minute, Acheson to Steel, 28 May 1948, CO 537/4400.　　　[42] Creech Jones to Anderson, 15 Sept. 1948, CO 537/4400.
[43] Clifford to Sir Thomas Lloyd (Under Secretary of State, Colonies), 8 Dec. 1947, CO 537/4400.

There was also some rather non-military concern. The Governor-General of the Falkland Islands believed that 'There are far too many larrikins with nothing to occupy their time after working hours and with compulsory service still in force at home compulsory part-time service here would be a reasonable contribution to Empire preparedness and a wholesome (and much needed) discipline for the young'.[44] In purely military terms one Colonial Office official minuted: 'The possibility of the Falkland Islands being in an active sphere of operations is very remote.'[45] While the Governor-General drew attention to a possible attack from Argentina, which he said was 'not beyond the bounds of possibility',[46] Creech Jones was reluctant to provoke Argentina (or Chile) and quietly let the matter drop.

Although consideration of Morrison's ideas continued into December, the Defence Committee saw no reason to reverse government policy. To have taken such a decision so shortly before an election would have certainly been seen as an irresponsible and cynical move. (Whether it would have worked in the election was a different matter.) Yet this was not the last attempt by a Labour minister to get rid of National Service. As has been noted, the new Minister of Defence, Shinwell, was keen to move to an all-regular army, and would make just such an effort. But Morrison's initiative was the last such attempt in Attlee's first government.

In the February 1950 election National Service was not an issue. Although the Liberals opposed it because it created inefficiency, weakened the economy, and impaired family life,[47] the opposition and the government still maintained a bipartisan approach on the issue. The Labour Party was not especially keen to advertise the subject; while there were general references to the duties and obligations of citizenship in the party manifesto there were no references to conscription.[48] The Conservatives, on the other hand, argued that with better administration it was possible to reduce the burden of National Service.[49]

[44] Ibid.
[45] Departmental Colonial Office minute by Edmonds, 23 Jan. 1948, CO 537/4400. [46] Clifford to Lloyd, 26 Apr. 1948, CO 537/4400.
[47] Liberal Party manifesto, *No Easy Way: Britain's Problems and the Liberal Answers* (1950).
[48] Labour Party manifesto, *Let Us Win Through Together* (1950).
[49] Conservative Party manifesto, *This is the Road* (1949).

The new Attlee government in March 1950 moved Shinwell to the Ministry of Defence. His doubts about National Service were of long standing. As one of those who had not occupied office during the war, he had criticized the idea of conscription in 1945. Despite this, in November 1949 he had accepted the arguments of the Adjutant-General, Sir James Steele, that it was unrealistic to consider abandoning National Service.[50] Nevertheless, he had long been reluctant in his acceptance of conscription and had taken every opportunity to press for an all-regular army. In addition he wanted to get to grips with the strategy and foreign policy that underpinned the defence policy for which he had been departmentally responsible. As Minister of Defence, with a seat in the Cabinet, he would now be in a much better position to do that. Having arrived at the War Office with the crucial decisions on National Service already taken, he had had little realistic hope of reversing policy. As a new Minister of Defence with growing experience and indeed a growing reputation, he would have a much better chance of achieving reform.

The problems that immediately confronted him and the government were considerable. The level of regular recruitment and re-engagement was low and getting worse. The Chiefs of Staff were becoming increasingly concerned with the unpreparedness of the armed forces for war in the near future. Yet Shinwell wasted little time before tackling the issue of National Service. By May 1950 he was arguing with the Chiefs of Staff in favour of an all-regular force along the same lines as he had done at the War Office.[51] A regular army would be more efficient. It would free from the task of training conscripts some 15,000 regulars who would then be available to provide additional fighting units. There would be corresponding reductions in the wastage of manpower in general. As he had previously suggested, the necessary reserves could be provided by a period of part-time training in the auxiliary forces.

In the long run, an all-regular army might (but only might) be cheaper. In the short term however, it would undoubtedly mean an increase in costs, since it would be necessary to increase regular emoluments and improve conditions before National Service could be deemed unnecessary and discontinued. From the

[50] AC/M (49) 5, 18 Nov. 1949, WO 163/63.
[51] COS (50) 77th, 17 May 1950, AIR 8/1588.

Treasury point of view short-term cost, even set against the promise of long-term saving, was not an endearing prospect, and if there was no certainty of savings, Treasury enthusiasm was unlikely. The idea that the additional expenditure involved should come from within the defence budget would have horrified the service chiefs, whose priorities lay in a wholly different direction.

Shinwell's initial action in May was to inform the Chiefs of Staff of his views and to ask the War Office and the Air Ministry to estimate first, the numbers of regulars that they would need to fulfil their existing commitments and second, how much the transition to all-regular forces would cost.[52] He also wanted to know whether the problem of providing the trained reserves could be met by the existing regular reserves being supplemented by a 'form of compulsory training in the Auxiliary forces alone'—an idea which he (and Morrison) had unsuccessfully advocated in the past. Indeed, Shinwell's initiative amounted to no more than a restatement of previous ideas and wishes (his own, Morrison's, and Harwood's) which had never before gained effective support within the government. Moreover, by the time the service departments had completed their preliminary investigations along the lines requested by Shinwell the Korean war had rendered the prospect of radical reform unthinkable.

The war notwithstanding, the Air Ministry and the War Office presented powerful arguments in favour of the retention of conscription. The Air Ministry replied to Shinwell on 30 June 1950 (in a letter from the Deputy Permanent Secretary, F. H. Sandford, to Sir Maurice Dean).[53] It was calculated that the provision of an all-regular force would allow the ministry to reduce its estimated manpower requirement from 205,000 to 192,000. The former comprised 131,000 regulars and 74,000 National Servicemen and assumed both an eighteen-month period of full-time service and a regular recruiting rate at existing levels. The figure of 192,000 assumed the same shape and size of embodied forces and that the men would serve the same average length of regular service. It made no provision for the basic training of National Servicemen either during a possible short period of embodied service or during a period of reserve liability as

---

[52] Sir Maurice Dean to Sir James Barnes (Air Ministry) and Sir George Turner (War Office), 20 May 1950, AIR 8/1591.
[53] Sandford to Dean, 30 Jun. 1950, AIR 8/1591.

envisaged by Shinwell. No attempt was made to calculate how much of the saving in manpower (some 13,000) would be taken up in providing either of those facilities.

By now the size of the National Service intake was determined primarily by the numbers required for active service, which meant more reserves than would be immediately needed. The value of men who had been trained only part-time and/or in the auxiliary forces would be limited, especially where they had not had sufficient experience in their service trade. The Air Ministry suggested that if National Service were radically reduced then the RAF might abandon its policy of training National Servicemen in skilled trades, as many of these would in any case be in reserved occupations in the event of war. Training conscripts in unskilled or only slightly skilled occupations would not require an increase in the training establishment or the manpower estimate of 192,000.

It would also be possible for some of the more skilled personnel, such as those for the Command and Reporting System, to be accommodated within the 192,000 figure. Here there was an additional problem. At this time the RAF trained some 300 National Servicemen a year to be pilots. In addition to their eighteen-month period of service, they were required to accept the full obligations of either the Royal Auxiliary Air Force (RAAF) or the Royal Air Force Volunteer Reserve, as opposed to the normal reserve liability of the ordinary conscript. These trainees constituted virtually the only manpower source for meeting future pilot requirements for the twenty fighter squadrons of the RAAF, a substantial part of the air defence of the country which, since mid-1948, had been an increasing defence priority. As the RAAF was currently manned largely by pilots trained in wartime, and as these would have to be replaced before long, the need for National Service pilots for the RAAF would grow accordingly. Thus some form of National Service would still be required (within the 192,000 figure) to provide for these and the Command and Reporting System.

At this stage the Air Ministry made no comment on the practicability of increasing the regular content, although it drew attention to the inevitable expense of the transition period and to the fact that as the average cost of a regular airman was higher than that of a National Serviceman, the anticipated financial saving would not be proportionate to the reduction in the size of the force. While this is what the Air Ministry told Shinwell, it privately held out no hope whatsoever of attracting and keeping the required number of regulars, although there was certainly some sympathy for the idea of an all-regular force. No attempt was made to suggest means of providing the additional regulars; nor—contrary to Shinwell's wishes—was there any costing of the transition period.

Slessor, now Chief of the Air Staff, recognized that the additional numbers could be found only with substantial inducements, but in his opinion even a spectacular increase in pay such as the Minister of Defence might contemplate was of doubtful recruiting value in the present period of full employment.[54] He had for some time favoured tackling the conditions and morale of the RAF (particularly its Pilot and Flying Officers) and had in the past proposed a variety of measures to improve the morale and *élan* of the service and particularly its officer corps. These ranged from uniform allowances to private glider flying (the modern equivalent of the hunting that he had enjoyed as a young officer) to an educational allowance designed to make it possible for RAF officers to send their sons (but not daughters) to public schools: 'If we want to continue to attract the type of officer who had made the service what it was in the past, we must make it possible for him to send his son to the type of school that he went to himself.' Nevertheless, he did not regard pay and taxation as unimportant. As he commented, 'It was a damned sight easier to have a spirit of adventure when income tax was five bob in the pound and one's Father had something to leave one instead of leaving it to the Chancellor.' These sentiments and values reflected the socially exclusive base of the officer class in peacetime. There was little sympathy with (or understanding of) Labour ministers compelled to impose a disquieting level of austerity (from rationing to pay policy) on their own working-class supporters and who remained at least nominally wedded to ideas of 'democratic armed forces'. What was apparent was the belief, certainly shared by Shinwell, that pay itself was not the whole answer to the recruiting problem.

[54] Slessor (then at the Imperial Defence College) to Sir Hugh Saunders, 25 Aug. 1949, AIR 8/1591.

The Army Council discussed the issue in June 1950. Shinwell received the War Office's reply on 19 July,[55] and on the following day the new Secretary of State for War, John Strachey, sent a personal and far more sympathetic response.[56] The War Office argued that an all-regular army was an 'undoubtedly attractive' conception for the purpose of fighting the Cold War but that while there were many other advantages of a more stable army, the case against the all-regular force was considerable. The problems remained: providing sufficient regulars to meet peacetime commitments and training the reserves for mobilization in war.

In order to remove the National Servicemen from the active army it would be necessary to phase out conscription by gradual reductions in the size of the intake or the period of service or indeed both. It was calculated that the reserve army would require a strength of some 100,000 men for an indefinite period. With a reduced intake there would be increasingly adverse effects on the strength of the reserve, which 'sooner or later would involve Selective Service which might be politically unacceptable'.[57] To reduce the period of full-time National Service would have very serious effects on the standard of training in the reserves, especially of officers, specialists, and tradesmen. The War Office argued that this would further retard the mobilization of the TA, which would then take some six months to become effective, twice as long as planned at present. Reinforcement of Europe and the Middle East would be seriously jeopardized. There would also be particularly serious effects on the state of readiness of the Anti-Aircraft Command.

In this situation, Turner explained, the active and reserve armies would have conflicting long-term requirements. Any advantages of an all-regular army were a long way off. The active army required some 350,000 soldiers (including women and National Servicemen) to meet its commitments. To meet those commitments with an all-regular army would need 310,000 men, a figure which did include provision for the basic training of National Servicemen prior to their entry into the reserves. The existing regular strength was only 180,000. Moreover, with current

[55] Turner to Dean, 19 Jul. 1950, AIR 8/1591.
[56] Strachey to Shinwell, 20 Jul. 1950, AIR 8/1591.
[57] Turner to Dean, 19 Jul. 1950, AIR 8/1591.

recruiting trends, it was anticipated that the regular strength would fall to 150,000 in the next few years.

Therefore, in order to provide an all-regular army capable of filling existing commitments it would be necessary to more than double the number of regular soldiers. As Turner noted: 'Any discussion on a long-term all-regular army is therefore bound to be largely academic. The real problem for the War Office at this time was the level of regular recruiting and re-engagement.' 'Considerable improvements' were necessary even to arrest the downward trend of recruiting. How these could be achieved was not clear. Actually increasing the regular strength would take a number of years to become effective, even on the most optimistic of War Office forecasts, and even if 'political, economic or financial considerations dictated an appreciable reduction in the size of the Active Army and even if improvements contemplated in conditions of service and other factors led to a dramatic improvement in recruiting'. During that time National Service would still be essential to provide the required numbers of troops for the active army.

Despite the force of these arguments and despite Army Council discussion of the whole issue, John Strachey, Shinwell's successor, was yet another Secretary of State for War who was less than happy with the War Office view, and he urged Shinwell to continue with the 'detailed study of the financial and other effects of the approach to all-regular forces'.[58] While recognizing that the matter needed a great deal of study, he nevertheless quoted £20 million as the figure which would be required to effect a dramatic change in the trend of regular recruiting. This figure had been picked up from the Army Council discussion and it was, as Strachey admitted, only a guess. If £20 million were the price of progressively reducing conscription to a training period of only three to five months, it strengthened the case for reform for Strachey and Shinwell.

Strachey did accept that a reduced period of full-time training would mean lengthening the time between the mobilization of the TA and its disembarkation overseas. It would also mean that the reserves would be short of skilled tradesmen and officers. This was recognized as serious, but he believed that the difficulties

[58] Strachey to Shinwell, 20 Jul. 1950, AIR 8/1591.

could be ameliorated by specific increases in the pay of the tradesmen or by giving special inducements to civilian tradesmen. In spite of these problems Strachey considered that an all-regular army would mean a substantial improvement in the quality of the active regular divisions available at the beginning of war: 'In other words the tendency would be to improve the force available at the very beginning of war but to postpone the arrival of efficient reinforcements for that initial force'—a view which had considerable political implications for the British contribution to West European defence.

The timing of Shinwell's initiative gave it little chance of serious consideration. Even before he had approached the War Office and the Air Ministry, he had reported to the Defence Committee that he and the service ministers were gravely concerned at present trends in regular recruiting and re-engagements, and he undertook a series of enquiries (through inter-service working parties) into various measures designed to improve recruiting. These would investigate such factors as career and trade structures, living conditions, and training. The purpose of the report to the Defence Committee was not in fact to advertise the regular recruiting issue, but to ensure that ministers refrained from making premature statements that would encourage hopes of service pay increases.[59] This caution arose from the fear of the Chancellor, Hugh Gaitskell, that any such public statement would damage the government's wages policy.

The development that put paid to Shinwell's efforts was the Korean war. This was not because additional troops were necessary. Initially the Chiefs of Staff were reluctant to send any British ground forces and when they did agree to do so, the commitment was only a token combat brigade, sent for purely political reasons. (None the less, when that did happen, they were hard put to raise the troops.) Initially the Chiefs of Staff did not believe that the North Korean attack on South Korea indicated an imminent Soviet attack on Western Europe. However, the heightened perception of the communist challenge (especially among ministers) did bring the existing inadequacies of the forces into sharp relief. The Chiefs of Staff were provided with an opportunity to press their case on a more receptive audience. In addition, the risk of

[59] DO (50) 29, 21 Apr. 1950, CAB 131/9.

a general war with the Soviet Union had increased, the service chiefs believed, and they warned the Cabinet that the Soviet Union 'might engineer another act of aggression in the near future in Germany or in Persia and an increase in the period of National Service would yield the forces needed to meet any threat of this character'.[60] Such acts of aggression would not necessarily involve all-out war. It was not until after the decision to extend National Service was taken that the full-scale Korean rearmament drive got under way and the government and the service chiefs began to take more seriously the prospect of a full-scale assault in Western Europe.

Extending National Service to two years with the colours would mean retaining 77,000 conscripts, of whom nearly 50,000 would be in the army. After strengthening various overseas garrisons this would allow for a strategic reserve comprising an infantry division, an armoured brigade, and an airborne regiment. It would, however, inevitably mean deferring entry into the TA, which would create the same sorts of problems as had arisen when conscription was last increased.

The RAF would retain 28,000 National Servicemen, enabling it to improve both the serviceability of its equipment and its ground functions, currently at only 50 per cent of their normal establishment, which was in 'an unsatisfactory condition'. While this would help the RAF it could not solve the basic need for long-service troops. The navy, maintaining its token intake of conscripts, noted that it would not directly benefit by the extension.

In the minds of a number of Cabinet ministers (including Shinwell and Bevin) the rationale for the longer period of service was the reinforcement of the defences of Western Europe. By increasing the strength of the forces of occupation in Germany back to three divisions, Shinwell hoped to set an example which the other Brussels Pact signatories might follow. If that happened the resulting forces 'would provide a useful deterrent against aggression',[61] even without the American commitment that ministers were now beginning to doubt, in the face of the Korean priority. It was also the case that if the British decision to extend conscription were co-ordinated with similar French, Belgian, and Dutch action, then it would be politically easier to effect

[60] CM (50) 53, 11 Aug. 1950, CAB 128/18.   [61] Ibid.

in Britain. Indeed, when the Cabinet first discussed the question on 11 August they decided to defer their decision until the French, Dutch, Belgian, and Luxemburg governments had been approached.

However, Bevin's preliminary soundings proved disappointing, as he reported to the Cabinet the following week.[62] The governments in question had all dwelt on the internal political problems of extending conscription. In particular, the French (with elections impending) argued that any action on their part would depend upon further American or British aid. Bevin concluded from this that it was increasingly evident that Britain should turn to NATO rather than to the Western Union for effective co-operation in defence.

It was his view that the Cabinet should take the decision to extend National Service without waiting for further European responses, in the hope that the force of Britain's example would lead the others in a similar direction. Shinwell concurred and held out the hope that at least the Dutch might be co-operative. There was, however, some feeling in Cabinet that unilateral action might make the Western Union countries even less willing to provide forces. As there would be more British troops available, more of these could be deployed in Western Europe, reducing the number of continental troops required. Unilateral action would also advertise the lack of cohesion and effective co-operation within the Western Union.

Bevin and Shinwell's view prevailed nevertheless. It would be potentially more embarrassing for the government if the other countries were to refuse publicly. In any case the European aspect was but one part of the reason for the increase in the length of service. Accordingly the Cabinet gave its approval on 16 August. A week later this decision was communicated to the armed forces in a broadcast delivered by the Prime Minister. On 12 September 1950 the House of Commons was recalled to discuss the Korean situation. On conscription, opposition to the government came only from the relatively small number of MPs who had previously opposed the government's policy on grounds of principle. National Service was now to be two years with the colours, which was the period of service that lasted until its abolition in 1957.

[62] CM (50) 54, 16 Aug. 1950, CAB 128/18.

The Korean rearmament programme represented an unprecedented peacetime defence effort and was intended to cost £4,700 million over three years.[63] Detailed analysis of the programme is beyond the scope of this study, but it is important to emphasize that the expansion of the defence budget involved a change in emphasis within the defence policy priorities between short- and long-term goals. Unlike previous changes in priorities, this was not at the expense of other objectives: indeed, as far as meeting peacetime foreign policy commitments was concerned, the opposite was the case. The extension of conscription provided the services with the extra resources they needed and when, for example, the government seriously contemplated military intervention at Abadan in 1951, manpower was not an obstacle. In addition, in January 1951 it was decided to recall up to 235,000 Z reservists (in the RAF known as Class G reserves) for fifteen days' refresher training.[64] The result was a further strengthening of Britain's ability to react, but one which nevertheless fell short of real preparedness for war, which the Chiefs of Staff do not appear to have considered imminent.

As the Cold War developed, attitudes changed. Opposition to the government's defence policy from within the Labour Party concentrated on its cost (and social implications) rather than its logic or its assumptions. Sentiment against conscription was still powerful, but public opposition on the issue had declined as the Cold War intensified from 1948. Abolishing conscription would have required bold and radical action to achieve a fundamental recasting of defence planning. With the rearmament programme under way, that was politically unthinkable for government and party alike.

[63] For a discussion of this see Philip Williams, *Hugh Gaitskell* (Cape, 1979), ch. 8.   [64] CM (51) 8, 25 Jan. 1951, CAB 128/19.

10
Conclusion

LABOUR lost the general election of October 1951. The new Churchill administration pursued policies in foreign and defence affairs that in the main followed from, and were based on the same assumptions as, those of the Attlee governments. However, the Conservatives did slow the Korean rearmament drive, and by 1955 they had developed a strategic nuclear capability that Harold Macmillan and Duncan Sandys were to use to justify ending conscription.[1] Nevertheless, the essentials of the National Service scheme remained the same, with the period of service fixed at two years, until in 1957 it was decided to phase out conscription altogether.

In opposition, Labour manœuvred for political advantage, urging reviews of the length of service and suggesting that Labour would be able to reduce the burden of conscription. Nevertheless, National Service continued on the bipartisan basis which had characterized the 1945–51 period. When the decision to end conscription was taken Labour supported it, although there was criticism of the Sandys doctrine of reliance on strategic nuclear weapons.[2] There was also a handful of Labour MPs, notably Crossman and Wigg, who argued against this bipartisan orthodoxy in favour of a scheme of selective military service. The vast majority of the party, however, was only too happy to see an end to conscription.

For British defence and foreign policy the post-war period has been characterized as 'the long retreat'.[3] One of the fundamental issues has been the search for a level of defence effort compatible

---

[1] Cmd. 9608, *National Service* (1955). For an analysis of Macmillan's decision to abolish conscription see Martin Navias, 'Terminating Conscription? The British National Service Controversy 1955–6', *Journal of Contemporary History*, 24 (1989), 195–208.   [2] Cmd. 124, *Defence: Outline of Future Policy* (1957).
[3] C. J. Bartlett, *The Long Retreat* (Macmillan, 1972). For a more critical and pessimistic overview see Christopher Coker, *A Nation in Retreat* (Brassey's, 1986).

with newly recognized social objectives in a changed and often inhospitable economic climate. Even with (until recently) a constantly rising level of economic growth, governments of all colours have sought to accommodate diverging objectives.

To suggest that resulting policies were unhappy compromises implies the existence of some rational or objective solution. Such a view has little foundation. Decisions about the allocation of resources and the pursuit of foreign policy are inherently subjective. A serious adjudication about the proportion of national effort that ought to have been allocated would require a detailed study of all the domestic and international circumstances involved. While this study has been concerned to show the overall dilemma as it was perceived (and as it affected a particular policy) at the time, it has barely touched upon either of those two conditions.

Domestic and foreign policy objectives have been taken largely for granted. Where some attention has been given to the wisdom of the government's planning (e.g. in respect of the Middle East), this reflects the contemporary debates. The underlying purpose of this form of analysis has been to balance the advantage of hindsight with a sympathetic approach to the position of decision-makers in order to understand the character of the government and the extent to which 'choices' were seen to exist. Implicit in this, and a central theme of the book, was that the allocation of resources for defence presented the government with a series of dilemmas.

The issue of National Service symbolized and was itself at the centre of these conflicts. Yet it has also been argued that, even within the parameters of foreign policy, conscription was not an effective long-term policy. The issue of compulsory military service cannot be divorced from the overall context and the overall dilemma. When defence budgets or manpower allocations were discussed they invariably involved consideration (and reconsideration) of the National Service scheme. This was the case, for example, with the 1947 convertibility crisis and with the long-term planning for future war.

The relationship between National Service and the broader issues is complex. National Service policy was influenced by the higher levels of policy. This was evident in the debates and changes of mind over the length of service, the size of the intake, the stoppage of releases, and the nature of exemptions. These aspects represented points on a political weather-vane—indicators of the alternating priorities accorded to domestic and foreign policy objectives. With the size of intake and nature of exemptions, this was in part due to the circumstances under which the National Service Act was designed, in turn a reflection of the government's failure to develop a considered and coherent manpower policy within an agreed strategic and financial framework. The length of the period of full-time service provided the focus for much of the debate throughout the Attlee governments. There was conflict over both the transitional scheme (for 1947 and 1948) and the long-term design of the new legislation; in the case of the latter, conflict was apparent both in government and in the Labour Party.

Although changes in these aspects indicated the alternating priorities of the government, the attachment to the principle of universal liability remained, albeit within limits prescribed by the prevailing norms of the political culture (*vis-à-vis* women, Ulstermen, and conscientious objectors). Moreover, although changes in policy did indicate changes in priorities, the length of service was nevertheless a compromise between service requirements and what the government could afford. Yet this was a compromise which neither side regarded as satisfactory.

When, in October 1946, the Chiefs of Staff argued for an eighteen-month period of service, that in itself represented their accommodation to what was economically and politically acceptable. The RAF and the navy ideally wanted a three- or four-year period of service but quickly recognized that this was politically impractical. The Chiefs of Staff estimated that a two-year period was required to provide all three services with what was needed, but they too saw that this was not politically acceptable. Even then a ministerial battle was needed before the eighteen-month option was chosen in preference to twelve. After that decision was abandoned in the wake of the PLP rebellions, the extensions of service in 1948 and 1950 were indicators of the increased priority accorded to defence; yet in 1948 even this did not provide the services with what they claimed was their essential minimum.

National Service policy was influenced by more general decisions. But to what extent did the acceptance of conscription determine the wider considerations? This cannot be answered easily in so far as National Service did not in itself determine the size of the armed forces or the amount spent on defence. Although the scheme was based on the principle of universal service, the number of conscripts and the size of the forces as a whole could be varied by adjusting such factors as the intake and the length of service.

The questions of conscription and the scale of the post-war defence burden were inevitably intertwined, but decisions about provision for defence and conscription were divorced. That was the case in 1945, when, but for Attlee, the principle of permanent conscription would have been accepted with virtually no analysis of the scale or consequences of the defence effort. And despite Attlee's and Dalton's awareness of the need to tackle the defence burden, the decision on the National Service scheme in October 1946 was divorced from a decision on the long-term defence budget. In February 1947 the latter was established at £600 million (a figure with which the services were simply unable to comply). In October 1947 it was made clear that National Service of eighteen months' full-time service entailed a budget of £750 million, which proved to be an underestimation. In his acceptance of that policy it was clear that Dalton and the Treasury saw the issues as separable.

The existence of conscription could not but influence the general situation. National Service provided for much larger forces than would have been possible with a purely voluntary system. The cost of the larger forces was dependent on a range of other factors (from training facilities to weapons procurement). Some indication of the cost can be gauged from the rough calculation that as defence budgets developed, 100,000 men cost £100 million. Therefore conscript forces of 300,000–400,000 meant expenditure of some £300–400 million on defence. The cost of conscripts was increased so long as they received the same or at least comparable rates of pay as the regulars. Yet the assumption that all-regular forces constituted a cheaper or indeed more cost-effective option in turn assumed that sufficient regulars could be found from the voluntary method.

To have rejected a long-term compulsory system would have required a radical reduction in the scope of Britain's foreign and defence commitments, as was graphically illustrated by the Harwood report. The impact of that reduction would have been dependent on a host of other factors, both strategic and financial.

Yet it is clear that a decision to abandon National Service would have imposed on the government and on the military a radical if arbitrary restraint within which they would have to plan. Without conscription, considerable reductions would have been necessary and harsh choices about strategy and foreign policy would have to have been faced. Yet having said that, it should be noted that even after conscription had been abandoned, Britain continued to maintain a role east of Suez and a standing army in West Germany.

This study of conscription has been in large part a study of British defence policy. It is important to note that certain fundamental aspects and fundamental criticisms have not been explored. The process whereby early contingency planning was translated into the actual long-term defence planning has not been examined. The question of when, or indeed whether, the Soviet Union should have been regarded as a long-term military threat has not been posed. It has been noted that decisions about the provision for defence predated the emergence of a perceived threat—a perception which, for the military, was not altered by the beginning of the Cold War or even the outbreak of hostilities in Korea. Preparation for defence proceeded on the assumption that it would be necessary to be in a position to wage war at the time when the Soviet Union would be in such a position, and that time was taken as 1957. Although the Soviet Union was believed to have 175–6 divisions in Eastern Europe, planning was based on the long-term potential of Soviet forces.[4]

Defence policy was required to perform three tasks. First, it had to provide the military basis for foreign policy in peacetime. Second, forces would be needed that were capable of fighting a major war by 1957—a date which was reviewed only in the wake of the allied negotiations and NATO planning in the context of the testing of the Soviet atom bomb and the Korean rearmament drive. Third, it would be necessary to fight with what was available should 'unpremeditated' war occur—a concern which occupied the services during the Berlin crisis, when they warned of the condition of the forces and eventually succeeded in getting the government to act, and during the Korean war, when the government embarked on a massive rearmament drive which enhanced

[4] For an account of Western intelligence estimates of Soviet conventional strength, see Mathew Evangelista, 'Stalin's Post-war Army Reappraised', *International Security*, 7 (1982/3), 110–38.

the ability to wage war in the short term. In terms of force structure and manpower provision, these three tasks were not mutually exclusive: particularly in the RAF and the navy, the forces that existed in peacetime represented a substantial part of the front-line strength in war.

National Service was nevertheless designed with these differing purposes in mind. Conscripts would be used to provide the regular soldiers and airmen until such a time as reduction in commitments allowed for all-regular service. However, as obligations persisted, and new ones arose, and as regular recruiting failed to reach its expected levels, conscription became a mathematical imperative. The army and the RAF could not reach their requirements without it. The increases in the length of service were demonstrations of the growing dependence on the compulsory system.

There were various options, canvassed at different times, designed to replace, or at least reduce, the need for British servicemen. These included the use of women, civilians, a foreign legion, or Colonial manpower. The first two were not ignored. But apart from the last of these it was clear, that at best, they could only ameliorate the manpower problem, not solve it. The use of Colonial manpower on the necessary scale would have required revision of the assumptions involved. Attlee did press the services on Colonial manpower, as indeed on the other proposals, but was not prepared to impose a policy which would have cut across traditions and, moreover, perceptions of the military value and (in some circumstances) political reliability of the troops. This was perhaps indicative of the cultural typology of a government which regarded India in such a different light from African and other Colonial territories when it came to decolonization.

In a different context there were manpower resources that could have replaced the need for large British forces in peace and war—those of the Commonwealth and the United States. The desire to get the Antipodean nations and South Africa to guarantee forces for the Middle East in wartime was a continuing concern of the Chiefs of Staff—albeit in the form of supplements to, rather than replacements for, British forces. As for the Americans, Bevin's foreign policy accorded the highest priority to getting the United States involved in international security (though he was reluctant to get them involved militarily in the Middle East). In so far as the provision of British forces was necessary to get the Americans involved, the need for embodied forces was actually reinforced. Alliance-building offered no short-term savings. As for British withdrawal in anticipation of US intervention, neither the government nor the Chiefs of Staff felt the necessary confidence in their ally to contemplate, for example, an abandonment of a Middle Eastern strategy in war.

It can be argued that the foundation of the armed forces was simply too large and the 'teeth to tail' ratio hopelessly out of balance. It is the case that embodied forces deployed overseas appear relatively small in relation to the size of the services as a whole. Ministers were bemused by the fact that with 700,000 men and women in the forces in the United Kingdom the War Office had to go to considerable lengths to send a single active brigade to Malaya in 1948. There can be little question that the forces were bureaucratically swollen as a result of their expansion in the war. Radical and extensive reorganization was required. Failing that, arbitrary cuts offered the only alternative.

However, from the perspective of practical policy-making, arbitrary cuts in administration for the forces as a whole did, in the short term, damage the efficiency and effectiveness of the services. The government made cuts in administration and pressed for overall economies, though the manpower economy reviews in 1948–9 made for dismal reading. These measures were not sufficient. Yet for the government and indeed for the services themselves, the problem did not yield to a painless bureaucratic solution. Without a breathing space of some years, the dislocation of massive cuts could not but jeopardize the provision of forces in being and seriously delay the long-term design. The chaos that had followed the Great War was not forgotten. And whereas then a breathing space had been granted, hope for a period of grace after 1945 soon evaporated.

The only other possibility was the reduction or elimination of overseas commitments to compensate for those administrative cuts that were undertaken. In examining this question it should be realized that only a relatively small proportion of troops was deployed overseas. Bevin did complain that the size of the armed forces was not attributable to his foreign policy. There was no straightforward relationship between the termination of commitments and the reduction of troops. When Palestine was evacuated, for example, the troops were redeployed in the Middle East theatre. However, it was clear that the maintenance of overseas responsibilities on a global scale required unprecedented numbers of servicemen. National Service was unavoidable so long as regular recruiting was unable to provide these numbers. It is almost impossible to determine which commitments would have to have been eliminated to reduce requirements to a level that could be met by voluntary methods alone. Withdrawal from the Middle East or even Europe would not necessarily, or at least immediately, have reduced peacetime requirements to the extent that could have been met by regular recruiting.

In each of these areas withdrawal required a particular view of wartime strategy and the deployment of troops at the outset of war. The second requirement of defence was the preparation for war in the long term; the third was the ability to react in an emergency. Each of these required mobilization at the start of war. The National Service scheme was originally designed for this purpose. However, conscription was not tied to a particular strategy. The need for trained reserves was shared by all three services and the importance of conscription in this was even recognized by the navy. For the RAF the shortage of regulars coupled with the transfer of various wartime functions to the auxiliary services increased the dependence of front-line strength on the reserves.

Although conscription was not tied to a specific strategy it was nevertheless evident that as the provision for defence fell short of what the Chiefs of Staff required, the development of an army designed to fight abroad in the early stages of a war in Western Europe did not constitute a prudent allocation of resources unless and until the overall strategic design fully encompassed that commitment.

The need for large numbers of adequately trained reserves was a lesson learned from 1939, when lack of preparedness had been painfully obvious. The particular inadequacies of the voluntary TA were recalled. The shadow of the 1930s lay across the whole of military and political thinking. Psychologically the desire to avoid (and in some quarters to make up for) the mistakes of the 1930s was every bit as powerful as the psychology that had helped form the attitude of appeasement and the unwillingness to rearm quickly or sufficiently. On this particular question, as perhaps in the more fundamental areas of British (and other) perceptions of

East–West relations, the psychology of decision-makers was a poor guide to wise and effective planning. The attitude of mind that sought to provide forces on the scale envisaged was the product of both appeasement and total war. Yet it is apparent that the need for trained reserves—at least in the army—became a psychological objective divorced from strategy, or at least from a financially realistic strategy.

It is neither surprising nor necessarily wrong that the experience of the six years of war played a crucial role in framing attitudes and influencing planning. The military was aware that, as Tedder put it, 'modern warfare renders the last war obsolete'.[5] Yet it was apparent that modern warfare incorporated atomic bombs only as an extension of wartime practices of strategic bombing. Policy was founded on the notion of deterrence, based on the nuclear-armed long-range bomber fleet. Yet atomic bombs would not replace conventional forces (armies, navies, air defence systems). This stance can be criticized as reflecting the failure to recognize the crucial significance of such a revolutionary change in warfare and, moreover, the failure to foresee the implications of this for defence resource allocation—views which justify later theories and policies of deterrence.

Detailed consideration of these issues is beyond this study; but these criticisms can be challenged on moral or pragmatic grounds. It can be argued that an adequate conventional defence was preferable to one based on nuclear deterrence. In so far as a long-term policy of National Service signalled such a preference, conscription can be defended. On the other hand, as became apparent during the Attlee government, there were grounds for not equating compulsory military service with an adequate conventional capability.

In this context there are two sorts of criticisms: those which attacked conscription on principle—views propounded by Liddell Hart and Martel and reinforced by the services' experience of training National Servicemen; and those which were rooted in administrative problems and the competition over resources. It became apparent that an economically or socially desirable defence effort drastically reduced the efficacy of universal conscription with the length of service that was deemed necessary. The Harwood

---

[5] Bartlett, *The Long Retreat*, 35.

report brought home the point that conscription was a mis-allocation of resources where resources were limited, as they were until the Korean rearmament programme.

It was also apparent that decisions about strategy and the allocation of resources were not adequately co-ordinated. The acceptance of conscription predated an agreed strategic doctrine including a decision on the nature of the commitment to Western Europe. In turn these developments predated collective decisions by Western nations on commitments in Europe and the Middle East. The decision on National Service in October 1946 predated agreement on the scale of the defence effort, and when agreement was reached at a ministerial level, the struggle with the services to get near that target was barely beginning.

It is easy to be critical with hindsight. Nevertheless, the failure to co-ordinate strategy, policy, and resources was evident. As has been apparent throughout the study, the government was more than aware of the problems involved and constantly tried to reconcile diverging objectives. Yet it is difficult to avoid the conclusion that the decision on a long-term scheme of conscription was taken too early. Attlee got it right in the spring of 1945, when he blocked Churchill's attempt to get the principle of permanent conscription accepted, but he got it wrong in 1946. And once it had been introduced as a long-term scheme the political difficulties of abandoning the principle of universal compulsion meant that a reversal of the decision was virtually unthinkable.

It should be noted that the government did not introduce permanent conscription. But it is clear that the acceptance of a time limit on the 1947 act was little more than a tactical concession to placate opposition in the PLP. Moreover, while there were fundamental problems with National Service as the long-term basis for defence policy, that did nothing to change the immediate and foreseeable need to provide troops in peacetime. With that in mind a National Service scheme of limited duration did, albeit inadvertently, represent the prudent policy. And so long as some conscripts were necessary, a universal scheme was politically unavoidable for a Labour government, whatever its other drawbacks.

The conflict between short- and long-term requirements was but part of what became a more general and identifiable problem for the government. As the Cold War began, and economic

constraints tightened, the government had to establish priorities
between short- and long-term objectives for defence; increasingly
it chose the former. National Service, initially justified on the
grounds of providing trained reserves, was increasingly defended
on grounds of mathematical necessity. That transition did not
follow any considered reappraisal of policy or strategy. Indeed, as
the government moved falteringly towards a long-term continental commitment, the need for trained reserves ready on mobilization began to translate into concrete strategic requirements.
It was only by 1955 that the Conservative government was able
to declare that 'in a nuclear age the conception of reserve forces
waiting to take part in large scale conventional war is out of
date', though conscripts were still necessary to 'supplement the
regulars and so provide sufficient active forces to meet the country's
needs'.[6]

Nevertheless, the need for National Service remained rooted in
the requirements of defence policy. To this there was added an
additional foreign policy dimension. Conscription was viewed as a
symbol of Britain's resolve and determination—a view which was
voiced increasingly at ministerial level from 1947. This sort of
consideration had been important in 1939, when French public
opinion had played a key role in the decision to introduce the 1939
Military Training Act. In 1945 Eden's Foreign Office paper to the
APW Committee had also strongly emphasized this symbolic
importance, and Churchill was to cite it as a principal reason for
his support of the government's policy. Bevin, likewise, spoke in
these general terms in October 1946; but it was when the prospect
of collective defence and in particular American military aid began
to take shape that a case for conscription on grounds that were
other than strictly military appears to have entered ministerial
calculation.

Abandoning conscription would have presented difficulties to
American as much as European opinion, while Britain was
manœuvring to get each of these to provide effective military
forces. It might well have hindered the process of forming an
effective West European defence. Yet, on the other hand, that
could have been compensated for by the contraction of extra-
European commitments and by the deployment and/or promise of

[6] Cmd. 9608, *National Service*, para. 18.

British divisions for the continent. Attempting to calculate how the abolition of National Service would have been viewed by friends and allies is difficult. Preserving French and American confidence in Britain's resolve, while abandoning compulsory service, would have had obvious difficulties, especially as the Americans had departed from their peacetime traditions in re-introducing the draft. Yet it would not have fundamentally affected the likelihood of America going to war with the Soviet Union if Stalin attacked Western Europe. It is significant that the decision to end conscription in 1957 followed the Suez débâcle, at a time when, first, the Western alliance had taken shape, and second, the feelings and sensitivities of Britain's allies did not rank very high in the priorities of defence policy.

It is worth emphasizing that National Service was designed and maintained solely for the purposes of foreign and defence policy. Advocacy on domestic grounds, such as instilling discipline or patriotism in the young, was confined to sections of the Conservative Party (and indeed public opinion) that were of little consequence to policy-makers. Occasionally ministers did speak, at least within the confines of Whitehall, of the intrinsic value of discipline or of 'regular meals and healthy exercise'; and Montgomery made no secret of the personal benefits which he believed that young men would receive. Yet he was also anxious to point to the inherent benefits of a voluntary system and, within Whitehall, sought to justify his policy in terms of military requirements. That is not to suggest that the military goal of a trained and disciplined nation could be without political consequences; nor is it to suggest that Montgomery did not have very definite views about social organization; but it is to emphasize that decisions were not taken on these grounds.

The nearest that any minister came to accepting conscription on non-military grounds was Bevin, whose argument that the rights of citizenship in a welfare state entailed duties and obligations predated the Labour government and was an argument for permanent conscription. Although this demonstrates the considerable change from Bevin's pre-war attitude, it does not in itself suggest that Labour's Foreign Secretary would have argued for conscription had there not been a military need. At least in 1947 Bevin specifically saw National Service as providing the best military system Britain had devised, comparing it favourably with the

Haldane system. It seems much more likely that the citizenship argument was a political gloss on the military case. It is clear that Bevin's attitude to the military became less sympathetic over the years while his foreign policy increased his dependence on them.

The non-military aspect is worth noting because, while the argument for conscription rested on defence policy requirements, opposition to conscription, particularly within the Labour Party, rested mainly on non- and indeed anti-military grounds. Opposition was spread across a wide spectrum of intellectual and political opinion. Pacifism and non-conformity had been traditional elements in forming Labour's attitude on issues of foreign and defence affairs. The pre-war notion of a socialist foreign policy, which Attlee himself had promulgated, had fused the party's domestic radicalism with a view of international affairs which rejected the armed camps of a balance of power. These sentiments were still evident in 1945. Domestically the vision of the New Jerusalem, and internationally the prospect of the collective security of a United Nations organization, reinforced one set of views just as the lessons of appeasement and the experience of office had changed those of Attlee's ministers, even if the Prime Minister himself sought radical solutions to Britain's fundamental problems in the period 1945–7.

Criticism of the government's conduct of foreign policy fuelled opposition to conscription, given that National Service was inextricably linked with Bevin's foreign policy. Yet although in most sections of the PLP the issues were closely connected, there were some, notably on the non-pacifist left, who, in 1946–7, clearly distinguished between them. Keep Left MPs were anxious to support the principle of conscription (even though they were involved in the revolt over the length of service), while they provided the leading backbench critics of the government's foreign policy.

Economic concerns were also apparent, although these were translated into opposition on the length of service, rather than on the principle of conscription. This was to form the main focus of conflict within Whitehall. Anxiety over the loss of productive manpower from industry increased with the publication of the 1947 *Economic Survey* and extended far beyond the Labour Party. This was a crucial part of the rationale for the twelve- as opposed to the eighteen-month period of service, and therefore a key factor in the backbench revolt of April 1947 that led to the dramatic volte-face by the government. The first reading rebellion in November 1946 had been confined to the opponents of the principle of compulsory military service; the more significant one on the second reading extended to those who objected to the longer period of service. The political perception of what was a reasonable length of service had occupied the government in the spring of 1946 when considering the interim arrangements for 1947 and 1948. Deciding what was reasonable reflected, in part, a political judgement. Yet, at least in economic terms, the length of military service could be directly translated into industry's manpower shortages.

Attitudes within the PLP comprised both long-standing objections and specific and immediate concerns, which in the particular circumstances of 1946–7 erupted into the largest public expression of dissent that the party was to see. Although for many criticism of Bevin's foreign policy was inextricably linked with this issue, conscription was a singular question, and one that even under a trusted Labour government could move a wide cross-section of the party to open and embarrassing disobedience. Conservatives have long claimed that issues of security can somehow be divorced from politics. Yet on this issue it is clear that whatever the merits of the case for the shorter period of service, the action of the government was taken purely because of internal party dissent. It was on this, and really only on this, that Attlee was prepared to subordinate the needs of the military to the feelings of his party.

Despite that reversal of policy, and despite party sentiment, a Labour government did introduce compulsory military service as the long-term basis for Britain's defence policy, and after the events of 1948 reversed its earlier change of mind. Conscription was introduced for an eighteen-month period, subsequently extended in the wake of the Korean situation to two years. The acceptance of National Service symbolized Labour's transition from a pre-war party of opposition to a post-war party of government.

It was a Labour government that took decisions on the provision of an independent strategic nuclear capability, on a Middle Eastern strategy, and on a formal Western military alliance. Acceptance of conscription was but one of a number of defence policy decisions which facilitated an enduring bipartisan approach to the central questions of Britain's security. National Service was a critical part of that consensus.

In 1939 Labour had not been able to support a measure that, whatever its military defects, symbolized Britain's willingness to commit its army to support the French against Nazi Germany. The PLP of 1939 was more pacifist than the post-war party and conscription touched other raw nerves, even among hard-headed anti-pacifists like Ernest Bevin. By August 1945 Attlee had consolidated his personal position in the party and the issue of National Service provided a test of his skills as party leader as well as Prime Minister.

The question does arise whether Labour in opposition would have supported conscription. This is bound up with a whole range of speculations about both the likely nature of the party's attitudes and the likely actions of a Conservative government. Churchill was highly critical of Labour's handling of defence issues, especially the demobilization scheme, and it should be noted that his 1951–5 government did slow down Attlee's rearmament programme. It is part of the logic of politics that parties of the right enjoy inherently better opportunities for taking fundamental and radical decisions about defence and security. Yet there is little to indicate any real willingness among senior Conservatives to tackle the basic problems of resource allocation and the fundamental imbalance between the self-image of great power status and an inadequate economic and industrial base (at least until after Suez). Moreover, Churchill was adamant in his support for conscription while in opposition, and whatever the platitudes about reducing the length of service through increased efficiency, the defence policies of his government were essentially continuous with those of the Attlee governments.

In 1945 Churchill had pressed for permanent conscription. Had he won the election it is difficult to see Labour accepting from him what it had barely accepted from Attlee. The bonds of loyalty to a Labour government—not least among ministers of the left who were initially opposed—would not have existed. In any case it is questionable whether Attlee would have survived electoral defeat, and even more doubtful whether he and Bevin could have exercised the sort of influence on the party's foreign (and defence) policies that their positions in power afforded them. Labour's attitude to Palestine and to the Middle East would without doubt have been fundamentally different out of office. If these views are correct, then, as in domestic policy, the existence of a post-war consensus depended on the existence of a Labour government in 1945.

The British are an island people with an ingrained tradition of voluntary military forces; the Labour Party is a coalition of forces and values each with particular reasons for opposing compulsory military service. That a Labour government chose to introduce National Service is an illustration of the political culture of the early post-war years and an indication of how lessons of the past, fused with perceptions of the future, were changing the basis of British defence policy. The fundamental and unresolved tensions inherent in that policy were part of the heritage that the Attlee government was to bequeath. Yet whatever its undoubted defects, conscription could provide a basis for conventional defence. As successive governments grappled with the dilemmas of defence policy, dependence on nuclear weapons increased. For that, if for no other reason, National Service was more than just an unfortunate necessity of the times.

Appendix 1

Strength of the Armed Forces and Women's Services and Expenditure on Defence, United Kingdom

TABLE A1.1. Strength of Armed Forces and Women's Services, 1938–1951[a] ('000)

	1938	1944	1945	1946	1947	1948	1949	1950	1951
Total	381	4,544	4,682	1,917	1,248	808	737	666	804
Royal Navy	113	790	789	350	190	135	137	129	136
Army	199	2,742	2,931	1,189	774	450	395	354	427
Royal Air Force	70	1,011	963	439	285	222	205	183	241
Total reserves	426				128	157	207	219	277
Territorial Army	168				19	43	69	78	110
Women's Services	1	467	437	138	64	39	33	24	23

[a] At 30 June each year.

Source: Annual Abstract of Statistics, 90 (1955).

TABLE A1.2.   Expenditure on Defence, 1946–1951 (£m)

	1946	1947	1948	1949	1950	1951
Defence spending	1,560	930	740	770	820	1,090
Total government spending	4,222	3,545	3,505	3,734	3,686	4,053

Source: Annual Abstract of Statistics, 92 (1955).

Appendix 2

Demobilization

The scheme of release from the forces after the end of hostilities provided for two classes: A, based on age and length of service, and B, out-of-turn release for those employed in essential occupations in reconstruction. There was also provision for release on compassionate or medical grounds. Class A began to be released from 18 June 1945; Class B from 16 July 1945.

The scheme terminated in March 1949 when all men and women called up by 31 December 1946 had been released, except those who voluntarily extended their service. Those conscripted after 1 January 1947 served for fixed periods.

TABLE A2.1.   Total numbers released, 18 June 1945–31 March 1949[a]

	Men	Women	Total
By period			
1945 (June–Dec.)	1,342,110	172,480	1,514,590
1946	2,545,210	231,050	2,776,260
1947	591,650	46,690	638,340
1948	505,210	24,650	529,860
1949 (Jan.–Mar.)	81,420	3,490	84,910
Total	5,065,600	478,360	5,543,960
By service			
Royal Navy	748,890	81,510	866,400
Army	3,207,310	229,650	3,436,960
RAF	1,073,000	167,200	1,240,600
Total	5,065,600	478,360	5,543,960
By category[b]			
Class A	4,369,000	421,170	4,790,170
Class B	288,150	4,220	292,370
Other releases and discharges	375,000	53,970	427,970
1947–8 National Service	33,450	–	33,450
Total	5,065,000	478,360	5,543,960

[a] The peak was reached at the end of 1945/beginning of 1946 when between
November 1945 and March 1946 1,957,000 were demobilized.
[b] Class A constituted about 87%, Class B 5% of releases. The Class B scheme was
substantially finished by the end of 1946 when 276,000 had been released. The
principal categories of Class B were: building/civil engineering: 154,300;
agriculture: 22,800; coalmining: 16,300; textiles: 9,500; police: 6,500;
schoolteachers: 9,000; students: 9,200.

Source: *Ministry of Labour Gazette*, 57/5 (May 1949).

Appendix 3

Summary of 1947–1948 National Service Scheme

All men were required to register at the local offices of the Ministry of Labour between the ages of seventeen years eight months and seventeen years eleven months, although provision was made for earlier registration and call-up at seventeen years six months. Those who were able to defer their service (see below) were required to register. Men were allowed to express preferences as to which service they would join. After medical examination which eliminated the unfit, the conscripts were called up, usually four to six weeks after registration. Men were called up at age eighteen until June 1948, when the age was raised to eighteen years three months; it remained thus until February 1951, when it was reduced to eighteen years two months.

The legislation applied to all British citizens resident in the United Kingdom, and to citizens or nationals of the Dominions (including Eire) who had been resident in the United Kingdom for at least two years and who chose not to return to their own countries. Liability for service was extended to the Channel Islands and the Isle of Man in 1949.

The period of full-time service was initially designed at twelve months; it was extended to eighteen months and eventually to two years. The total liability was initially seven years with the part-time service consisting of a total of sixty days. As full-time service was extended, reserve liability was reduced to three and a half years by 1950.

Liability for service extended up to age twenty-six. This was raised by the 1948 Amendment Act to thirty years to 'catch' doctors and dentists. Those who were able to defer their service beyond this time were thus exempted. Certain industrial categories were exempted, particularly coalminers. So were agricultural workers, although after December 1951 the conditions under which they were allowed to defer their service were tightened. Merchant seamen were able to avoid military service, together with, after June 1950, seagoing fishermen who were prepared to join the Royal Naval Reserve. Men were also exempted on grounds of individual hardship (e.g. only sons of dependent widows) which had traditionally applied. Provision for exemption on grounds of conscientious objection remained as under wartime legislation.

Although not entitled to avoid service, apprentices, students, and those undertaking courses of professional training were allowed to defer their military training until their studies were completed.

Appendix 4

Breakdown of National Service Intake, 1929–1933[a]

	1929	1929	1930	1930	1931	1931	1932	1932	1933	1933
Posted to HM Forces or entered as volunteers	183,400	234,900	171,500	231,000	154,200	219,000	146,800	212,400	145,700	209,800
Found unfit for service	28,700	38,200	30,900	41,200	36,600	50,700	43,600	60,900	35,500	54,400
Available for HM Forces or awaiting medical examination	3,900	–	3,900	300	3,300	300	3,000	300	3,100	100
Application for deferment under consideration	500	–	600	–	600	–	400	–	1,700	300
Call-up deferred:										
Apprentices	41,400	–	52,200	–	51,800	–	53,000	–	52,100	–
Articled pupils and others training for professional qualifications	–	–	–	–	5,500	–	6,300	–	6,400	–

Appendix 4 (*cont.*)

	1929	1929	1930	1930	1931	1931	1932	1932	1933	1933
Agricultural workers	18,400	13,300	19,900	14,400	19,200	14,100	18,400	13,800	5,200	3,800
Coalmining workers	8,400	6,100	8,700	6,900	8,500	7,400	9,400	8,500	10,600	8,500
Seamen	5,300	3,300	3,800	5,000	4,200	5,300	4,300	4,100	3,700	5,100
Scientific workers on high-priority work	nfg^b	600	nfg	700	nfg	1,100	nfg	1,300	nfg	1,600
Boys at school taking GCE etc.	100	–	500	–	1,000	–	900	–	800	–
University students, student teachers, etc.	7,000	100	7,600	400	9,100	600	9,900	700	10,200	400
Migrants and others gone abroad	nfg	2,000	nfg	2,500	nfg	2,500	nfg	2,800	nfg	2,700
All others (inc. hardship cases, COs, etc.)	1,900	500	2,100	600	1,900	800	2,000	1,100	2,100	1,300
TOTAL	299,000	299,000	301,700	303,000	295,900	302,000	298,000	306,000	277,100	288,000

^{a} Two figures for each year are given. This is to show the effect of the system of deferment. Men who were deferred were not medically examined until called up. Those listed as deferred in the second of the columns had passed the age of 26 and were almost all exempted.
^{b} nfg = no figures given.

Source: Ministry of Labour Gazette, 55–67 (1948–59).

Appendix 5

Army Organization: Pre-war and Post-war Comparisons

TABLE A5.1.   Numbers of formations (by brigades)

	1938	1948 (30 Nov.)
United Kingdom	2 cavalry	–
	1 tank	–
	14 infantry	1 (with a second by 1 Apr. '49)
BAOR	–	4 infantry
		1 parachute
		1 armoured
Trieste		1 infantry
Austria		1 infantry
Egypt	1 cavalry	4 infantry
	2 infantry	–
Palestine	4 infantry	–
Far East	2 infantry	1 infantry
		3 Anglo/Gurkha
Total UK	17	1
Total overseas	9	16 (plus 1 by Apr. '49)

In addition there were 2 anti-aircraft brigades in 1938; by 1948 there were 38. The regular element of these amounted to some 7 brigades. Therefore the total number is 28 in 1938 (excluding India), compared with 25 (plus 1 by 1 Apr. 1949) in 1948.

Source: Brief for Prime Minister from Director General Manpower Planning (Gen. Woodall), 30 Nov. 1948, DEFE 7/506.

TABLE A5.2.   Comparison of Arms (excluding India)

	1938 Strength	% of army strength	1948 (30 Nov.) Strength	% of army strength
Cavalry[a]	9,586	5.3		
Royal Tank Regiment	5,325	2.9		
Royal Armoured Corps	–	–	23,789	6.0
Royal Artillery	42,051	23.1	58,436	14.6
Infantry	79,479	43.6	85,317	21.3
Royal Engineers	7,067	3.9	35,380	8.8
Royal Signals	5,849	3.2	24,355	6.1
Royal Army Service Corps	8,345	4.6	42,255	10.5
Royal Army Medical Corps	4,609	2.5	16,163	4.0
Royal Army Ordnance Corps	4,569	2.4	28,788	7.1
Royal Electrical & Mechanical Engineers	–	–	35,731	8.9
Miscellaneous	18,642	10.2	46,700	12.7
Total	182,642		396,800	

[a] excluding Household Cavalry

Source: Brief for Prime Minister from Director General Manpower Planning (Gen. Woodall), 30 Nov. 1948, DEFE 7/506.

Appendix 6

Principal Persons

ALEXANDER Albert Victor Alexander, later 1st Earl (1885–1965). Labour and Co-operative MP for Hillsborough 1922–31, 1935–50. Parliamentary Secretary at the Board of Trade 1924; First Lord of the Admiralty 1929–31, 1940–6; Minister of Defence 1947–50; Chancellor of the Duchy of Lancaster 1950–1.

ANDERSON Sir John Anderson, later Viscount Waverley (1882–1958). National MP for Scottish Universities 1938–50. Secretary of State for Home Affairs and Minister of Home Security 1939–40; Lord President of the Council 1940–3; Chancellor of the Exchequer 1943–5.

ATTLEE Clement Richard Attlee, later 1st Earl (1883–1967). Labour MP for Limehouse 1922–50; West Walthamstow 1950–5. Under Secretary of State for War 1924; Chancellor of the Duchy of Lancaster 1930–1; Postmaster-General 1931; Lord Privy Seal 1940–2; Deputy Prime Minister 1942–5; Secretary of State for Dominion Affairs 1942–5; Prime Minister 1945–51; Minister of Defence 1945–6; Leader of the Labour Party 1935–55.

BELLENGER Frederick John Bellenger (1894–1968). Labour MP for Bassetlaw 1935–68. Financial Secretary to the War Office 1945–6; Secretary of State for War 1946–7.

BEVAN Aneurin Bevan (1897–1960). Labour MP for Ebbw Vale 1929–60. Minister of Health 1945–51; Minister of Labour and National Service 1951; Deputy Leader of the Labour Party 1959–60.

BEVIN Ernest Bevin (1881–1951). Labour MP for Central Wandsworth 1940–50; East Woolwich 1950–1. General Secretary of the Transport and General Workers' Union 1921–40; Minister of Labour and National Service 1940–5; Foreign Secretary 1945–51; Lord Privy Seal 1951.

BROOKE Sir Alan Francis Brooke, later Viscount Alanbrooke (1883–1963). Commander II Corps, British Expeditionary Force 1939–40; CinC Home Forces 1940–1; Chief of the Imperial General Staff 1941–6.

CALLAGHAN Leonard James Callaghan (b. 1912). Labour MP for South Cardiff 1945–50; South-east Cardiff 1950–83; Cardiff South and Penarth 1983–7. Parliamentary Secretary at the Ministry of Transport 1947–50; Parliamentary and Financial Secretary at the Admiralty 1950–1.

Chancellor of the Exchequer 1964–7; Home Secretary 1967–70. Foreign Secretary 1974–6. Prime Minister 1976–9; Leader of the Labour Party 1976–80.

CHAMBERLAIN Arthur Neville Chamberlain (1869–1940). Conservative MP for Birmingham Ladywood 1918–29; Edgbaston 1929–40. Postmaster-General 1922–3; Paymaster-General 1923; Minister of Health 1923, 1924–9, 1931; Chancellor of the Exchequer 1923–4, 1931–7; Prime Minister 1937–40; Lord President of the Council 1940.

CHURCHILL Winston Leonard Spencer Churchill, later Sir Winston (1874–1965). Conservative MP for Oldham 1900–4; Liberal MP for Oldham 1904–6; North-west Manchester 1906–8; Dundee 1908–22. Conservative MP for Epping 1924–45; Woodford 1945–64. Parliamentary Under Secretary at the Colonial Office 1905–8; President of the Board of Trade 1908–10; Home Secretary 1910–11; First Lord of the Admiralty 1911–15, 1939–40; Chancellor of the Duchy of Lancaster 1915; Minister of Munitions 1917–19; Secretary of State of War and Air 1919–21; Secretary of State for the Colonies 1921–2; Chancellor of the Exchequer 1924–9; Prime Minister 1940–5, 1951–5; Minister of Defence 1940–5.

CRIPPS Sir Richard Stafford Cripps (1889–1952). Labour MP for East Bristol 1931–50; South-east Bristol February–October 1950. Solicitor-General 1930–1; Ambassador to the Soviet Union 1940–2; Lord Privy Seal and Leader of the House of Commons 1942; Minister of Aircraft Production 1942–5; President of the Board of Trade 1945–7; Minister of Economic Affairs 1947; Chancellor of the Exchequer 1947–50.

CROSSMAN Richard Howard Stafford Crossman (1907–74). Labour MP for East Coventry 1945–74. Assistant Editor of the *New Statesman and Nation* 1938–55; Editor of the *New Statesman* 1970–2. Member of the Anglo-American Palestine Commission 1946; Minister of Housing and Local Government 1964–6; Lord President of the Council and Leader of the House of Commons 1966–8; Secretary of State for Social Services 1968–70.

CUNNINGHAM, A. Sir Andrew Cunningham, later Viscount (1883–1963). CinC Mediterranean Fleet 1939–43; First Sea Lord 1943–6.

CUNNINGHAM, J. Sir John Cunningham (1885–1962). Fourth Sea Lord 1941–3; CinC Levant 1943; CinC Mediterranean 1943–6; First Sea Lord 1946–8.

DALTON Edward Hugh John Neale Dalton, later Baron (1887–1962). Labour MP for Peckham 1924–9; Bishop Auckland 1929–31, 1935–59. Parliamentary Under Secretary of State for Foreign Affairs 1929–31; Minister of Economic Warfare 1940–2; President of the Board of Trade 1942–5; Chancellor of the Exchequer 1945–7; Chancellor of the Duchy of Lancaster 1948–50; Minister of Town and Country Planning 1950–1; Minister of Local Government and Planning 1951.

DURBIN Evan Frank Mottram Durbin (1906–48). Labour MP for Edmonton 1945–8. Member War Cabinet Secretariat and Personal Assistant to Deputy Prime Minister Attlee; Parliamentary Secretary at the Ministry of Works 1947–8.

EDEN Robert Anthony Eden, later Sir Anthony, 1st Earl of Avon (1897–1977). Conservative MP for Warwick and Leamington 1923–57. Parliamentary Private Secretary to the Foreign Secretary 1926–9; Parliamentary Under Secretary for Foreign Affairs 1931–3; Lord Privy Seal 1933–5; Minister Without Portfolio, League of Nations Affairs 1935; Secretary of State for Foreign Affairs 1935–8, 1940–5, 1951–5; Secretary of State for Dominion Affairs 1939–40; Secretary of State for War May–December 1940; Leader of the House of Commons 1942–5; Deputy Leader of the Opposition 1945–51; Prime Minister and Leader of the Conservative Party 1955–7.

GAITSKELL Hugh Todd Naylor Gaitskell (1906–63). Labour MP for South Leeds 1945–63. Principal Private Secretary to Dalton as Minister of Economic Warfare 1940–2; Principal Assistant Secretary, Board of Trade 1942–5; Parliamentary Secretary, Minister of Fuel and Power 1946–7; Minister of State for Economic Affairs 1950; Chancellor of the Exchequer 1950–1; Leader of the Labour Party 1955–63.

HALL George Henry Hall, created Viscount 1946 (1881–1965). Labour MP for Aberdare 1922–46. Civil Lord of the Admiralty 1929–31; Parliamentary Under Secretary of State for the Colonies 1940–2; Financial Secretary to the Admiralty 1942–3; Parliamentary Under Secretary of State for Foreign Affairs 1943–5; Secretary of State for the Colonies 1945–6; First Lord of the Admiralty 1946–51; Deputy Leader of the House of Lords 1947–51.

HENDERSON Arthur Henderson, later Baron (1893–1968). Labour MP for Cardiff South 1923–4, 1929–31; Kingswinford 1935–50; Rowley Regis 1950–66. Joint Parliamentary Under Secretary of State for War 1942–3; Financial Secretary to the War Office 1943–5; Parliamentary Under Secretary of State for India and Burma 1945–7; Minister of State for Commonwealth Relations 1947; Secretary of State for Air 1947–51.

HOLLIS General Sir Leslie Chasemore Hollis (1897–1963). Military Assistant Secretary of the Committee of Imperial Defence 1936–40; Military Assistant Secretary to the War Cabinet 1940–5; Secretary of the Chiefs of Staff Committee 1940–5; Chief Staff Officer to the Minister of Defence and Deputy Military Secretary to the Cabinet 1947–9.

HORE-BELISHA Isaac Leslie Hore-Belisha (1893–1957). MP for Plymouth Devonport 1923–45 (Liberal 1929–31, Liberal Nationalist 1931–42, National Independent 1942–5). Parliamentary Secretary to the Board of Trade 1931–2; Financial Secretary at the Treasury 1932–4; Minister of Transport 1934–5; Secretary of State for War 1937–40.

ISAACS   George Alfred Isaacs (1883–1979). Labour MP for Gravesend 1923–4; Southwark North 1929–31, 1939–50; Southwark 1950–9. Minister of Labour and National Service 1945–51; Minister of Pensions 1951.

ISMAY   General Sir Hastings Lionel Ismay, created Baron 1947 (1887–1965). Chief of Staff to the Minister of Defence 1940–5; Deputy Military Secretary to the War Cabinet 1940–5; Additional Secretary to the Cabinet 1945; Viceroy of India 1947; Secretary-General of the North Atlantic Treaty Organization 1952–7.

JAY   Douglas Jay (b. 1907). Labour MP for Battersea North 1946–83. Personal Assistant to Prime Minister Attlee 1945–6; Parliamentary Private Secretary to Chancellor of the Exchequer 1947; Economic Secretary to the Treasury 1947–50; Financial Secretary to the Treasury 1950–1.

LAWSON   John James Lawson, later Baron (1881–1965). Labour MP for Chester-le-Street 1919–49. Financial Secretary to the War Office 1924; Parliamentary Secretary at the Ministry of Labour 1929–31; Secretary of State for War 1945–6.

LIDDELL HART   Sir Basil Henry Liddell Hart (1895–1970). Writer and journalist. Military correspondent, *Daily Telegraph*, 1925–35. Military correspondent, *The Times*, 1935–9.

MARTEL   General Sir Giffard Le Quesne Martel (1889–1958). Writer on military affairs. Assistant, then Deputy Director of Mechanization at the War Office 1936–9; Commander of the Royal Armoured Corps 1940.

MONTGOMERY   Bernard Law Montgomery, later Viscount (1887–1976). Commander Eighth Army 1942–4; CinC Land Forces, Operation Overlord, 1944; CinC British Forces of Occupation 1945–6; Chief of the Imperial General Staff 1946–8; Chairman of the Commanders-in-Chief Committee of the Western Union 1948–51; Deputy Supreme Allied Commander Europe 1951–8.

MORRISON   Herbert Stanley Morrison, later Baron (1888–1965). Labour MP for South Hackney 1923–4, 1929–31, 1935–45; East Lewisham 1945–50; South Lewisham 1950–9. Minister of Transport 1929–31; Minister of Supply 1940; Home Secretary and Minister of Home Security 1940–5; Member of the War Cabinet 1942–5; Deputy Prime Minister 1945–51. Lord President of the Council and Leader of the House of Commons 1945–51; Foreign Secretary March–October 1951; Deputy Leader of the Opposition 1951–5.

NOEL-BAKER   Philip John Noel-Baker, later Baron (1889–1982). Labour MP for Coventry 1929–31; Derby 1936–50; Derby South 1950–70. Member of League of Nations Section of British Delegation to the Paris Peace Conference 1919; Member of League of Nations Secretariat 1919–22; Parliamentary Private Secretary to the Foreign Secretary 1929–31; Principal Assistant to the President of the Disarmament

Conference at Geneva 1932–3; Parliamentary Secretary at the Ministry of War Transport 1942–5; Minister of State at the Foreign Office 1945–6; Secretary of State for Air 1946–7; Secretary of State for Commonwealth Relations 1947–50; Minister of Fuel and Power 1950–1. Winner Nobel Peace Prize, 1959.

SHINWELL   Emanuel Shinwell, later Baron (1884–1986). Labour MP for Linlithgow 1922–4, 1928–31; Seaham 1935–50; Easington 1950–70. Financial Secretary to the War Office 1929–30; Parliamentary Secretary at the Department of Mines at the Board of Trade 1924, 1930–1; Minister of Fuel and Power 1945–7; Secretary of State for War 1947–50; Minister of Defence 1950–1.

SINCLAIR   Sir Archibald Henry Macdonald Bart Sinclair, later Viscount (1890–1970). Liberal MP for Caithness and Sutherland 1922–45. Secretary of State for Scotland 1931–2; Secretary of State for Air 1940–5; Leader of the Liberal Parliamentary Party 1922–45.

SLESSOR   Sir John Cotesworth Slessor (1897–1979). Director of Plans, Air Ministry, 1837–40; Assistant Chief of the Air Staff (Policy) 1942–3; CinC Coastal Command 1943–4; Deputy CinC Allied Forces Middle East 1944–5; Air Member for Personnel 1945–8; Commandant of the Imperial Defence College 1948–50; Chief of the Air Staff 1950–2.

SLIM   William Joseph Slim, later Viscount (1891–1970). Commander Fourteenth Army 1943–5; Commandant of the Imperial Defence College 1946–8; Chief of the Imperial General Staff 1948–52.

STRACHEY   Evelyn John St Loe Strachey (1901–63). Labour MP for Aston 1929–31; Dundee 1945–50; West Dundee 1950–63. Parliamentary Under Secretary of State for Air 1945–6; Minister of Food 1946–50; Secretary of State for War 1950–1.

TEDDER   Arthur William Tedder, later Baron (1890–1967). CinC RAF Middle East 1941–3; CinC Mediterranean Air Command 1943; Deputy Supreme Commander, Operation Overlord, 1944; Chief of the Air Staff 1945–9.

WIGG   George Edward Cecil Wigg, later Baron (1900–83). Labour MP for Dudley 1945–67. Parliamentary Private Secretary to Shinwell 1945–51; Paymaster-General 1964–7.

WILKINSON   Ellen Wilkinson (1891–1947). Labour MP for Middlesborough East 1924–31; Jarrow 1935–47. Parliamentary Secretary at the Ministry of Home Security 1940–5; Minister for Education 1945–7.

Bibliography

PRIMARY SOURCES

Official Papers

The following papers are all held in the Public Records Office, Kew (London).

Ad Hoc Cabinet Committee: Minutes and Papers (CAB 130 series), 1945–51.

Armistice and Post-war Planning Committee: Minutes and Papers (CAB 87/69), 1945.

Cabinet: Minutes (CAB 128 series) and Papers (CAB 129 series), 1945–51.

Chiefs of Staff Committee: Minutes (CAB 79 series) and Papers (CAB 80 series), 1944–5; Minutes (DEFE 4 series) and Papers (DEFE 5 Series), 1946–51.

Defence Committee: Minutes and Papers (CAB 131 series), 1946–51.

Lord President of the Council's Papers: CAB 124/131, 124/591–5.

Ministerial Manpower Committee: Minutes and Papers (CAB 134/509–10), 1945–6.

Prime Minister's Papers: PREM 8/280, 8/600, 8/609, 8/610, 8/659, 8/748, 8/833, 8/834, 8/1021, 8/1154, 8/1158; CAB 21/2069, 21/2071.

War Cabinet: Minutes (CAB 65 series) and Papers (CAB 66 series), September 1944–July 1945.

Departmental Files

Admiralty: ADM 1/20965, 116/5651, 167/126, 167/127, 167/129, 205/70.

Air Ministry: AIR 8/799, 8/800–1, 8/1473, 8/1587–8, 8/1591, 8/1612, 19/582–5, 20/660.

Colonial Office: CO 537/4400.

Foreign Office: FO 371/50812, 371/95976, 371/96115.

Foreign Secretary: FO 800/451–4, 493.

Ministry of Defence: DEFE 7/1, 7/4, 7/62–5, 7/144–6, 7/505–6.

Treasury: T 225/72–5, 247/71.

War Office: Minutes of the Army Council 1945–9, WO 163/63.

Minutes of the Executive Committee of the Army Council, 1945–51: WO 163/76–81.

Minutes of the Standing Committee on Army Post-War Problems, 1945–51: WO 163/239–42.

CIGS Files: WO 216/192, 216/216, 216/233–7, 216/239, 216/248, 216/270, 216/297, 216/300–1, 216/313–14, 216/316–17, 216/348.

Private Papers

Papers of General Sir Ronald Adam, Liddell Hart Centre for Military Archives, King's College, London.

Diaries and Papers of Viscount Alanbrooke, Liddell Hart Centre For Military Archives, King's College, London.

Papers of Viscount Alexander, Churchill College, Cambridge.

Papers of Earl Attlee, Bodleian Library, Oxford.

Diaries and papers of Hugh Dalton, British Library of Political and Economic Science, London School of Economics.

Papers of Sir P. J. Grigg, Churchill College, Cambridge.

Papers of Baron Ismay, Liddell Hart Centre for Military Archives, King's College, London.

Labour Party Defence Papers, 1947–59, Labour Party Archives, London.

Labour Party National Executive Committee Minutes and Papers, 1945–51, Labour Party Archives, London.

Papers of Sir Basil Liddell Hart, Liddell Hart Centre for Military Archives, King's College, London.

Papers of Sir Giffard Martel, Imperial War Museum, London.

Papers of Viscount Montgomery of Alamein, Imperial War Museum, London.

Papers of Herbert Morrison, Nuffield College, Oxford.

Government Command Papers

All the following were published by HMSO, London.

Cmd. 6715, *Post-war Code of Pay, Allowances and Service Pensions and Gratuities for Members of the Forces Below Officer Rank*, December 1945.

Cmd. 6743, *Statement Relating to Defence*, February 1946.

Cmd. 6750, *Post-war Code of Pay, Allowances, Retired Pay and Service Gratuities for Commissioned Officers of the Armed Forces*, March 1946.

Cmd. 6831, *Call-up to the Forces in 1947 and 1948*, May 1946.

Cmd. 6923, *Central Organisation for Defence*, October 1946.

Cmd. 7042, *Statement Relating to Defence*, February 1947.

Cmd. 7046, *Economic Survey for 1947*, February 1947.

Cmd. 7327, *Statement Relating to Defence 1948*, February 1948.

Cmd. 7588, *Pay and Marriage Allowances of Members of the Forces*, December 1948.

Cmd. 7607, *Pay, Retired Pay, Service Pensions and Gratuities for Members of the Women's Services*, January 1949.

Cmd. 7608, *Report of the Army and Air Force Courts-martial Committee 1946*, January 1949.

Cmd. 7631, *Statement of Defence 1949*, February 1949.

Cmd. 7883, *Collective Defence under the Brussels and North Atlantic Treaties*, February 1950.

Cmd. 7895, *Statement on Defence 1950*, March 1950.

Cmd. 8026, *Increase in the Length of Full-time National Service with the Armed Forces*, August 1950.

Cmd. 8027, *Service Emoluments*, August 1950.

Cmd. 8094, *First Report of the Committee Appointed to Consider the Administration of Justice under the Naval Discipline Act 1950*, November 1950.

Cmd. 8119, *Second Report of the Committee Appointed to Consider the Administration of Justice under the Naval Discipline Act 1950*, January 1951.

Cmd. 8141, *Courts-martial Procedure and Administration of Justice in the Armed Forces*, January 1951.

Cmd. 8146, *Defence Programme: Statement Made by the Prime Minister in the House of Commons on Monday 29 January 1951*, February 1951.

Cmd. 9608, *National Service*, October 1955.

Cmnd. 124, *Defence: Outline of Future Policy*, April 1957.

Cmnd. 545, *Advisory Committee on Recruiting*, October 1958.

Party and Trade Union Documents

Labour Party Annual Conference Reports, 1944–51.

Co-operative Party Congress Reports, 1945–51.

Trades Union Congress Reports, 1945–51.

National Union of Mineworkers Conference Reports, 1945–51.

Labour Party manifestos
 Let us Face the Future, 1945.
 Let Us Win Through Together, 1950.
 Labour Party Election Manifesto, 1951.
Conservative Party manifestos:
 Mr Churchill's Declaration of Policy to the Electors, 1945.
 This is the Right Road, 1949.
 The Manifesto of the Conservative and Unionist Party, 1951.

Liberal Party manifestos:
20 Point Manifesto of the Liberal Party, 1945.
No Easy Way: Britain's Problems and the Liberal Answers, 1950.
The Nation's Task, 1951.
Communist Party: *Towards a People's Army*, 1946.

SECONDARY SOURCES

Place of publication is London unless otherwise stated.

ADDISON, P., *The Road to 1945* (Cape, 1975).
ALDERMAN, D. K., 'Discipline in the Parliamentary Labour Party 1945–51', *Parliamentary Affairs*, 18 (1965), 293–305.
ATTLEE, C. R., *As It Happened* (Heinemann, 1954).
——, *The Labour Party in Perspective* (Gollancz, 1937).
——, 'Introduction', in L. Clive, *The People's Army* (Gollancz, 1938).
BARKER, R., *Conscience, Government and War* (Routledge & Kegan Paul, 1982).
BARTLETT, C. J., *The Long Retreat* (Macmillan, 1972).
BECKETT, I., and GOOCH, J., eds., *Politicians and Defence: Studies in the Formulation of British Defence Policy* (Manchester University Press, 1981).
BERGER, M., *Engels, Armies and Revolution: The Revolutionary Tactics of Classical Marxism* (Harvard University Press, 1977).
BERRINGTON, H., *Backbench Opinion in the House of Commons 1945–55* (Pergamon, 1973).
BOND, B., *British Military Policy between the Wars* (Oxford University Press, 1980).
——, *Liddell Hart: A Study of his Military Thought* (Cassell, 1977).
BULLOCK, A., *The Life and Times of Ernest Bevin*, ii: *1940–5* (Heinemann, 1967).
——, *Ernest Bevin: Foreign Secretary* (Oxford University Press, 1985).
BURNS, J. M., 'The Parliamentary Labour Party in Great Britain', *American Political Science Review*, 44 (1950), 855–71.
BURRIDGE, T., *Clement Attlee: A Political Biography* (Cape, 1985).
BUTLER, D. E., *The British General Election of 1951* (Macmillan, 1952).
CANTRIL, H., ed., *Public Opinion 1933–1946* (Princeton: Princeton University Press, 1951).
CEADEL, M., *Pacifism in Britain 1914–45* (Oxford University Press, 1980).
CLARK, I., and WHEELER, N. J., *The British Origins of Nuclear Strategy 1945–55* (Oxford University Press, 1989).

COKER, C., *A Nation in Retreat* (Brassey's, 1986).

CROSSMAN, R. H. S., 'Labour and Compulsory Military Service', *Political Quarterly*, 10 (1939), 309–21.

DALTON, H., *Memoirs*, ii: *The Fateful Years 1931–45* (Muller, 1957).

——, *Memoirs*, iii: *High Tide and After 1945–60* (Muller, 1962).

DARBY, P., *British Defence Policy East of Suez 1947–68* (Oxford University Press, 1973).

DAWSON, R. V., *The Conscription Crisis of 1944* (Toronto: University of Toronto Press, 1961).

DENNIS, P., *Decision By Default* (Routledge & Kegan Paul, 1972).

DEVEREUX, D., *The Formulation of British Defence Policy in the Middle East 1948–56* (Macmillan, 1990).

DONOUGHUE, B., and JONES, G., *Herbert Morrison: Portrait of a Politician* (Weidenfeld & Nicolson, 1973).

DOWSE, R. E., 'Clement Attlee', in J. P. MACKINTOSH, ed., *British Prime Ministers in the Twentieth Century*, ii: *Churchill to Callaghan* (Weidenfeld & Nicholson, 1978).

EATWELL, R., *The 1945–51 Labour Governments* (Batsford, 1979).

EDEN, A., *The Reckoning: Memoirs of Anthony Eden* (Cassell, 1965).

EVANGELISTA, M., 'Stalin's Post-war Army Reappraised', *International Security*, 7 (1982/3), 116–38.

FISK, R., *In Time of War: Ireland, Ulster and the Price of Neutrality 1939–45* (Paladin, 1985).

FITZSIMMONS, M. A., *The Foreign Policy of the British Labour Government 1945–51* (Indiana: Notre Dame University Press, 1953).

FLETCHER, R. T., 'Pulheems: A New System of Medical Classification', *British Medical Journal*, 1949, i. 83–8.

FOOT, M. M., *Aneurin Bevan*, i: *1897–1945* (MacGibbon & Kee, 1962).

——, *Aneurin Bevan*, ii: *1945–1960* (Davis-Poynter, 1973).

FOOT, M. R. D., *Men in Uniform* (Weidenfeld & Nicolson, 1961).

GADDIS, J. L., *The United States and the Origins of the Cold War, 1941–7* (New York: Columbia University Press, 1971).

GALLUP, G. H., ed., *Gallup International Public Opinion Polls: Great Britain 1937–75*, i (New York: Random House, 1976).

GIBBS, N. H., *History of the Second World War*, i: *Grand Strategy* (HMSO, 1976).

GORDON, M. R., *Conflict and Consensus in Labour's Foreign Policy 1914–65* (Stanford: Stanford University Press, 1969).

GOWING, M., *Independence and Deterrence: Britain and Atomic Energy 1945–52*, i: *Policy Making* (Macmillan, 1974).

——, *Independence and Deterrence: Britain and Atomic Energy, 1945–52*, ii: *Policy Execution* (Macmillan, 1974).

GROVE, E. J., *Vanguard to Trident: British Naval Policy since World War II* (Bodley Head, 1987).

HAMILTON, N., *Monty*, iii: *The Field Marshal 1944–76* (Sceptre, 1987).

HARRIS, K., *Attlee* (Weidenfeld & Nicolson, 1982).

HARROD, R. F., 'The Conscription of Wealth', *Political Quarterly*, 10 (1939), 322–37.

HAYES, D., *Challenge of Conscience: The Story of the Conscientious Objectors of 1939–45* (Allen & Unwin, 1949).

HENNESSY, P. *Whitehall* (Fontana, 1990).

HOWARD, M. E., *The Central Organisation of Defence* (Royal United Services Institute, 1970).

——, *The Continental Commitment* (Temple Smith, 1972).

——, *War and the Liberal Conscience* (Temple Smith, 1978).

JACKSON, R. J., *Rebels and Whips* (Macmillan, 1968).

JAY, D., *Change and Fortune* (Hutchinson, 1980).

JENKINS, M., *Bevanism—Labour's High Tide: The Cold War and the Democratic Mass Movement* (Spokesman, 1979).

LEWIN, R., *Slim: The Standard Bearer* (Leo Cooper, 1976).

LEWIS, J., *Changing Direction: British Military Planning for Post-war Strategic Defence 1942–7* (Sherwood Press, 1988).

LIDDELL HART, B., 'The Question of Conscription', *World Review*, 2 (1947), 21–4.

——, *Defence of The West* (Cassell, 1950).

LOUIS ROGER, *The British Empire in the Middle East 1945–61* (Oxford University Press, 1984).

McCALLUM, R. B., and READMAN, A., *The British General Election of 1945* (Frank Cass, 1947).

McKENZIE, R. T., *British Political Parties* (Heinemann, 1955).

MACKINTOSH, J. P., *The British Cabinet* (Stevens, 1962).

MARTEL, G., *The Problem of Security* (Michael Joseph, 1945).

——, *An Outspoken Soldier* (Sifton Praed, 1949).

MEARSHEIMER, J. J., *Liddell Hart and the Weight of History* (Brassey's, 1988).

MOGGRIDGE, D., *The Collected Writings of J. M. Keynes*, xxiv: *Activities 1944–6: The Transition to Peace* (Macmillan, 1979).

MONTGOMERY, B. L., *The Memoirs of Field-Marshal The Viscount Montgomery of Alamein* (Collins, 1958).

MORGAN, J., *The Backbench Diaries of Richard Crossman* (Hamish Hamilton, 1981).

MORGAN, K. O., *Labour People* (Oxford University Press, 1987).

——, *Labour in Power, 1945–51* (Oxford University Press, 1984).

MYERS, F., 'Conscription and the Politics of Military Strategy in the Attlee Government', *Journal of Strategic Studies*, 7 (1984), 55–73.

NAVIAS, M., 'Terminating Conscription? The British National Service Controversy 1955–6', *Journal of Contemporary History*, 24 (1989), 195–208.

NAYLOR, J. F. *Labour's International Policy* (Weidenfeld & Nicolson, 1969).

NEUMANN, S., and VON HAGEN, M., 'Engels and Marx on Revolution, War, and the Army in Society', in P. PARET, ed., *Markers of Modern Strategy* (Princeton: Princeton University Press, 1986).

NICHOLAS H. G., *The British General Election of 1950* (Macmillan, 1951).

NORTON, P., *Dissension in the House of Commons 1945–74* (Macmillan, 1975).

OVENDALE, R., *Britain, the United States, and the End of the Palestine Mandate, 1942–1948* (Royal Historical Society, 1989).

——, *The English-speaking Alliance: Britain, the United States, the Dominions and the Cold War 1945–51* (Allen & Unwin, 1985).

——, *The Foreign Policy of the British Labour Governments* (Oxford University Press, 1984).

PEDEN, G. G., *British Rearmament and The Treasury 1932–1939* (Scottish Academic Press, 1979).

PIMLOTT, B., *Hugh Dalton* (Cape, 1985).

POCOCK, J. G. A., *The Machiavellian Moment: Florentine Political Thought and the Atlantic Republican Tradition* (Princeton: Princeton University Press, 1975).

RAE, J., *Conscience and Politics* (Oxford University Press, 1970).

ROBERTS, A., *Nations in Arms* (Chatto & Windus, 1976).

ROSE, R. 'The Relation of Socialist Principles to British Labour Foreign Policy', D.Phil. thesis, Oxord University, 1961.

ROTHSTEIN, A., *The Soldiers' Strikes of 1919* (Journeyman, 1980).

SCOTT, L. V., 'The Classical Marxist Tradition and its View of War', MA thesis, London University, 1980.

——, 'The Labour Government and National Service', D.Phil. thesis, Oxford University, 1983.

SELDON, A., *Churchill's Indian Summer* (Hodder and Stoughton, 1981).

SHINWELL, E. S., *Conflict without Malice* (Odhams, 1955).

SMITH, R., and ZAMETICA, J., 'The Cold Warrior: Clement Attlee Reconsidered, 1945–7', *International Affairs*, 61 (1985), 237–52.

SNYDER, W. P., *The Politics of British Defense Policy 1945–62* (Columbus, Ohio: Ohio State University Press, 1964).

TAYLOR, A. J. P., *English History 1914–45* (Pelican, 1975).

WIGG, G., *George Wigg* (Michael Joseph, 1972).

WILLIAMS, P. M., *Hugh Gaitskell* (Cape, 1979).

——, *The Diary of Hugh Gaitskell, 1945–1956* (Cape, 1983).

WINTER, J. M., *Socialism and the Challenge of War* (Routledge & Kegan Paul, 1974).

WYATT, W., 'Conscription: A Defence', *Political Quarterly*, 21 (1950), 288–300.

Index

Shinwell, Emanual (*cont.*):
  extension of National Service (1950) 257–8
  Military Training Act (1939) 5
  National Service 11, 108, 180–2; *see also* extension of National Service (1948 and 1950)
  opposes conscription (1945) 36–7, 39
  as Secretary of State for War 77–8, 91, 186–7
  seeks abolition of conscription 195, 198, 206, 210, 239, 245, 249–56
Sinclair, Sir Archibald:
  APW committee 16, 19–20, 32
  Military Training Act (1939) 5
Slessor, Air-Marshal Sir John 78, 84–7, 143, 147–8, 182, 222, 253
Slim, Field-Marshall Sir Bill 78, 181, 194, 205–6, 213, 253
socialist foreign policy 8–9, 39–40, 272
Sorenson, Revd Reginald 127
Soviet Union 9, 12, 23–4, 34, 37, 38, 42–3, 51–3, 67–9, 82–3, 87–9, 95, 97, 108–9, 125, 127–8, 152, 186, 191, 216, 217, 218, 219–20, 222–3, 228, 235, 256–7, 264, 271
Smith, Ellis 36
Speed, Sir Eric 75, 176, 194–5
Steele, General Sir James 78, 194, 250
Stephen, Campbell 62
Strachey, John 58–9, 254–6

Tedder, Air-Marshal Lord 84, 86, 147–8, 166, 172, 174–5, 182, 192, 204–6, 212–3, 215, 268
Templer, General Sir Gerald 194–5
Territorial Army 18, 83, 87–9, 115–16, 161, 168, 173, 175, 198, 210, 213, 223–4, 231–4, 244, 254–5, 257, 267
Times, The 135
Tizard, Sir Henry 175, 233
Trades Union Congress 33, 37–8, 99, 138

Trieste 51, 165, 168, 186, 202, 215, 221, 283
Truman doctrine 26, 67, 81, 152
Turner, Sir George 254–5

United Nations 35, 40, 69, 97, 117, 127–8, 272
United States 24, 26, 37, 38, 52, 83, 97, 109, 125, 127–8, 157, 166, 179, 201, 220, 222, 226–7, 230, 233, 235–8, 265–6, 270–1
  commitment to Western Europe 87, 97, 154, 198, 202, 214, 219, 223, 235, 247, 257
  reintroduction of draft 209, 214, 241
  see also Truman doctrine
Ulster/Northern Ireland 37, 100–4, 262

Venezia Guilia 38, 49, 51, 70, 114, 137

Warnock, Edmund 102
Wavell, Field-Marshal Lord 181
Webb, Sydney 8
Welsh and conscription 123, 152
Western Union 12, 186, 198, 224, 229, 231, 234, 237–8, 258
  see also Brussels Treaty
Wheeler, Nicholas 82
Whiteley, William 63
Wigg, George 93, 132, 260
Wilkinson, Ellen 26, 98, 108
Wills, Edith 124
Wilmot, John 56–7
Wilson, Harold 199
Women:
  permanent forces 60–1, 73, 79–80, 105–6, 227, 265, 276
  WRNS 227
  see also conscription of women
Wood, Richard 74, 183–4
Wyatt, Woodrow 93

Yates, Victor 121, 127–8

Zilliacus, Konni 95, 123